INDONESIA, ISLAM, AND DEMOCRACY

AZYUMARDI AZRA

INDONESIA, ISLAM, AND DEMOCRACY

DYNAMICS IN A GLOBAL CONTEXT

A. Azra
To Bill Tucheello
with respect and gratitude
Jakarta 5/6/06.

The Asia Foundation

SOLSTICE
JAKARTA SINGAPORE

ICIP
International Centre
for Islam and Pluralism

Solstice Publishing
an imprint of Equinox Publishing
Menara Gracia, 6th floor
Jl. H.R. Rasuna Said Kav. C-17
Jakarta 12940
Indonesia

ISBN 979-99888-1-0

© 2006 Azyumardi Azra

Produced with the support of The Asia Foundation, Jakarta

Printed in Indonesia.

10 9 8 7 6 5 4 3 2 1

TABLE OF CONTENTS

PART THREE
The Dynamics of Islamic Movements

PREFACE

O ver the last few years, a number of friends and institutions have suggested that I collect my articles that have been published in a number of journals as well as unpublished papers presented at various conferences, mostly abroad. Due to my heavy workload as Rector of Syarif Hidayatullah State Islamic University and other engagements, the publication of this collection has been delayed. Fortunately, as a result of the persistence of Dr. Syafi'i Anwar, Director of the International Center for Islam and Pluralism (ICIP), and feelings of guilt, I have done something about it.

This particular collection is entitled *Indonesia, Islam, and Democracy: Dynamics in a Global Context*. This title perfectly reflects the content of the book. In the first instance, this book is about Indonesia, the most populous Muslim nation in the world today. And, since the sudden fall of President Soeharto in May 1998, Indonesia is in transition from authoritarianism to democracy. During the crucial period of transition, issues relating to the place of Islam in democracy and the Indonesian political system have once again come to the forefront.

In addition, on the basis of my research since the late 1980s, I strongly believe that Indonesian Islam cannot be separated from the development of Islam elsewhere, particularly in the Middle East. The dynamics of Islam therefore, in one way or another, have intense ramifications for the Muslim world and the international order. The latest religious and political developments outside Indonesia also have certain impacts on Indonesian Islam.

The publication of this book has not been possible without the support of many friends and colleagues. I would therefore like to thank all of them; particularly, Syafi'i Anwar and others at ICIP; and, of course, Ahmadi who prepares all the texts, and Idris Thaha who assists him.

I am also grateful to Mark Hanusz of Equinox Publishing who – with his great love of Indonesia -- is bringing works of Indonesian scholars like mine to the international audience through persistent efforts. No doubt he contributes a great deal in this respect. I am also indebted to my proofreader, Chris Stewart, who tirelessly refined my English.

My greatest debt is, of course, to my family: my wife Ipah Farihah, our sons Raushanfikr Usada Azra, Firman el-Amny Azra and M. Subhan Azra, as well as our daughter Emily Sakina Azra who have, over the years, sustained my scholarly spirit with their love and understanding, especially when I have had to travel across the continents from time to time attending and presenting papers at various conferences. May God bless all of them.

Azyumardi Azra
UIN Campus, Ciputat
April 2006

PART ONE
INDONESIA, ISLAM, AND DEMOCRACY

ISLAM AND THE INDONESIAN TRANSITION TO DEMOCRACY

O ne of the most evident tendencies in the post-cold war period in the approach towards the new millennium is the rapid growth in the number of nation-states are becoming democratic. This trend does not seem to be taking place in dominantly or pre-dominantly Muslim states in the Islamic world as a whole. According to a report entitled *Freedom in the World 2000: The Democracy Gap,* there is a noticeable lack of democracy in the Arabic core of the Muslim world.

Since the early 1970s, when the third major historical wave of democratization began, the Muslim world, or more precisely its Arab core, has seen little significant evidence of improvements in political openness, respect for human rights, press freedom and transparency. The democracy gap between the Muslim world and the rest of the world is indeed dramatic. Of the 192 countries in the world today, 121 are electoral democracies; but in countries with a Muslim majority, only eleven of forty-seven (or twenty-three per cent) have democratically elected governments. In the non-Islamic world, there are 110 electoral democracies out of 145 states, or over seventy-six per cent. The report concludes that a non-Islamic state is more than three times more likely to be democratic than an Islamic state.

In contrast, however, the report also mentions some "bright spots" of democracy in a number of predominantly and least Arabicized Muslim countries such as Albania, Bangladesh, Djibouti, the Gambia, Indonesia, Mali, Niger, Nigeria, Senegal, Sierra Leone, Turkey and Iran. Despite its shaky foundation and development, democratic ferment is considerable in these countries. Of thirty-one non-Arab countries, eleven are electoral democracies, while of the sixteen Arab-majority countries, one (Tunisia) has an authoritarian presidential system; two (Libya and Iraq) are one party dictatorships; four (Algeria, Egypt, Syria and Yemen) are states with a dominant ruling party that faces thwarted and severely circumscribed political opposition; while the nine remaining states are monarchies.

Despite these "bright spots" of democracy among Muslim countries, there is little doubt that the old question about Islam and democracy; whether or not Islam, for instance, can play a more positive role in the new wave of democracy, remains a subject of heated discussion both from within Islam and from without. It is important to point out, however, that despite the "democracy gap" in many – if not most – Muslim countries, the Freedom House report believes that recent history shows that Islam is not inherently incompatible with democracy and democratic values. Indeed, if one takes into account the large Muslim populations of such countries as India, Bangladesh, Indonesia, Nigeria, Turkey and the Muslim populations of North America and Western Europe, the majority of the world's Muslims live under democratically constituted governments. The "bright spots" of democracy among Muslim countries, therefore, raise hopes for democracy in the Muslim world.

Indonesia, particularly under the two presidents during the so-called "reform period" (*masa reformasi*), Abdurrahman Wahid and Megawati Soekarnoputri, is still in the transition to democracy. If the presidencies of Presidents Habibie and Wahid can be said to be the first (preparatory) phase, the presidency of President Megawati can be regarded as the period of democratic consolidation. During the preparatory stage, one might observe that prolonged and inconclusive political conflicts continued to strongly color the Indonesian political scene. During the period of Megawati's presidency, there are already some signs to show that there is a deliberate decision on the part of political leaders to institutionalize some crucial aspects of democratic process, which, in the end, will result in a "consolidated democracy", which is one stage in the democratic transition in which all the major political actors, parties, organized interests, forces and institutions consider that there is no alternative to democratic processes to gain power, and that no political institution or group has a claim to veto the action of democratically elected decision makers.

During this stage towards the consolidation of democracy, however, discussion and debate on the relationship of Islam and democracy has once again come to the forefront of Indonesian society both at the level of discourse and the realities of Indonesian politics in the aftermath of President Soeharto's fall from grace. The fact that there have been a number of conflicting political trends since Indonesia entered the democratic transition during the *interregnum* of President B.J. Habibie, has only created further confusion about the relationship between Islam and democracy. The process of political liberalization that has been initiated by President Habibie has, therefore, created mixed signals.

As one might observe, on the one hand, Muslim groups have played an important role in the fall of Soeharto, ending a long period of autocratic rule and, therefore, providing an impetus for the growth of democracy. Prominent Muslim leaders, such as M. Amien Rais, Nurcholish Madjid and Abdurrahman Wahid, had been at the forefront of the opposition movement in the last years of Soeharto's power. On the other hand, however, with the new opening of democracy in Indonesia, "political Islam" – among which there exists some radical groups – also gained new momentum and, in fact, appears to be one of the most visible political developments in post-Soeharto Indonesia. The rise of "political Islam" has worried some, for it could be incompatible with democracy.

The rise of political Islam can be clearly observed in several tendencies. First, the establishment of a large number of "Islamic parties" which have mostly replaced *Pancasila* with Islam as the basis for their organization. Second, the increasing demands from certain groups of Muslims for the official adoption and implementation of *shari'ah*. Third, a proliferation of Muslim groups considered by many as radicals at both the religious and political levels. These groups include the Jihad Troops (*Lasykar Jihad*), the Islamic Defense Front (*Front Pembela Islam* – FPI), the Party of Liberation (*Hizb al-Tahrir*), the Indonesian Jihad Council (*Majelis Mujahidin Indonesia*) and some other smaller groups (cf. Bamualim et. al., 2001).

These three developments – by no means exhaustive – appear to some to represent the return of the idea of an Islamic state in Indonesia, and this could allegedly bring the future of democracy and pluralism in Indonesia into question. I would argue, however, that despite the apparent recent tendencies among Indonesian Muslims to cling to political and formal Islam, it remains difficult to imagine that Indonesia would and could be transformed into an Islamic state. The three new tendencies could be very alarming for those who are concerned with the future of democracy in this country, but one should not overestimate them since there are also a number of factors that are at work in Indonesian society that make the realization of an Islamic state in Indonesia only a remote possibility.

Indonesia is undergoing very complex developments. One of the most important questions to answer is in regard to the feasibility and viability of an Islamic state in Indonesia. In addition, and not the least in importance, is, of course, the discussion on the future of democracy in the country in relation to all the recent tendencies towards political and formal Islam.

MODERN NATION-STATE, KHILAFAH AND DAWLAH AL-ISLAMIYYAH

Before going any further, it should be clear that any discussion of Muslim politics should avoid any sweeping generalizations. In fact, there is no single Muslim politics; Islam as a political reality and Muslims as a group are not a monolithic entity. Hefner has persuasively argued that there is no single, civilization-wide pattern of Muslim politics, but a variety of competing organizations and ideals. In his opinion, the modern era's nation making and market globalization have, if anything, only increased pluralism and political contestation and struggle in the Muslim world. As a result, the most significant "clash of cultures" today and in the new millennium is not that between distinct civilizations, but rival political traditions within the same Islamic country (Hefner, 1999:41).

The contest and rivalry among a variety of Islamic political traditions are becoming increasingly complex with the contemporary Islamic revival. At almost the same time as the rising waves of democracy, the so-called revival of religion – including Islam – has also swept many parts of the globe. The increased attachment to Islam has led some Muslims to believe in, and practice, Islam in the way they consider to be the comprehensive holistic manner (*kaffah*). In the political field, their understanding of *kaffah* Islam means the unity of religion (*al-din*) and the state (*al-dawlah*) as had been proposed by some Muslim jurists and political thinkers in the classical and medieval periods of Islam. In short, this is one of the signs of the return of traditional Islamic political concepts and doctrines (*fiqh siyasah*) that actually have little, if any, relevance to democracy and the realities of modern political concepts and systems.

The tendency among some Muslims to return to traditional Islamic politics contributes significantly to renewed tension between Islam and democracy. This tendency once again revives the old debates on relations between Islam and politics. Both at the theoretical and practical levels, Muslim intellectuals, scholars, *ulama*, and leaders have engaged in discussing such issues as the compatibility or incompatibility of Islam and contemporary ideas and practices of democracy, civil society and human rights. Again, there is no single and monolithic answer to these questions. The tendency among Muslims to return to traditional politics, furthermore, produces further complexities of the possible forms of the state where Muslims constitute the dominant or pre-dominant population. As a result, there are at least three forms of state that currently exist or are being conceived among Muslims, each of which has a certain conceptual and practical framework for relations between Islam and the state as well as the place of democracy in the respective form of the state.

The first is the modern nation-state in the form of a republic. A majority of Muslims have accepted this modern form of nation-state based mostly on Western concepts and practice. While most nation-states have adopted secularism, most modern Muslim nation-states view Islam in a different context. A limited number of Muslim countries, like Turkey, have also adopted secularism or quasi-secularism, but most of them have accepted Islam as the official religion while in practice adopting certain secular ideologies. As a result, there is a great deal of difference among modern Muslim nation-states, for instance, on the kind and level of democracy implemented in their respective countries.

It is clear that even though most Muslim countries adopt the modern republic form of nation-state with secular or quasi-secular ideologies, many of them – as can be seen from the Freedom House report – are not yet democratic and are mostly autocratic, repressive and dictatorial in nature. In addition, these Muslim nation-states with secular or quasi-secular ideologies have apparently failed to deliver their promises of modernity and better welfare for their people. This failure has not only eroded the credibility of secular regimes in the eyes of the "Islamists", but also strengthened skepticism of the viability of modern nation-states.

A loss of credibility is also faced by the self-proclaimed "Islamic states" (*al-dawlah al-Islamiyyah*) in the form of traditional monarchies such as Saudi Arabia and the Gulf states. Even though these Islamic states take the Qur'an as the basis of their constitution and *shari`ah* as their legal system, these monarchies are not unlike secular Muslim states in that they are also autocratic, suppressive and dictatorial. Therefore, modern Muslim thinkers criticize these monarchies mainly for their apparent incompatibility with democracy, since all of them disregard basic democratic values such as equality, plurality, free association, press freedom and respect for human rights. On the other hand, the Islamists – as we will discuss below – bitterly criticize the monarchies, because monarchy is incompatible with Islam. They believe that the kingship (*al-mamlakah*) runs contrary not only to the Islamic emphasis on the equality of all believers before God, but also with the principle of *shura* (deliberation) exhorted by the Qur'an.

Despite the unsatisfactory realities of certain existing "Islamic states", the idea of *al-dawlah al-Islamiyyah* continually circulates among certain Muslim groups. In contrast with the very concept of the *khilafah* that proposes a single and universal Islamic political entity transcending the existing Muslim nation-states – as outlined below – the *dawlah Islamiyyah* is an Islamic state in one single country. The very term *al-dawlah al-Islamiyyah* is of course very problematic, because the term had never been used in the classical and medieval periods of Islam. There is no reference to the term in the Qur'an, nor in the classical Islamic political concepts (*fiqh siyasah*) as formulated by such *ulama* as al-Mawardi, al-Ghazali and others. Therefore, the term and concept of *al-dawlah al-Islamiyyah* is a modern invention among Muslims, as an alternative to both the concepts of *khilafah* and modern-nation states based on a Western model.

At the same time, the declining credibility of secular Muslim nation-states and monarchies combined with the renewed attachment to Islam have led certain groups of Muslims, regarded by many as radicals (such as the Hizb al-Tahrir, Gama'ah Tafkir wa al-Hijrah and other splinter groups of the Ikhwan al-Muslimun), to carry out serious attempts to replace secular nation-states and monarchies with the classical model of "Islamic political entity", better known as the caliphate (*al-khilafah*), which in their contemporary discourse is called "universal caliphate". The proponents of the universal caliphate believe that this kind of Islamic political entity led by a single caliph is the answer and the only answer to resolve Muslim disunity and powerlessness vis-à-vis the Western powers (Dekmejian, 1995; Abu-Rabi`, 1996; Lawrence, 1998).

The contemporary revival of the idea of a single and universal caliphate is undoubtedly very problematic. I would argue that the idea is mostly based on historical and religious romanticism as well as a misconception of not only the very meaning of the caliphate but also of the historical development of the caliphate itself in the post-Prophet Muhammad period. Supporters of the caliphate have confused, and have failed to distinguish, between the original and genuine caliphate during the Four Rightly Guided Caliphs (*al-khulafa' al-rashidun*) and the despotic monarchies of the Umayyads, Abbasids and the Ottomans. While at least the first two caliphs i.e. Abu Bakr and Umar ibn al-Khattab were elected on their merit, the subsequent "caliphs" in the post-*al-khulafa' al-rashidun* period were essentially kings (*muluk*) with all their uncontested rights and privileges over all other Muslims. Therefore, modern thinkers of the caliphate such as Jamal al-Din al-Afghani, `Abd al-Rahman al-Kawakibi, Rashid Rida, Sayyid Qutb, and Abu al-A`la al-Mawdudi have all refused to recognize the credibility and legitimacy of those Muslim kings as "caliphs" (cf. Azra, 1996:153ff).

One should be aware, however, that these thinkers proposed different, if not conflicting ideas, on some main themes of the caliphate. al-Kawakibi and Rida, for instance, insisted that the caliph should be an Arab of the Quraysh tribe. Al-Mawdudi on the other hand strongly refutes this idea; to him the caliph should be democratically elected among all Muslims on the basis of merit by a special electing body called "*ahl al-halli wa al-`aqd*", or *Majlis al-Shura*. According to al-Mawdudi the lofty position of the caliph must not be reserved for an Arab, since Arabs have no special privileges over other non-Arab Muslims (cf. Thaib, 1995:79-80).

Despite all the conceptual and practical problems surrounding the feasibility and viability of the caliphate today and in the new millennium, the idea seems to have continually attracted certain Muslim elements throughout the world. In Southeast Asia, particularly in Indonesia, the idea of the caliphate has been put into circulation by such organizations as Hizb al-Tahrir (Party of Liberation) and Jamaah Tarbiyah (the groups for Islamic education) since at least the 1980s. It is important to note that during the Soeharto New Order, these movements had been very careful not to invite the regime to take firm action against their activities. As a result they survived the harsh rule of Soeharto and made their presence more pronounced in the post-Soeharto period.

The Hizb al-Tahrir, that was initially established in Jordan in 1952 by Shaykh Taqi al-Din al-Nabhani and began to spread in Indonesia in the early 1980s, is, no doubt, more prominent in Indonesia since the fall of Soeharto. Calling openly for the establishment of the universal caliphate, the movement held an international conference on *khilafah* in Jakarta in early 2000. Even though the conference invited a number of prominent leaders of the Hizb al-Tahrir from overseas, there were reportedly not many local Muslims in attendance at the conference. The Indonesian Hizb al-Tahrir makes itself even more visible, militant, and vocal with its demonstrations, protesting certain policies of the Indonesian Government such as the plan of President Abdurrahman Wahid to open trade relations between Indonesia and Israel. The Hizb al-Tahrir also actively took to the streets in Jakarta when the Megawati government increased the price of fuel. The Hizb al-Tahrir's largest demonstration was arguably against the US' military operation in Afghanistan in the aftermath of the September 11 attacks on the World Trade Center, New York and the Pentagon in Washington DC. The Hizb al-Tahrir's staunch anti-Americanism is no surprise, since its leaders firmly believe that the US is the mastermind of the so-called "Western conspiracy" to destroy Islam and Muslims (Azra, 2002; Solahuddin, 2002).

Apart from its increased visibility, it is doubtful that the Hizb al-Tahrir's appeals for the establishment of the *khilafah* would be able to win significant support from Indonesian mainstream Muslims, represented by large organizations such as the NU (Nahdlatul Ulama) and Muhammadiyah, and most Muslim political parties basically ignore the issue. The discourse on *khilafah* is conspicuously absent from public discourse. And this clearly indicates that mainstream Muslims are simply not interested in the *khilafah*, let alone in supporting its establishment.

INDONESIAN CASE: THE *PANCASILA*

As mentioned earlier, polemics and debates among Indonesian and foreign observers on the relationships of Islam and politics, and Islam and democracy in the nation-state of Indonesia have once again come to the forefront in Indonesia in the aftermath of the fall of Soeharto. This has a lot to do with the rise of "political Islam" which appears to be one of the most visible political developments in post-Soeharto Indonesia. Many believe that the rise of political Islam represented by so many "Islamic parties" would create serious political repercussions for the future of the Indonesian state that has, until now, been based on *Pancasila* (or Five Pillars).

In that regard, it is worth pointing out that despite the fact that the first pillar of *Pancasila* is belief in the One Supreme God, many foreign observers view this basis of the Indonesian state as primarily secular. This argument is further supported by the fact that Indonesia has not adopted any religion – particularly Islam as the religion to which most Indonesians adhere – as the official religion of the state.

On the other hand, a majority of Muslims would love to argue that Indonesia is neither a secular nor a theocratic state. For them *Pancasila* is in accord with Islamic belief and teachings. The first pillar of *Pancasila*, for instance, in their opinion, is simply another reformulation of the Islamic belief in the One Supreme God (*tawhid*). The case is also the same with the other four pillars of *Pancasila*; just and civilized humanity; unity of Indonesia; democracy which is guided by the inner wisdom of its leaders; social justice for the entire people of Indonesia (cf. Taher, 1997:1-16).

In spite of the Muslim acceptance of *Pancasila*, certain Muslim groups have in the past attempted to replace *Pancasila* with Islam as the basis of the Indonesian state. In the 1950s the Masjumi Party, for instance, struggled in the national parliament to replace *Pancasila* with Islam. Then came the Darul Islam (Islamic State) rebellions under the leadership of Kartosuwirjo in West Java, and Daud Bereueh in Aceh that attempted to establish the Indonesian

Islamic State (*Negara Islam Indonesia* – NII). But as we already know, all these efforts – legally and illegally – failed. It is important to note that non-Muslim groups, mainly Christians and secular circles, retain strong suspicions that Muslims will continue their struggle to establish an Islamic state in Indonesia at the expense of other groups of citizens (cf. Azra, 2000c).

As a result, both the Soekarno and Soeharto regimes took harsh measures not only against any potential Muslim group that subscribed to the idea of Islamic state, but also against any dangerous manifestation of political Islam. Thus, the period from the last years of President Soekarno in the late 1950s and early 1960s, through much of the Soeharto era was marked by the demise of political Islam. For more than forty years, therefore, Islamic political forces were the subject of state repression and manipulation. The New Order regime of Soeharto, in particular, provided no room for political Islam to breathe. Soeharto, in fact, carried out the systematic de-politicization of Islam, the peak of which was the forced adoption of the *Pancasila* as the sole ideological basis of any organization in 1989 (cf. Effendy, 1998).

The opposition to the forced adoption of *Pancasila* as the sole ideological basis of any organization came, of course, not only from many Muslim organizations; most, if not all, Christian organizations opposed the move even more bitterly. Given their past history, however, Muslims became the main subject of suspicion. Therefore, potential Islamic political forces remained under tight control even after their adoption of *Pancasila* as the sole ideological basis.

The retreat of political Islam during much of the New Order period, however, provided a momentum for the rejuvenation of cultural Islam. This began with Soeharto's more accommodative and conciliatory attitude towards Islam and Muslims in the period after Muslims' acceptance of *Pancasila* as the sole ideological basis of any organization in 1989. Conflict, mutual suspicion and hostility between President Soeharto and many Muslim groups had diminished significantly. Soeharto's more conciliatory gestures, some argued, were initiated because he believed that there was nothing to worry about with Islam and Muslims since he had been able to co-opt them. But, by the same token, for certain personal reasons, Soeharto seemed to have instilled a genuine leaning towards Islam, creating closer links with Muslims. As a result, others could also argue that Soeharto had indeed been co-opted by Muslims.

The fact that Soeharto's newly found leaning towards Islam had contributed to the re-flowering of cultural Islam is evident, for instance, from the enactment of the 1989 law establishing an Islamic Court and the 1989 Law of National Education which recognizes the existence of Islamic education on a par with "secular" education. This was followed by the establishment of the All Indonesian Muslim Intellectuals' Association (*Ikatan Cendekiawan Muslim se-Indonesia* – ICMI) chaired by B.J. Habibie, then Minister of Research and Technology; the founding of Islamic banks (Bank Muamalat Indonesia/BMI, and Bank Perkreditan Rakyat Syariah/BPR-Syariah), and the like.

Soeharto undoubtedly had miscalculated and underestimated the far-reaching implications of the so-called "cultural Islam". Not unlike Snouck Hurgronje, the most prominent Islamic Advisor of the Dutch Netherlands Indies government, who advised the Dutch to allow "Islam as cultural phenomenon" to express itself more freely at the expense of political Islam that must be suppressed by any means necessary, in the final analysis, Soeharto had apparently been slowly contained and even dictated to by the growing political repercussions of the cultural Islam. There was a lot of discussion in public of course about whether or not Soeharto with his newly found Islamic leaning was co-opting Islam, or, conversely, whether it was Soeharto who had been co-opted by Muslims.

The most widely discussed example of the political repercussions of the "cultural Islam" is, of course, ICMI. Even though ICMI is formally an association of "Muslim intellectuals" only, there is no doubt that it had played a significant political role since its establishment in 1990. By way of Habibie – often called the "super minister" – ICMI had allegedly engineered an increase in the number of Muslim ministers in the last two Cabinets of Soeharto at the expense of the Christians. It was also assumed that ICMI had played a significant role in the appointment of high-ranking government officials such as provincial governors and the like. The end result of all these new revelations was what some observers called the "honeymoon" between Soeharto and Islam.

Having considered the role of Habibie in the ICMI political maneuvers, it is not surprising that many Muslims considered Habibie and ICMI to be the representatives of Islam and Muslims in general. Habibie's personal piety had only added to this sentiment. Therefore, when Soeharto resigned from the presidency on 19 May 1998, and was replaced by Habibie following the monetary, economic and political crises that had plagued Indonesia since the end of 1997, President Habibie was defended by certain Muslim groups from the attacks of his opponents who questioned the legitimacy of his accession to the presidency in such an unusual way.

Even though President Habibie had abolished the Mass Organization Law that had forced the adoption of *Pancasila* as the sole ideological basis of any organization and abolished the notorious *Pancasila* Training Courses (P4), the *Pancasila* had admittedly won a bad name. There remains a lot of resentment from the Indonesian people, not only against the forced adoption of *Pancasila*, but also against its monopolistic interpretation by the Soeharto regime. As a result, *Pancasila* has been markedly absent from public discourse since the time of Habibie's *interregnum* and his successor Abdurrahman Wahid, and even during the period of President Megawati who replaced Wahid following his impeachment by the Peoples' Consultative Assembly (*Majelis Permusyawaratan Rakyat* – MPR) on 23 June 2001. It is important to point out that there is no significant public discourse among Islamic political parties and mainstream Muslim organizations on the possible replacement of *Pancasila* with any other ideology. There are, of course, smaller groups that appeal for the reintroduction of the "Jakarta Charter" – see below – into the Preamble of the 1945 Constitution – thus allowing for the possible transformation of Indonesia from a *Pancasila* state into an Islamic state; but again – as will be explained below – there is no solid support for this move. All this indicates that *Pancasila* is still regarded by the majority of Indonesian Muslims as the most acceptable, common political platform for a plural Indonesia.

THE RISE AND FALL OF ISLAMIC PARTIES

The Habibie presidency lasted for only fifteen months. Despite his relatively short *interregnum*, one of the most significant contributions of Habibie was the liberalization of Indonesian politics. Following his appointment, Habibie not only freed most political prisoners, abolished restrictions on press freedom and lifted the forced adoption of *Pancasila* as the nation's sole ideology, but also abandoned the three-party system of Indonesian politics as represented by Golkar (Functional Groups), the United Development Party

(*Partai Persatuan Pembangunan* – PPP), and the Indonesian Democratic Party (*Partai Demokrasi Indonesia* – PDI). As might be expected, this last policy has led to the rise of a great number of "Islamic political parties". The abolition of the 1985 Mass Organization Law that made it obligatory for all organizations to adopt *Pancasila* as their sole ideology has only added further momentum to the cause of political Islam. Without such a legal obligation, it was reasonable to expect that many Muslims would seek a return to an Islamic basis for their political parties (Azra, 2000a).

The extent of political euphoria among Muslims can be clearly seen in the proliferation of Islamic parties. There were some forty "Islamic parties" among the 141 parties that formally registered with the Ministry of Justice in the lead-up to the June 1999 general election. After vetting by the Team of Eleven (Tim 11), the committee entrusted with selecting the political parties that would contest the election, forty-eight parties – of which around twenty were Islamic – were deemed eligible to take part (Salim, 1999:7-8). This was far more than the ten Islamic parties that had participated in the 1955 general election.

There has been a lot of discussion of what "Islamic parties" are meant to be. I would propose that there are at least two major elements that identify a party as "Islamic". First, in their documentation, many such parties have officially adopted Islam as their ideological basis. Examples include the United Development Party (*Partai Persatuan Pembangunan* – PPP); the Star and Crescent Party (*Partai Bulan Bintang* – PBB); the United Party (*Partai Persatuan* – PP); Indonesian Islamic Political Party of Masyumi (*Partai Politik Islam Indonesia Masyumi* – PPIIM); Indonesian Islamic Association Party (*Partai Syarekat Islam Indonesia* – PSII); Indonesian Islamic Association Party of 1905 (*Partai Syarekat Islam Indonesia 1905* – PSII 1905); Islamic Nation Party (*Partai Umat Islam* – PUI); and New Masyumi Party (*Partai Masyumi Baru*). There is one party, the KAMI, that has adopted the Qur'an and the Sunnah of the Prophet Muhammad as its basis. Taken together, there are ten parties that have adopted Islam or the original sources of Islamic teachings, instead of *Pancasila*, as their sole ideological basis. This group of Islamic parties, as Fealy proposes, might also be best categorized as "formalist Islamic parties" since those parties have formally adopted Islam or the Qur'an and the Sunnah as their sole ideological basis (Fealy, 2000:3).

The second group of "Islamic parties" are Muslim parties that have retained *Pancasila* as their basis but, at the same time, employ obvious Islamic symbols such as Arabic scripts, the star and crescent, the *ka'bah* (cubic building in Mecca that is the direction faced by Muslims whilst praying), and other symbols that are widely associated with Islam. While these parties are perceived to be "pluralist parties" by adopting *Pancasila*, they are in fact Muslim-based parties for, in some cases, they are supported mostly by members of certain non-political Muslim organizations such as the NU and Muhammadiyah. The parties included in this group are the National Awakening Party (*Partai Kebangkitan Bangsa* – PKB) supported by the NU; the National Mandate Party (*Partai Amanat Nasional* – PAN), many of whose members have backgrounds in Muhammadiyah; Fathers of the Orphans Party (*Partai Abul Yatama*); New Indonesia Party (*Partai Indonesia Baru* – PIB); United Indonesia Solidarity Party (*Partai Solidaritas Uni Indonesia* – Partai SUNI); the Peace-Loving Party (*Partai Cinta Damai* – PCD); Democratic Islam Party (*Partai Islam Demokrasi* – PID); and Indonesian Muslim Nation Party (*Partai Umat Muslimin Indonesia* – PUMI). To this group, one might add two "splinter" parties among the NU members: Nation Awakening Party (*Partai Nahdlatul Ummat* – PNU) and Nation Awakening Party (*Partai Kebangkitan Ummat* –PKU). Both parties have *Pancasila* and Islam as their ideological bases. According to Fealy, all of the parties included in this group might be best described as "pluralist Islamic parties" (Fealy, 2000:4; cf. Kadir, 2001:10-14).

Several months before the June 1999 elections (Azra, 2000a), I predicted that the prospects of these Islamic/Muslim parties were very doubtful. The prediction was mainly based on at least three arguments: First, these parties have caused acute political fragmentation, schisms and conflicts among both the Muslim leadership and the masses. They have created confusion and tension among Muslims at the grass-roots level. As a result, there have been cases of open fighting among fanatical supporters of the Islamic parties, even among members of the NU supporting different parties.

Second, these Islamic/Muslim parties have mostly been trapped in romantic notions of Islamic politics and the "illusion" of the numerical superiority of Muslims among the Indonesian population rather than in political realism. Many Muslim political leaders have based themselves in religious idealism and normativism, believing that all of Indonesia's Muslim population would automatically support them, and would cast their votes for Muslim parties in the election.

Third, they seemed to have underestimated both the PDI-P and Golkar. Many Muslim political leaders believed that Megawati's PDI-P would not achieve a high vote for several reasons; Megawati's gender, her unproven leadership capability, a belief that her influence stems mainly from the charisma of her father, Soekarno and the predominance of non-Muslim and secular figures in the PDI-P leadership. All these proved wrong. They were not able to stop Megawati's PDI-P from winning the election, in spite of appeals from many Muslim *ulama* and leaders to Muslims not to cast their votes for PDI-P. On the other hand, Golkar had also been underestimated because of its past close affiliation with the Soeharto regime. Since the fall of Soeharto, Golkar has come under continued attack as the status-quo party which should be disbanded. The fact is that while most of the Islamic parties have struggled to establish branches in many parts of Indonesia, Golkar was able to keep most of its political machine intact. As a result, to the surprise of many, Golkar became the second winner of the election, finishing second only to the PDI-P.

All of these arguments can perhaps explain why Islamic parties were defeated in the June 1999 election. Taken together, all twenty Islamic parties could only take 37.1 per cent of the total votes. This is a significant decrease compared with the result of the 1955 election, when Islamic parties won 43.9 per cent of the total national vote. In contrast, PDI-P and Golkar were able to win more than half of the total vote at 33.76 per cent and 22.46 per cent respectively and, thus became the winners of the election. Worse still, of the twenty Islamic parties, only four were able to meet the required minimum threshold of two per cent of parliamentary seats (precisely ten seats); these are PPP, PKB, PAN, and PBB.

The fact that Islamic parties were able to gain only a relatively small share of the total vote in the 1999 election worried many Muslims, who believe that it marked the end of political Islam. Certain external factors such as PDI-P's complacency and insensitivity to Muslims' aspirations have, however, provided the stimulus for the fragmented Islamic parties to forge their loose coalition, which was initially called "*Fraksi Islam*" (the Islamic faction) and later known as the "*Poros Tengah*" (Middle Axis). The growing unresolved conflict among supporters of Habibie and Megawati had created an unexpected opportunity for the *Poros Tengah* to propose Abdurrahman Wahid as its presidential candidate in the MPR general session in October 1999.

Considering the fragmentation of Islamic parties, the election of Abdurrahman Wahid as the fourth president of Indonesia, I would argue, was more a result of political expediency rather than of real strength of Islamic/ Muslim political parties. Before long, however, President Wahid proved to be a major disappointment for the Islamic political parties. Wahid showed that he was elected more because of his own personal credentials rather than anything else, including the initial support for his candidacy by the *Poros Tengah*. Through his controversial statements and policies, he soon came into open conflict with the *Poros Tengah*. His erratic attitude and unorthodox management style, that resulted in the so-called scandals of "Bulogate I" and "Bruneigate", and his declaration of martial law, finally led to his impeachment in the Special Session of the MPR on 23 June 2001, to be replaced by Vice President Megawati Soekarnoputri as the fifth president of the republic.

In the light of these dismal recent events, what is the prospect for the Islamic parties, or even political Islam? How viable is the idea of stronger and formal connections between Islam and the Indonesian nation-state?

First of all, the result of the 1999 election once again confirmed that Islamic parties have never been very popular among Indonesian Muslims. One of the most important reasons for this is that most of the Muslim population are leaning more towards what I call "substantive Islam" rather than towards "formalistic Islam" (Azra, 2000a). Although there is a continued tendency among Muslims to undergo some kind of "*santrinization*", this seems to have more to do with ritualistic or cultural Islam at best rather than with the political Islam or Islamic parties. The tendency among Muslims to become more devout (*santri*), at least formally, therefore has not been necessarily translated into a more Islamic political orientation. To put it in a more simple way, belief and rituals is one thing, and political behavior is something else.

At the level of political behavior and political praxis, therefore, there is no convincing sign that Muslims, as represented by Islamic parties, support the idea of formal Islamic politics. Again, this attitude is hardly surprising, since no prominent Muslim political leader subscribes to the idea and aim of establishing an Islamic state in Indonesia at the expense of *Pancasila*. Prominent leaders of Muslim politics such as Abdurrahman Wahid, Amien Rais, Yusril Ihza Mahendra, Deliar Noer, Ahmad Sumargono, Muhaimin Iskandar, Nur Mahmudi Ismail, A.M. Fatwa, Salahuddin Wahid, and many others have declared openly that they and their political parties do not aim at establishing an Indonesian Islamic state (Salim, 2000:10). To this list one might also add the leaders of the largest Muslim socio-religious organizations, such as KH Hasyim Muzadi (General Chairman of the NU) and Ahmad Syafii Maarif (chief national leader of Muhammadiyah), who also dismiss the idea of establishing an Islamic state in Indonesia.

One of Indonesia's most prominent Muslim leaders, Amien Rais, former chief leader of the Muhammadiyah who is the Speaker of the MPR, has, since long before the rise of political Islam, considered the idea of an Islamic state as having no precedent in Islamic history. He therefore argues that there is no religious obligation for Muslims to establish one. Nur Mahmudi Ismail, president of the Justice Party (*Partai Keadilan* – PK) considered to represent the new spirit of contemporary Islamic political revival, also maintains that the most important facet of Islam is the substance, not the label or formalism. He therefore accepts the *Pancasila* as the sole foundation of the Indonesian state. He recognizes that his party is indeed based on Islam, but this does not necessarily mean that it would lead to the struggle of establishing an Islamic state (Salim, 2000:10).

Certain Islamic parties may campaign for an Islamic state. As Liddle and Mujani (2002:2-3) have shown, however, the largest declaredly Islamic party (PPP), won only eleven per cent of the national vote at the 1999 general election and holds twelve per cent of the seats in the Parliament (*Dewan Perwakilan Rakyat* – DPR) and ten per cent of the seats in the MPR, which has the authority to amend the constitution. The campaign is supported by the PBB, which won only two per cent of the 1999 vote and has three per cent of the seats in the DPR and two per cent in the MPR. All the remaining parties with a total of eighty-two per cent of the national vote, seventy-five per cent of the DPR and seventy per cent of the MPR seats will be very unlikely to support the idea of an Islamic state and, in all likelihood, will support the maintenance of the Indonesian state in its current form.

Furthermore, as I argued elsewhere, the adoption of Islamic political formalism and symbolism by Islamic/Muslim parties in post-Soeharto Indonesian politics seems not to have been motivated to any significant extent by "Islamic ideology", but rather by a power struggle, or, to put it more blatantly, by a lust for power among Muslim political leaders. More than anything else, political pragmatism is the most important feature of political behavior of most Muslim political leaders. One example of this political pragmatism can be seen in the acceptance of Hamzah Haz, chairman of the PPP, to be vice president to President Megawati in the 2001 MPR Special Session. This is clearly in contradiction with the PPP and Hamzah Haz's earlier stance in 1999, that opposed the presidential candidacy of Megawati for gender reasons; claiming that Islam prohibits women from holding leadership positions. Therefore, the so-called "Islamic ideology" has, in many cases, no clear relevance to political realities and development.

Another obvious indication of this tendency can be seen in the current split of Islamic/Muslim parties. The split within political parties is, of course, not unique among Islamic parties, since non-Islamic parties such as the PDI-P and Golkar are also afflicted by such divisions. But given the Islamic teachings on Islamic solidarity (al-ukhuwwah al-Islamiyyah), the split of Islamic parties for some people is a baffling phenomenon.

The current split within Islamic parties can be observed clearly in the PBB. The intense conflict between Yusril Ihza Mahendra, chairman of the party, on the one hand, and Hartono Mardjono, on the other, resulted in the expulsion of the latter from the PBB. Hartono finally established his own party, Partai Islam Indonesia (PII, Indonesian Islamic Party) in the middle of March 2002, at the same time losing his case in court against Yusril Ihza Mahendra.

A much more intense conflict and split has taken place within the PKB. The root cause of the split in the PKB was the unsupportive attitude of Matori Abduldjalil, chairman of the party, towards the embattled President Abdurrahman Wahid, one of the most important founders of the PKB, who was later impeached. Joining the Special Session of the MPR in June 2001 that unseated President Wahid, Matori was expelled by Wahid from the PKB. But Matori refused to accept the decision, and kept the chairmanship of the PKB while Wahid appointed Alwi Shihab as the caretaker of the party. Various attempts to settle the case and reconcile the two camps proved futile, and each camp finally held their own extra-ordinary congress in early 2002.

The PPP is also afflicted by division. The main cause was the decision of the PPP national leadership under Hamzah Haz, who is also vice president of the republic, to postpone the national party congress from 2002 to 2004. Certain elements in the PPP opposed this move, believing that it was simply an attempt by Hamzah Haz to maintain his power in the PPP in order to pursue his own political agenda in the general election of 2004. The dissenting elements in the PPP finally broke away from Hamzah Haz's PPP and established the PPP-Reformasi (Reform-PPP) under the leadership of Zainuddin MZ, the most popular *da`i* (preacher), who has been dubbed the *"kiyai sejuta ummat"* (preacher to millions of *ummah*) in contemporary Indonesia.

It is important to mention that, in addition to the splits in and between Islamic parties, new parties are continuously being founded in anticipation of the 2004 general election. Many of them are Islamic parties. According to the Ministry of Justice and Human Rights, there are now almost 300 parties registered with the department. One might wonder how difficult it will be for the National Election Commission to reduce the number of these parties to a more a reasonable one, so that they will not be counterproductive for the development of a healthy democracy in Indonesia.

THE PROSPECT OF ISLAMIC FORMALISM

The failure of Islamic parties, again, is a clear indication of the unpopularity of formal Islam among Indonesian Muslims. Such is the case with the growing appeals by certain groups of Muslims for the application of the *shari`ah* (Islamic law) in Indonesia. The idea and appeal of the *shari`ah* is, of course, not new. It can be traced back to the days surrounding Indonesian independence when Indonesian leaders formulated the original 1945 Indonesian constitution. At the initial stage of the formulation of the 1945 constitution, Muslim leaders introduced to the Preamble a phrase stating that "the Indonesian state is based on the belief in the One, Supreme God with the obligation for the adherents of Islam to implement the *shari`ah*". The final seven words of this stipulation are known in Indonesia as "the seven words" of the *Piagam Jakarta* (Jakarta Charter).

Before long this stipulation was dropped because of the objections of Christian leaders and secular nationalists. They argued that the national constitution should not give preferential treatment to any religious group. Furthermore, the constitution should maintain the commitment to national plurality. Because of these reasons, Muslim leaders agreed to omit the "seven words" of the Jakarta Charter (Taher, 1998:38-9), however the debate on the application of the *shari`ah* continued. Muslim leaders once again brought their case before the Constituent Assembly in 1959 which ended with the Decree issued by President Soekarno on 5 July 1959 mandating a return to the Indonesian Constitution of 1945. This meant that the Jakarta Charter, the basis for the application of the *shari`ah*, was abandoned.

It is clear that the issue is far from being resolved. The issue of the application of the *shari`ah,* arose again in both the post-Soekarno and post-Soeharto era. The sessions of the MPR-S in 1966 and 1967, following the fall of Soekarno, were tense with rumors of Muslim proposals to bring forward the Jakarta Charter for deliberation. As one might expect, however, this aspiration was suppressed by the army-backed Soeharto regime. In the post-Soeharto period, some of the newly-founded Islamic parties – discussed above – once again demanded the legalization of the Jakarta Charter as an integral part of the Preamble of the 1945 Constitution (Salim, 2000:13-14).

The appeal for the application of the *shari`ah* gained momentum with the adoption during the Habibie presidency of Islamic law in the province of Aceh as an integral part of the proposed solution of the Aceh unrest. There are at least three main reasons behind this move; firstly, that the majority of the population of Aceh province – as well as Indonesia as a whole – are Muslims; secondly, it is the *shari`ah* that would be able to resolve the breakdown of law and order in the post-Soeharto era, and; thirdly, it is only the *shari`ah* that could overcome the increase in such social ills afflicting Indonesian society as drug abuse, crime and the like.

The adoption of Islamic law in Aceh was finally approved by the central government when President Megawati signed the Law of Negeri Aceh Darussalam in early 2002 which includes the special provision for the province to implement *shari`ah*. The official enactment of the *shari`ah* by the Aceh provincial government in conjunction with the celebration of Islamic new year of 1423 AH on 15 March created mixed feelings both in Aceh and other circles at the national level. Many are doubtful that Islamic law could be enforced successfully since there exist many constraints within the *shari`ah* as well as in Acehnese society itself. It seems so far that the implementation of *shari`ah* simply means the adoption of the Muslim dress-code, particularly the requirement for Muslim women to wear the *jilbab* (headcover). It remains to be seen whether the implementation of *shari`ah* will include such penalties as the amputation of hands or legs for thieves, or stoning to death for those committing adultery.

Support for the application of the *shari`ah* peaked in the period surrounding the 2000 annual session of the MPR this year. Certain Islamic parties, particularly the PPP, have openly declared their intention to reintroduce the Jakarta Charter in the MPR session, thus allowing for the application of Islamic law. It seems unnecessary to provide a detailed account of the debates surrounding this. What is important is that the move is strongly opposed by a majority of MPR members, and the issue of the application of the *shari`ah* once again failed in the highest Indonesian political institution. The issue was not on the agenda of the Special MPR Session of 2001; and it is very doubtful, therefore, whether the issue will appear on the MPR agenda in the near future.

Despite the ill-fated response, the aspiration of Islamic law appears to continue to attract certain circles of Muslims. In late October 2000, some Muslims in South Sulawesi province appealed for the *shari`ah* in their region. Later the supporters of the *shari`ah* formed a special committee to prepare for the implementation of *shari`ah* in South Sulawesi province but, thus far, there has been no concrete result from this move. The districts of Cianjur and Tasikmalaya in West Java have also attempted to implement *shari`ah* and have apparently developed a clear and comprehensive concept and framework of how the implementation could work. It seems that the implementation of *shari`ah* – as is the case in Aceh – is ad-hoc and partial, related only to the Islamic dress-code for Muslim women. In the end, *shari`ah* is treated simply like an elixir to heal all kinds of social ills.

Apart from the problematic implementation of *shari`ah* in these areas, one important trend now worth watching are the attempts by proponents of the *shari`ah* to achieve their aims by taking advantage of the decentralization processes now taking place in Indonesia as a whole. They are taking this

approach because of their failure at the national level through the DPR and
MPR. Whether this new approach through the provinces and districts will
be successful remains to be seen. One thing is clear, however: these moves
at the provincial and district level will result in more complications for the
local autonomy and decentralization processes.

The case is the same with the worrisome phenomenon of the Lasykar
Jihad and other similar groups that are also seeking the implementation of
Islamic law. Worse still, in the name of Islamic law they attack nightclubs,
discotheques and houses allegedly used for prostitution. These radical groups
have also been very active in mass demonstrations against the US when the
US was conducting military operations in Afghanistan in the aftermath of
the September 11 tragedy. The slow and indecisive response of the Megawati
government to both US policies as well as to these groups has damaged
the image of Indonesian Islam. When the government finally took harsh
measures to put an end to mass-demonstrations against the US that could
have threatened Indonesia's political stability, the image of Indonesian Islam
worsened further.

I believe that the rise of these radical groups has more to do with the
failure of the government to enforce the law, thus providing them with a
vista or *raison d'etre* to take the law into their own hands. As long as the
government is, therefore, weak and indecisive, these groups will hold sway
at certain times and places to do what they call "*amar ma'ruf nahi munkar*"
– enjoin good and prohibit evil in their own way, including holding mass
rallies and demonstrations against any side, either in Indonesia or abroad,
that they consider has disregarded Islam and Muslims.

In conclusion, the keys to addressing the issue, including the appeals by,
and attempts of, certain groups of Muslims for the implementation of *shari'ah*
as well as increased radicalism among certain splinter groups are; firstly, re-
strengthening of the state and good governance; secondly, enhancement of
democracy and civil society; thirdly, reinforcement of law and order; and
lastly, speeding up economic recovery. If these solutions are not addressed,
Indonesia will continue to face serious consequences relating to all of the
issues outlined above.

There has been intense discussion on certain factors that have contributed
to the weakness of democracy in Indonesia as well as in many parts of the

Muslim world. These factors are the challenges that would greatly affect the development and enhancement of a democratic culture in this, the most populous Muslim country.

The first factor is the weakness in infrastructure or the prerequisites that are crucial and instrumental in the development and consolidation of democracy.

Indonesia, like most Muslim countries, is less developed in terms of education and economic prosperity. Not only that, but Indonesia can be classified as a Weberian "soft state", in which patrimonialism, corruption, cronyism and nepotism are rampant and significantly inhibiting economic development and distorting socio-cultural improvement.

A second factor is the continued tendency among Muslims to believe in the unity and merger of religion and politics. This belief owes its origin to the classical Islamic political theory that religion and the state are not separate or separable institutions. Even though, in practice, Indonesia – like many other Muslim countries – has made a distinction between the two, there are Muslim groups that remain insistent on the merger of religion and state. Furthermore, in Indonesia, this nostalgia translates into Islamic formalism in politics as is evident in the formation and proliferation of Islamic parties in the post-Soeharto period.

A third factor is the almost total absence of a democratic culture, not only among the Indonesian Muslim masses but also among the Islamic political elite. This tendency can be clearly seen in the fact that the dominant culture among certain segments of Muslims, particularly among the so-called traditionalists, is the uncontested loyalty to *kiyai* (traditional *ulama*) or other charismatic leaders. These *kiyai*s not only elicit an almost blind loyalty from their supporters, but also misuse and abuse traditional Islamic political concepts such as *bughat* (dissension), *jihad* against any political opponents, *bay'ah* (oath of loyalty) and other related concepts in order to support an undemocratic culture and the policies of the ruling elite.

A fourth factor is the weakness or dysfunction of civil society groups or organizations. Indonesia has a great number of Islamic civil society institutions in the form of voluntary organizations and groups that have been in existence since colonial times. Despite its existence, it must be admitted that Islamic civil society has not been able to play its crucial role effectively in

the development and consolidation of democracy. In fact, Indonesian Islamic
civil society had been made dependent on, or been co-opted by, the Soeharto
regime. In the post-Soeharto period, many – if not most – Indonesian Islamic
civil society institutions seem to suffer from some kind of disorientation,
and worse still have been pulled into practical politics.

There is no doubt that democratic ferment is considerable among the
bulk of Indonesian Muslims; this augurs well for the enhancement and
empowerment of the democratization process. Indonesia is now in transition
to a more authentic and genuine democracy. The process is, at times, very
painful and costly but the ferment for democracy in the form of political
parties, a free press, free association and civil society should be kept alive
and enhanced.

Enhancement of these important institutions for democracy to work will
surely contribute greatly to the efforts to establish good governance. The
construction of democratic, credible and accountable governance will restore
the faith of Muslims in democracy and, thus, will bring them to accept the
realities of modern politics rather than contemplating romantic ideals of the
past that are unworkable in contemporary times.

Finally, it is also imperative to reconcile the "Islamicness" of many
Muslims with the supposed unity between *din* and *dawlah* through a
kind of "substantification" of politics with the universal values of Islam
in contemporary politics. "Substantification" of politics simply means the
adoption of universal values of Islam such as *al-musawa* (equality), *al-'adal*ah
(justice), *shura* (deliberation), *tasamuh* (tolerance of plurality) as well as
Islamic ethics – that had been emphasized time and again by Muslim political
thinkers – in contemporary political concepts, systems and practice. With
this kind of "substantification", the opposition of some Muslims who consider
democracy to be a mere translation of secularism could be reduced.

CHAPTER 2

THE ISLAMIC FACTOR
IN POST-SOEHARTO INDONESIA

*20 years of Islamic resurgence have not created a Muslim political consensus.
Nor have those years united Muslims around a common leader. But it is
important to recognize this much in Muslim Indonesian politics: years
of struggle against Soeharto's dictatorship deepened the mainstream's
commitment to democracy, constitutional law, civil independence, and
peaceful reformation (Hefner, 1999: 64).*

The fall of Soeharto from power in May 1998 following the country's
monetary and economic crises heralded a new phase of Indonesia's
history. This new phase was marked not just by the transfer of power
from Soeharto to B.J. Habibie, his vice president, but more importantly
by a number of significant changes that took place soon after Habibie's
installation as president.

As mentioned in the previous chapter, one of the most obvious of these
was the rise of a great number of Islamic parties when Habibie formally
decided to abandon the three-party system which had been implemented
forcefully by Soeharto. The formation of Islamic parties was given added
momentum by the abolition of the 1985 Mass Organization Law, that had
made it obligatory for all organizations to adopt *Pancasila* as their "sole

ideological basis". Without such a legal obligation, it was reasonable to expect that many Muslims would seek a return to an Islamic basis for their political parties.

Although religious parties are not confined to Islam, and there are Catholic and Protestant parties as well, the establishment of Islamic parties has opened up a heated public debate. Many intellectuals and political observers have questioned the motives and logic of the rise of so many Islamic parties, as well as debating the political implications and the repercussions for the future of Indonesian politics. Minority Catholic and Protestant groups, supported by secular groups, have also voiced their concerns. They feel that the existence of Islamic parties is cause for anxiety and are worried that such parties will increase what they call "political sectarianism". In their opinion, the rise of Islamic parties could eventually lead to national disintegration (*Republika*, 27 July 1998).

The existence of such strong feelings among Christians is not surprising. It is no secret that for many years Christians have believed that Muslims generally still support the establishment of an Islamic state in Indonesia at their expense. The truth of this sweeping generalization has long been contested by many Muslims. Nurcholish Madjid's idea of "Islam yes, *partai Islam* no" or Abdurrahman Wahid's "indigenization of Indonesian Islam" are good examples of the thinking of Indonesian Muslim scholars who are, in principle, opposed to the idea of an Islamic state in Indonesia. Such scholars have attracted a large following among Indonesian Muslims, a fact that tends to be overlooked by many non-Muslims.

The replacement of *Pancasila* with Islam as the ideological foundation of some political parties has only increased the suspicions of non-Muslims. Within this context, it is necessary to discuss briefly the possible attitude of Islamic parties to the old idea of establishing an Islamic state in Indonesia.

POLITICAL FRAGMENTATION

As indicated above, the appearance of numerous Islamic parties has created public discussion among non-Muslims and Muslims alike. Among the central questions discussed are the motives and aims of these parties; whether, for example, they have been established for genuinely Islamic motives, in a bid for power, or as an expression of political euphoria, and whether they would ultimately aim to establish an Islamic state in Indonesia.

Many Indonesian Muslim scholars argue that the rise of Islamic parties in the post-Soeharto era is simply an expression of *era reformasi*, which is generally understood by the Muslim elite to mean political freedom and democracy. The explosion in the number of Islamic political parties is merely the expression of an almost uncontrollable political euphoria among the Muslim political elite, who had been suppressed or at least marginalized for most of the Soeharto era. The existence of so many Islamic political parties could be counterproductive for the unity and welfare of Indonesian Muslim society at large.

I have put forward a similar argument, saying in the media that the establishment of so many Islamic parties has been motivated more by the lust for power of the Muslim political elite than by genuinely religious motives (*The Jakarta Post*, 19 November 1998). The Muslims involved in establishing the parties have shown a strong tendency to promote their own interests and those of their group. As an illustration of this, it is only necessary to look at the proliferation of political parties within both the traditionalist (NU) and modernist (Muhammadiyah) wings of Indonesian Islam, and the competition between their leaders. If the elite of these two wings were more serious about promoting religious interests, they would have established fewer Islamic parties – preferably just one for the traditionalist and another for the modernist spectrum.

The contest for power among the Muslim leadership has led to much wider fragmentation of the Islamic-oriented political camp. This is clear from the split that has occurred among the supporters of the Islamic parties that participated in the general election of 1955. On the modernist wing, support for the old Masyumi Party is now split among at least three parties: the PBB, led by Yusril Ihza Mahendra; the New Masyumi Party (PMB), led by Ridwan Saidi; and the Political Party of Indonesian Islam Masyumi (PPIIM), led by Abdullah Hehamahua. To these, one should also add the Muslim Nation Party (PUI), led by Deliar Noer; the PK, led by Nur Mahmudi Ismail and the PAN, led by Amien Rais, former Chair of Muhammadiyah. Though PAN is not formally an Islamic party, its main constituency is the Muhammadiyah.

On the traditionalist wing, support for the NU is split among at least four parties: the PKB, founded by Abdurrahman Wahid, leader of the NU; the PKU, led by Yusuf Hasyim; the Party of the Awakening of the Muslim Nation (PNU), led by Syukron Makmun; and the Indonesian National Solidarity Party (SUNI), led by Abu Hasan.

Other remnants of smaller Islamic parties that existed in 1955 are also deeply divided. The PSII is divided into two parties: the PSII and the PSII 1905. Then there is the Association of Islamic Education (Perti), which has split into four parties; and the Party of the Islamic Sufi Brotherhood Association (PPTI), which is now divided into three parties. In addition to these, one must include the PPP, a remnant of the New Order political institution, which is now led by Hamzah Haz, an NU member. As indicated earlier, not all of the forty-odd Islamic parties registered with the Ministry of Justice were able to participate in the June 1999 general election. After selection by the Team of Eleven, forty-eight parties were found eligible to participate, of which around twenty were Islamic parties. Even though their number had been significantly reduced, it must be admitted that they were still too numerous.

There are no great differences among Islamic parties as far as their religious tendencies are concerned; they all belong to either the modernist or the traditionalist wing of Indonesian Islam. Neither are there any significant religious quarrels among them, as there were during the 1955 election campaign; the issue of *khilafiyyah*, or differences on petty religious issues are almost absent in the discourse of contemporary Islamic parties. Thus what becomes clear is that a political struggle is under way among party leaders to win the support and loyalty of the Muslim masses.

For this purpose, each of the Islamic parties includes Muslim religious scholars (*ulama*) in its leadership. A number of *ulama* were involved in the campaign of 1999. Some made use of religious themes, quoting verses of the Qur'an, for example, for their own political ends. The conflicting interpretations among the *ulama* of each party led not only to socio-religious controversy, but also to open conflict; violence erupted among supporters of the PKB and PPP, for instance, in several places in Central and East Java.

A RETURN OF ISLAMIC POLITICS?

The rise of Islamic parties has once again revived the old discussion among Muslims about the nature of the relationship between Islam and politics. Furthermore, it has created concerns among some Muslim scholars, such as Kuntowijoyo and Nurcholish Madjid, that "cultural" Islam, which was predominant in the Muslim approach during the Soeharto era, is being replaced by the "political" Islam represented by these Islamic parties (cf. Azra, 1999a).

It is necessary to recollect that, as a result of Soeharto's repression of Islamic politics, Muslims, whether they liked it or not, had to employ "cultural" Islam in order to advance Islam and Muslim interests. Although he was clearly not a supporter of Soeharto's policy, Nurcholish Madjid provided a strong impetus to the rise of "cultural" Islam through his famous slogan, "Islam yes, partai Islam no".

The end result of "cultural" Islam has been the renaissance of Islamic religion and culture in Indonesia. Among the indicators that are often quoted in this respect are the increased number of mosques, madrasah (Islamic schools) and hajj pilgrimages to Mecca. Others are the establishment of ICMI (the Indonesian Association of Muslim Intellectuals), Bank Muamalat Indonesia (the Islamic Bank), Islamic insurance (takaful) and the like since the early 1990s. All these developments have also had political implications. ICMI, for instance, has played an important political role since its establishment in 1990, bringing Islam into the power center in the last years of the Soeharto era.

The rise of Islamic parties has thus brought the continued existence of "cultural" Islam into question. There is concern among Muslim scholars that "political" Islam could not only lead to schisms and conflicts among the Muslim leadership, but also result in the formalization of Islam in Indonesian politics. But how likely is such a formalization? In my opinion, the "formalization" of Islam by way of Islamic parties does not necessarily signal the return of an authentic Islamic politics or, more exactly, of an Islamic ideology that aims to establish an Islamic state of the type mooted in the 1950s.

This argument is based on the fact that the new Islamic parties have not so far questioned the validity of Pancasila as the basis of the Indonesian state.

There is not a single statement in their official documents to indicate that they wish to replace *Pancasila* with Islam. Leaders of Islamic parties have never voiced any objection to *Pancasila* as the state ideology. The fact that Muslim and non-Muslim politicians alike wanted the People's Consultative Assembly (MPR) to lift the decree requiring political parties to use *Pancasila* as their sole ideology was to counteract former President Soeharto's efforts to retain power and influence. Similarly, the validity of *Pancasila* was not questioned during the 1999 election campaign. In short, the agenda of Islamic parties in the post-Soeharto era appears to be centered, not on Islamic ideology, but on power politics.

Furthermore, it is important to point out that parties with a religious affiliation are not popular among the masses. The results of the 1999 election show that most voters voted for secular parties such as the Indonesian Democratic Party of Struggle (PDI-P) and Golkar. Islamic parties, such as the PPP, PBB and PK, gained far fewer votes. It is not surprising that many Muslims felt that this marked the end of "Islamic politics". But the failure of Islamic parties at the poll can be viewed as a blessing in disguise for Muslim political leaders. It led not only to much soul searching among them, but also to a search for ways to put aside their differences and create a unified vision.

The leaders of Islamic parties increasingly realized that they would have to forge their own political front, known as *Poros Tengah* (the central axis). As their failure at the general election proved, however, a simple coalition of Islamic parties would not be sufficient to gain them the political influence they desired. It is only through coalition with the PKB and PAN – which are not formally Islamic parties – or with other groups in the MPR, such as the Golkar axis or the PDI-P axis, that these Islamic parties can hope to have a say in the presidential election and in the future development of Indonesian politics.

THE CENTRAL AXIS

As I have argued above, whether Islamic parties will play a significant political role depends greatly both on the internal unity of Islamic parties and on external factors, particularly political developments within Golkar and the PDI-P. Indeed, it was external factors that provided the stimulus for the Islamic parties to unite and establish their own political front, initially called *Fraksi Islam* (the Islamic faction), and consisting of the PPP, PBB, PK, PNU and other Islamic parties.

The fact that Islamic parties gained only a small share of the vote at the 1999 election worried many Muslims, who believed that it marked the end of Islamic politics. This pessimism is, I would suggest, based mainly on the false assumption that Islamic political aspirations are represented only by Islamic parties. Muslims forget that there are other parties, such as the PAN, PKB and even Golkar, which in one way or another take Muslim aspirations into serious consideration. They also tend to forget the important political role that the two largest socio-religious Islamic organizations, the NU and Muhammadiyah, could play.

The PDI-P's political insensitivity to Muslim aspirations provided an important stimulus to the establishment of a unified front for Islamic parties (Azra, 1999b). Muslims were very suspicious of the PDI-P, first, because most of its candidates were non-Muslims; second, because it intended to establish official diplomatic relations with Israel; and third, because if the PDI-P were to gain power it would "secularize" Indonesian politics by, for instance, abolishing the Ministry of Religious Affairs. All these issues were, of course, very sensitive ones for Indonesian Muslims. It was fair to expect that Megawati and other PDI-P leaders would be sensitive to Muslim concerns and clarify these issues. Unfortunately, however, Megawati failed to do so when she delivered her long-awaited speech in August 1999. To the dismay of many Muslims, she used the opportunity mainly to criticize President Habibie, not to address the above-mentioned issues.

Meanwhile, political tension escalated rapidly between the Habibie and Megawati camps in the contest for the presidency. Many people felt alarmed and threatened when Megawati's fanatical supporters launched a "blood oath" campaign in various cities in Java to show their resolute support for her quest for the presidency. As one might expect, the Habibie camp responded quickly by organizing and consolidating Muslim groups who considered Habibie to be the representative of Islam; they were ready to meet the challenge, and even to raise the banner of *jihad*, in defense of Habibie.

This has encouraged many concerned citizens to propose alternative presidential candidates. Among the leading figures most often mentioned in public discourse are Nurcholish Madjid and Abdurrahman Wahid. Madjid has repeatedly stated his unwillingness to become a candidate, on the grounds that it is inappropriate for someone like himself who is not involved in party politics to stand as a presidential candidate. He argues that if Indonesians are serious about democracy, they need to propose someone who is already involved in politics.

With Madjid's refusal, Abdurrahman Wahid has increasingly become the only alternative candidate. At the outset, Wahid seemed to have little interest in the position. On more than one occasion he has said that he preferred to support Megawati for the presidency. But Wahid is indeed interested in the job, and has given only qualified support to Megawati. He often says that even though he supports her, the NU *ulama* do not, and he cannot force them to do so. On one occasion, during a public lecture in Singapore, he pointed out that even though he personally supported Megawati, Islamic law (*shari'ah*) did not allow a woman to hold such a high office; and he could not change the *shari'ah*. Wahid is proving himself to be a politician *par excellence*.

The momentum for Wahid's candidacy has been boosted by the rise of the *Poros Tengah*, which is in effect an extension of the *Fraksi Islam*. This axis was initially proposed by the leaders of several Islamic parties, especially Hamzah Haz of the PPP and Nur Mahmudi Ismail of the PK. The crucial figure behind the central axis is, of course, Amien Rais of the PAN, who has strongly and unceasingly promoted Wahid's candidacy for the presidency. The central axis seems to be an important factor in the General Session of the MPR. This can be seen in the election of Amien Rais as Chair of the MPR after beating a coalition of the PDI-P and PKB. Interestingly, Golkar also supported Amien Rais. This was followed by the election of Akbar Tanjung, the head of Golkar, as Chair of the People's Representative Assembly (DPR). These developments signal the possibility of the central axis forging a coalition with Golkar in the presidential election.

There is, however, skepticism among some PKB leaders, particularly Matori Abdul Djalil (General Chair of the PKB) and a number of NU leaders (kiyai), about the seriousness and solidarity of the central axis in supporting Wahid's candidacy. They are suspicious that, in particular, Amien Rais, Yusril Ihza Mahendra of the PBB and Hamzah Haz of the PPB are supporting Wahid in order to achieve their own ends. It is also no secret that Hamzah

Haz is a strong supporter of Habibie. At this juncture, one has to admit that the central axis remains a fragile coalition.

CONCLUSION

It is clear that the Islamic factor has played an important role in the power struggle leading up to the presidential election. One could reasonably expect that Islam would play a similar role in Indonesian politics in future, simply because Islam is too important to ignore. But, as Hefner (1999) points out, it is sanguine to expect that Islam will become a permanent and united political force under a single leadership. Although the "Muslim force" appears to be united under the banner of the central axis, this coalition is unlikely to last for long.

Furthermore, it is important to note that the events of the MPR General Session have shown that the Islamic factor has not played an important role in formal Islamic politics, as represented by the Islamic parties. The more influential form of Islamic politics has been expressed through Islamic substantive politics, as represented in the emergence of personalities such as Amien Rais, Abdurrahman Wahid, or even Akbar Tanjung.

EPILOGUE

As I predicted in my chapter, which was written before the General Session of the MPR, the central axis did indeed play a crucial role in the election of Abdurrahman Wahid as the fourth president of the Republic of Indonesia. There is no doubt that the prospects for Wahid's candidacy improved greatly with the rejection, by a slim majority of MPR members, of President B.J. Habibie's accountability speech. Deeply disappointed by this rejection, Habibie withdrew from the presidential race. Golkar, his main supporter, was left in disarray. The party was left with little choice but to support Wahid, who had been nominated by the Muslim reform group (*Fraksi Reformasi*, consisting of the PAN and PK), and by the PKB and the PPP. With Golkar's support, Wahid's ascendancy to the presidency was virtually guaranteed.

The election of Megawati as vice president was in large part influenced by the non-parliamentary "direct action" of her fanatical supporters. On learning that Megawati had been beaten in the MPR, the PDI-P masses who had surrounded the MPR buildings from the beginning of the General Session quickly expressed their anger and frustration (see Chapter 3). They took to the streets in Jakarta, Solo, Bali and other places, burning and destroying buildings and other public utilities. Alarmed by the almost uncontrollable mass riots, Wahid, TNI commanders and leaders of other parties agreed to give the vice presidential post to Megawati.

A week after the election, President Wahid formed his first cabinet. Generally regarded as a cabinet of national reconciliation and integration, its composition has nevertheless caused disappointment in some quarters. The cabinet contains a significant number of military members, and some ministers are regarded as inappropriate for their appointed ministry. Perhaps even more damaging, some members of the cabinet are survivors of the New Order regime.

It is too early to predict the future of the Wahid government. In addition to the mixed feelings of the public in general about the cabinet, it can fairly be assumed that Indonesian economic recovery will not be as rapid as most Indonesians expect, and may be a very slow process indeed. President Wahid, of course, faces the daunting task of rebuilding democracy in Indonesia, as well as promoting national and social integration.

It remains to be seen how President Abdurrahman Wahid will manage to keep together the disparate Islamic alliance both within and outside government. Thorny and longstanding issues, such as the possible opening of trade relations with – even official recognition of – Israel, have divided Muslims. Similarly, the president has harshly criticized the Ministry of Religious Affairs, which he views as having favored Muslims at the expense of non-Muslims. These two issues have created strong criticism, not only from non-NU Muslim groups such as *Komite Indonesia untuk Solidaritas Dunia Islam* (KISDI), but also from Salahuddin Wahid, the president's younger brother, who is active in the PKU.

It is, therefore, apparent that the viability of the Islamic coalition is, in fact, mainly dependent on Wahid himself. If he continues to promote issues that are sensitive for most Muslims, he is certain to face opposition from within this coalition.

CHAPTER 3

CIVIL SOCIETY AND DEMOCRATIZATION DURING THE PRESIDENCY OF ABDURRAHMAN WAHID

With the fair and peaceful election of 2004, the Indonesian transition to democracy appears to have been completed. The complex, long and tiring election year in Indonesia is finally over in a surprisingly peaceful manner. The general elections began with the legislature elections on 5 April, followed by the First Round of the presidential election on 4 July, and ended with the Second Round of the presidential election on 20 September. Despite the bomb blast on 9 September in front of the Australian embassy in Jakarta, the final run-off of the presidential election ran smoothly with Susilo Bambang Yudhoyono and Muhammad Jusuf Kalla, presidential and vice-presidential candidates respectively, defeating Megawati Soekarnoputri, the incumbent president, and Hasyim Muzadi, her vice-presidential candidate.

The completion of the election and the formation of a new government has accelerated the peaceful transition of Indonesia from authoritarianism to democracy. The fall of authoritarianism under President Soeharto in May 1998, after thirty-two years in power, brought not only new optimism about the future of democracy in this country, but also seemingly endless political euphoria. The acute political fragmentation that followed the implementation of multi-party politics by President B.J. Habibie, which resulted in no single party gaining a majority in parliament in the aftermath of the 1999 general election in the midst of continued economic crisis and social disintegration, however, took its toll.

There is little doubt that civil society played an important role in the eventual fall of the Soeharto regime. The consolidation of civil society that regained momentum in the last decade of the Soeharto era resulted in the involvement of many civil society leaders and organizations in the newly-found democracy. This new tendency has, however, created a kind of unmaking process of civil society, particularly during the presidency of Abdurrahman Wahid. The relatively stable political situation during the era of President Megawati Soekarnoputri has not been able to create a conducive environment for the reconsolidation of civil society. It remains to be seen whether civil society will be able to reconsolidate itself in the next five years during the period of the new government of Yudhoyono and Kalla. This paper is an attempt to discuss civil society in Indonesia during the period of democratization since the fall of the Soeharto regime.

THE MAKING AND UNMAKING OF CIVIL SOCIETY

The hopes of Indonesians for a peaceful transition to, and consolidation of, democracy ran high when Indonesia, under the leadership of President B.J. Habibie, was able to conduct relatively free and fair general elections in June 1999. Moreover, the election in October 1999 of Abdurrahman Wahid, a national civic leader who was also the leader of the Democratic Forum (Forum Demokrasi/Fordem), further boosted hopes. But it is important to point out, as some scholars believe, that the successful transition to democracy depended not only on free elections and a good balance of power among government bodies, but also on a strong civil society that is instrumental in the building of civility, freedom and dignity, and on a civic culture in parliament and in society as a whole.

Given that the vast majority of the Indonesian population is Muslim, it is only fair to expect Muslims and Islam to play a positive role in the enhancement of civil society and, in turn, democracy. As the Japanese scholar Mitsuo Nakamura points out, however, there remains a serious question concerning the relevance of Islamic civil society for civility and democracy and whether or not the growth of Muslim civil society is conducive to democratization (Nakamura, 2001:13).

Nakamura is right. There are still doubts among Western scholars in particular regarding the compatibility of Islam and democracy, and Islam and civil society. Among them is Harvard political scientist Samuel Huntington who asserts that Islam is incompatible with democracy (Huntington, 1997).

Recent studies on civil society in Muslim societies, however, tend to refute Huntington's views. A number of studies conducted in the Middle East have shown that civil society in various forms has existed among Middle Eastern Muslims in the course of their history (Norton, 1995; 1996). Sullivan, who found a thriving civil society in Egypt in the form of various Muslim private voluntary organizations, appealed for the rectification of the conventional Western approach to the Muslim world based on the assumption of the absence of civil society. He urges that outside observers should look at "a continuing Islam, a deeply rooted, tradition-bound Islam" from which numerous voluntary organizations have sprung up today, instead of radical Islam (Sullivan, 1994:8-9).

Sullivan's argument and implicit definition of civil society in Muslim society are a perfect reflection of the current and continuing debates in Indonesia on the concept of "civil society". The debates on the meaning of civil society circling among Indonesian Muslims have divided scholars into two basic groups. The roots of their differences on the concept of civil society largely lie in the positions and relationship of civil society vis-à-vis the state.

The first group of scholars, the most prominent of whom is Mohammad Hikam, is influenced by post-Hegelian and post-Marxian thinkers such as Ernest Gellner, Hannah Arendt, Juergen Habermas, David Ost, Andre Arato, Fernando Cardoso, Antonio Gramsci and Alexis de Tocqueville. This group basically defines civil society as voluntary groups or organizations of citizens outside the state that provide a balancing force between the state and individuals, or the public in general. To express this more clearly, civil society is the realm of organized social life that is voluntary, self-generating, largely self-supporting, autonomous from the state and bound by legal order or set of shared rules. As a consequence of these definitions, this group of scholars, influenced by the "democracy revolution" in Eastern Europe, tend to place civil society in an opposing position vis-à-vis the state, as a "counter-hegemony" or "counter discourse" against the state, and even as the "alternative" to the state (Baso, 1999:173-219; cf. Karni, 1999; Culla, 1999). This first group, furthermore, puts a strong emphasis on the "universality" of the concept and practice of civil society. They, therefore, translate the very term "civil society" in the Indonesian language as "*masyarakat sipil*" or "*masyarakat kewargaan*". Both translations clearly do not have a religious, that is an Islamic, connotation.

In contrast, the second group of scholars, explained briefly below, translates the term "civil society" as "*masyarakat madani*" which has a strong Islamic connotation. The term "*madani*" refers to "Madinah", the city where the Prophet Muhammad established the first Islamic political entity which recognized religious, social and cultural plurality among its citizens. The term "*madani*" is also associated with "*madaniyyah*" (civility) and "*tamaddun*" (civilization, or civilized order). The second group of scholars, of whom the most prominent are Nurcholish Madjid and M. Dawam Raharjo, employs the term "*masyarakat madani*" interchangeably with "civil society". According to Madjid, civil society or *masyarakat madani* is the "house" where a variety of associations, groups, clubs, guilds, federations, political parties and the like become "a shield" between society and state. He admits that civil society played an instrumental role against despotic rule in Latin America, and Eastern Europe, but the aim of civil society is not to topple the government, since civil society might have certain weaknesses and negative excesses.

Despite their differences, both groups seem to agree that Islamic organizations have a great potential to function as civil society institutions in Indonesia. Their argument has, in fact, been supported by foreign observers and scholars, like Mitsuo Nakamura mentioned above and Robert Hefner. They have also shown that Islamic civil society has been in existence for many years. Hefner, for instance, makes it clear that Indonesian Islam has a wealth of civic resources. He maintains that, whether we are speaking of mass-based Muslim organizations like the 'neo-traditionalist' Nahdlatul Ulama (NU), the modernist Muhammadiyah, or the proudly independent University Muslim Student Association (*Himpunan Mahasiswa Islam* – HMI), Indonesia has the strongest civic-based Muslim society in the world. He notes that, since colonial times, most of these organizations have taken care to distance themselves from the state bureaucracy. He concludes that 'Muslim leaders recognized in action, if not always in word, that to fuse religious leadership with the state is itself the most profane of secularization, ending as it inevitably does with Islam's subordination to the short-sighted political interests' (Hefner, 2001:3; cf. Hefner, 2000).

Japanese scholar Mitsuo Nakamura argues that the roots of civil society in Indonesia lie in a variety of voluntary associations that have existed since colonial times (Nakamura, 2001:9). Muslim voluntary organizations that exerted nation-wide influence were undoubtedly among the earliest established civic organizations in the country. The most prominent among them were (and still are), the Muhammadiyah (founded in 1912), and the Nahdlatul Ulama (NU, founded in 1926). In addition, there are a lot of other Muslim organizations operating at provincial level throughout the country.

The Muhammadiyah and NU in particular have a number of nation-wide affiliated organizations; each has a youth, student and women's affiliate. Both organizations are very active in various programs of societal empowerment in the field of religious and "secular" education, social service, cultural enhancement and the like. While the Muhammadiyah has been able to disengage itself from direct political involvement, the NU became a political party from 1955 and was an important part of President Soekarno's "Guided Democracy" (*Demokrasi Terpimpin*). Relegated to only a marginalized faction in the PPP when President Soeharto forced all Islamic parties to merge in 1973, the NU in 1984 decided to return to its original *raison d'etre* of 1926 (*Khittah 1926*) as a civic organization. Despite Soeharto's repressive measures, these Muslim organizations have not only been able to keep their very existence in civil society intact, but also played an important role in supporting the pro-democracy movements.

In addition to Muslim civil society organizations, one might also observe at least two other groups of civil society groups in the last decade of the Soeharto period. The first group was advocacy and pro-democracy NGOs that sought to empower society in democracy, human rights, gender equity and other forms of social values. The second group was professional associations such as labor movements, educational associations, and the like. All of these organizations and groups within civil society were, to a large extent, supported financially by the rising middle class that had begun to form in the last decade of the Soeharto regime.

The dramatic political changes that have been occurring since 1998 deserve special attention. Following the fall of President Soeharto in disgrace in May 1998, the then Vice President B.J. Habibie replaced him. Before long President Habibie relaxed restrictions on press freedom and liberalized Indonesian politics by adopting a multi-party political system. To him all these changes were necessary to achieve one of the most important aims of *reformasi* (reforms), that is the formation of *masyarakat madani* (civil society) (Azra, 2000b; Nakamura, 2001).

The support of civil society by President Habibie during his *interregnum* is an important shift in the attitude of government. In the past the formation and enhancement of civil society in Indonesia had been accomplished through non-state voluntary organizations. During Habibie's presidency, however, the state began involving itself in the discourse of civil society. Furthermore, the election of Abdurrahman Wahid, as Nakamura argues, represented a dramatic turn-about in which a civil society leader was made the head of state. The newly reborn democracy in Indonesia, however, still faced the challenge of whether a civil society leader in power was capable not only of implementing the agenda of *reformasi*, but of also promoting civil society. President Wahid, during his brief tenure in office, has, to a limited degree, been able to provide a greater leeway for civil society to play their role in the building of democracy. Introducing the concept that "the best government is the least government", he put a lot of trust in civil society. His erratic, unpredictable personal style and lack of management skills, however, cost him dearly and he was soon impeached and removed from the presidency.

It is important to point out that the election of Wahid was the result of the 'political expediency' of the fragmented Islamic political forces, which at the last minute endorsed a fragile coalition of the *Poros Tengah* (Middle Axis) that was initiated by Amien Rais who had been the national chairman of the Muhammadiyah and chairperson of the National Mandate Party (*Partai Amanat Nasional* – PAN). Indeed, his election was a great surprise, since his party, the *Partai Kebangkitan Bangsa* (PKB/National Awakening Party), gained only eleven per cent of the vote in the 1999 general elections. If real democracy prevailed, Megawati Soekarnoputri would have been elected since her Indonesian Democratic Party of Struggle (PDI-P) topped all other candidates with thirty-four per cent of the total votes (Azra, 2000a).

Abdurrahman Wahid was considered by some to be a most ardent proponent of democracy and civil society (Falaakh, 2001), especially during his long tenure as the national chairman of the Nahdlatul Ulama (NU, lit. "the Awakening of Muslim Scholars", established in 1926), one of the largest Muslim organizations in the country. Elected as the new president in a general session of the MPR (*Majelis Permusyawaratan Rakyat* – Peoples' Consultative Assembly, the highest democratic institution in Indonesia) in October 1999, he, by and large, failed to meet public expectations. He created a lot of problems, not only by his lack of management skill and statesmanship, but also by his controversial statements and policies. These resulted in his losing credibility and social and moral legitimacy, which finally led the DPR (*Dewan Perwakilan Rakyat* – Peoples' Representative Council or parliament) to censure him. This followed the so-called "Bulogate" and "Bruneigate" scandals – explained in details below – that were used as the justification for the two part censure motions, "Memorandum I" and "Memorandum II", on 1 February and 30 March 2001 respectively. Responding to the president's controversial attitude and policies, the DPR finally proposed a motion to the MPR to hold a special session on 1 August which would impeach President Wahid.

In response, the president, who regarded the DPR's moves as illegal, issued a decree of civilian emergency in the early morning of 23 July. The decree in effect "froze" the MPR, DPR and the Golkar (Functional Group) party and proposed an early general election in 2002. In a quick counter move, however, the MPR refused to recognize the legality of the decree, and held the special session of the MPR on that very day. As had been expected, the Session unanimously impeached President Wahid, and elected Vice President Megawati Soekarnoputri as the new president, and Hamzah Haz, chairman of the United Development Party (*Partai Persatuan Pembangunan* – PPP, a Muslim party) as the new vice president.

In short, the tensions in Indonesian politics increased significantly during the short-lived Abdurrahman Wahid presidency. The anti- and pro-Wahid demonstrations in various cities became more and more worrying, with the constant threat of outright violence between opposing camps. Given this highly unsettled situation, it is not surprising that more and more people had become skeptical and disillusioned about the future of democracy in Indonesia.

There was much loss of civility among fanatical supporters of various parties both before and after the general elections as well as before and after the general session of the MPR. The election of Wahid by the MPR took place only because of the escalation of violence among fanatical supporters of Habibie and Megawati Soekarnoputri. Despite his frail health and the view of some that he was an unlikely presidential candidate, Wahid's acceptability among many groups – given his track record as one of the most prominent civic leaders and champions of democracy – made him the ideal choice to prevent further bloodshed. Sponsored initially by the *Poros Tengah* (Middle Axis), Wahid's candidacy suddenly loomed large with the rejection of Habibie's accountability speech by a slim majority of MPR members (Azra, 2000a; cf. Kadir, 2001).

A deeply disappointed Habibie withdrew from the presidential race, and the Golkar party – the dominant party during President Soeharto's period – that had been his main supporter, was flung into disarray. Golkar was left with little choice but to back Wahid, whose support base in the Middle Axis was mainly from the Islamic parties. With Golkar's support, Wahid's ascendancy to the presidency was virtually guaranteed. The PKB, which was founded by Wahid but initially cool to his bid, finally joined the Middle Axis and Golkar to almost guarantee that the National Chairman of the NU would win the presidency.

The election of Wahid did not stop outbreaks of violence in several cities. Megawati Sukarnoputri was subsequently elected vice president, in part due to the violent protests by her avid supporters. Supporters of her PDI-P surrounded the MPR building in Jakarta and vented their anger and frustration. They also took to the streets in Surakarta, Denpasar, and other party strongholds, burning and destroying buildings, including public facilities. Alarmed by the almost uncontrollable unrest, Wahid, military commanders, and leaders of other parties agreed that the vice presidential post should go to Megawati.

Even though the election of Wahid to the presidency was later virtually accepted by PDI-P, a problem soon loomed. A week after his election, Wahid formed his first cabinet. Generally dubbed a cabinet of national reconciliation and integration, its composition nevertheless caused disappointment in some quarters. The cabinet contained a significant number of military personnel, and some ministers were regarded as inappropriate for their appointments. Perhaps even more damaging, some members of the cabinet, particularly some generals, were connected to the Soeharto New Order.

Thus, the seeds of opposition to Wahid began to grow, even from the camps that supported his presidency. Before long, in addition to questions related to his cabinet, President Wahid made statements and implemented policies which disappointed not only the Middle Axis, but also Muslim society as a whole. Among them was the sudden replacement of Hamzah Haz, the Chairman of the United Development Party (PPP) and the strongest pillar of the Middle Axis, as the Coordinating Minister for People's Welfare. This became a sign of things to come, as Wahid subsequently replaced many ministers in his cabinet. Up to his impeachment on 23 July, no fewer than twenty-five ministers have been sacked and replaced by Wahid, creating instability and ineffectiveness in his government.

The president also dismayed members of the Middle Axis and many Muslims in the way he tackled both new and longstanding issues, ranging from his statements of possibly opening trade relations and even official diplomatic ties with Israel; his comments that violence in Maluku originated from the unjust treatment of Christians by Muslims; and his insistence on the lifting of the ban on communism, Marxism and Leninism, which were outlawed in the MPRS Decree No. 25/1966. While many in the Middle Axis believed that Wahid owed them a debt for his election, it seems that the president believed it was the Axis which needed him more (Azra, 2000c:151-2).

With his controversial statements and policies, President Wahid created ever-increasing opposition to himself. As a result he became involved in head-on collisions with Parliament (DPR). The DPR used the so-called "Bulogate" and "Bruneigate" scandals as a means to challenge the president. The "Bulogate" case refers to President Wahid's alleged embezzlement of non-budgetary funds of the Indonesian logistics agency (*Badan Urusan Logistik* – Bulog) for his own purposes, while "Bruneigate" refers to the president's alleged misappropriation of a five million Brunei dollar grant given by the Sultan of Brunei. For the purpose of investigating President Wahid's involvement in the cases, the DPR formed Special Committees, which finally concluded that there were strong reasons to suspect that the president had been involved in this misappropriation of state funds. The DPR issued Memorandum I and Memorandum II to censure him, which resulted in plans to hold the Special Session of the MPR in early August 2001 to demand his accountability report.

Responding to the "hostile" DPR, President Wahid made a number of moves that further cornered him. First, he seemed to condone violent acts by his fanatical supporters, who ran amok, mostly in East Java, in the aftermath of the issue of DPR Memorandum I. The violence included attacks on, and destruction of, the assets of Muhammadiyah organizations such as schools, offices and – even worse – mosques. Second, he appeared to condone the abuse by certain NU *ulama* of classic Islamic political concepts such as *jihad* against his opponents who were Muslims, particularly modernist Muslims. Third, he stated that if he were unseated in the Special Session of the MPR, a number of provinces would proclaim themselves independent from Indonesia. Fourth, he asserted that if the Special Session of the MPR was held, he would issue a martial law decree that would disband the DPR and the MPR. Fifth, he fired the national police chief without consulting the DPR as required by the Decree of the MPR and, in fact, tried to take command over the national police force.

Finally, on 23 July, President Wahid issued a decree of martial law, which finally led the MPR to hold an early special session the very same day. This resulted in the impeachment of President Wahid and the election of Megawati Soekarnoputri as the new president as mentioned earlier. Thus, the further unmaking of civil society in post-Soeharto Indonesia was the work of President Wahid who, ironically, was the national leader of the NU, the largest civil society organization in the country (Falaakh, 2001; Bush, 2001). Nonetheless, his fanatical supporters engaged in conflicts and violence against the Muhammadiyah, another Muslim civil society organization (Abdullah, 2001).

Wahid thus brought a lot of problems on himself. With his tendency to stir up controversy and his frequently startling comments, many are confused about the man behind the image. One of his most well-known personal traits is his eclecticism, which can be observed on at least two levels. First, it is evident in intellectual discourse in his synthesis of various intellectual traditions and tendencies – Islamic traditionalism, with its roots in the Islamic *pesantren*

(Muslim traditional schooling), Islamic liberalism, Javanese syncretism and Western secularism. Clearly, not all of these intellectual traditions are compatible with each other; in certain respects they are from conflicting perspectives. Second, in daily practicalities, he seems to be able to reconcile various, sometimes conflicting roles. He is an *ulama* or *kiyai* (traditional Muslim religious scholar), with all the religious connotations these entail, but he can also be a liberal, albeit not a radical; a non-governmental organization leader; a judge of a film contest; and a sports commentator. Several of these have a secular, if not a profane, connotation.

President Wahid is undeniably a complex, mercurial man, playing a variety of roles which are sometimes at odds with each other. There is also no denying that he is a Muslim scholar par excellence, brought up in the Islamic *santri* (strict and practicing Muslim) tradition. Perhaps there is some truth in the criticism that he ran the country like an Islamic boarding school (*pesantren*). Still, since his appointment to head the NU, Wahid has also displayed political savvy. As a politician, he remained heavily influenced by his background in social and political activism, such as his leadership of the opposition pro-democracy group, Democracy Forum. It remains part and parcel of Wahid's personality, leaving many confused when his statements sound more like an activist from an NGO than a president.

Some would argue that the controversial statements and policies are "shock therapy", designed to put an end to the status quo and the ills of Indonesian bureaucracy and society. They compare Wahid to a "bulldozer" clearing away the encumbering baggage of the past. I would argue, however, that although the shock therapy may have done some good, it has also taken its toll. It has spawned endless public debates and controversy, impacting on the work of the cabinet and bureaucracy as a whole. His ministers have appeared preoccupied in attempts to head off controversy resulting from his statements instead of focusing on what needs to be done to put Indonesia back on its feet. Worse still, his "shock therapy" – if one accepts this has been responsible in a large part for the unmaking of civility, tolerance, respect for pluralism, democracy, or, in short, of civil society.

The election of President Megawati and Vice President Hamzah Haz, however, is able to revive new hopes among Indonesians in general of political and economic recovery. The two new leaders are considered to represent a good coalition of national and Islamic political forces respectively, which in the past had been involved in bitter struggles for power. Their election undoubtedly has eased political tension that will allow them to implement programs of political stability and economic recovery.

CONSOLIDATION OF DEMOCRACY

It is clear from the Indonesian experience during President Wahid's period of office that peaceful transition from authoritarian rule to democracy is no easy process. On the other hand, the transition to, and consolidation of, democracy in many other countries in Eastern Europe, has been as uncertain as in Indonesia. At the same time, however, public expectation runs very high, and therefore the transition to democracy is everywhere very demanding. The problem is more complicated in Indonesia not only because of the unpredictability of the top leadership which resulted in the continued escalation of political conflict among fragmented and opposing political groups, but also because the economic crisis remains unsolved (Azra, 2000b). Because of the continued escalation of political uncertainty during the Abdurrahman presidency, some economic observers had already talked about the possibility of a "second economic crisis", following the first economic and political crises of 1998.

Worse still, the Abdurrahman Wahid regime has shown, throughout its period in office, a proclivity to deteriorate through self-exhaustion. Much of the damage was self-inflicted. It became sluggish and inefficient, and was unable to resolve the crisis of public confidence. Confronting this situation, the regime sought a re-equilibration, resorting even to repression – as in Wahid's final resort to "freezing" the DPR and MPR, and to his declaration of a civilian emergency in the aftermath of Memorandum I and II, which in the end led to the Special Session of MPR – to resolve the crises of his regime. It was also clear, however, that such efforts at re-equilibration and repression proved very costly and inconclusive, not only for democracy, but also for civil society. It is surprising indeed that such undemocratic moves by President Wahid were supported by many independent NGOs which lost their patience with the allegedly continuing influence of elements of Soeharto's New Order regime. Nevertheless, in the end, such actions did not help the regime to survive.

In short, all the hard data of improving political and economic trends in Indonesia does not speak in favor of democracy. It was always reasonable to expect that concerned citizens would seek ways in which to bring about a peaceful transition to democracy in Indonesia. The MPR Special Session proved to be the best way to resolve the political impasse, accomplishing, as it did, the unseating of Wahid from the presidency and his replacement by Vice President Megawati Sukarnoputri. If this helps the country to regain its political stability and to carry out programs of economic recovery, Indonesia could rebuild its disoriented civil society.

Looking at the Indonesian experience during President Wahid's brief period, it is clear that he failed not only to consolidate democracy but also civil society. Initially, he had brought a lot of hope for the empowerment of civil society by his dismantling of military hegemony; he not only sacked the strong man General Wiranto as Coordinating Minister of Politics and Security, but also dictated harsh measures against military abuses. In this last regard, President Wahid has been compared to a "bulldozer" who clears the ground for civilian supremacy at the expense of the military. Using Sorensen's stages of transition to democracy, President Wahid's period was the preparatory stage of democracy (Sorensen 1973).

The next stage of the transition to democracy is the consolidation stage. A number of political tendencies since the accession of Megawati to the presidency seems to be leading to the consolidation of democracy. First of all, she has been able to consolidate fragmented political forces into a broad based coalition. This, in turn, leads to a more stable politics which allows government not only to function in a better way, but also to find ways to resolve conflicts and violence that continue to ravage certain areas in Indonesia such as Maluku (Ambon), Central Sulawesi (Poso) and Aceh and Irian Jaya (West Papua) provinces which are struggling to gain independence from Indonesia.

Another crucial set of problems faced by President Megawati's government is the economy. Initially, the election of Megawati received a favorable response from the financial markets and some economic indicators gave encouraging signs. These soon faded away, however, in the aftermath of the September 11, 2001, terrorist attacks in the US which resulted in a great deal of domestic political repercussions in Indonesia. Mass demonstrations, threats of "sweeping" foreigners and appeals for the breaking of diplomatic relations with the US had escalated political tension. It is only as a result of the firmer policies of President Megawati towards both the US and Muslim hardliner groups that the political situation returned to normal. Nevertheless, further damage to the Indonesian economy has been done.

In this regard, employing Di Palma's arguments, Indonesia today – like many other nations facing democratization – falls short of the qualities classically associated with Western democracy. With the ongoing crises these qualities in fact slipped out of our hands. These qualities generally fall into three categories: first, economic prosperity and equality; second, a modern and diversified social structure in which a non-dependent middle class occupies center stage; and third, a national culture that, by tolerating diversity and exhibiting a preference for accommodation, is implicitly democratic (Di Palma, 1990:3).

These qualities are also often called the requisites or even prerequisites or preconditions of democracy. Improved wealth and socio-economic welfare will undoubtedly always be accompanied by a number of factors conducive to democracy: higher rates of literacy and education, urbanization, and the development and spread of mass media. Moreover, wealth and socioeconomic welfare will also provide the resources needed to mitigate the tensions brought on through political conflicts. This has been an important conclusion of a large number of studies. As early as 1959, Lipset concluded that 'the more well-to-do a nation, the greater the chances that it will sustain democracy' (Lipset, 1959:75). In 1971, Robert Dahl, another prominent political scientist, pointed out that it is 'pretty much beyond dispute that the higher the socio-economic level of a country, the more likely that it would be a democracy' (Dahl, 1971:65).

The second set of prerequisites that will help develop and sustain democracy is associated with the social structure of society, that is, the specific classes and groups making up society. The groups that play a crucial role in the development and maintenance of democracy are, among others, independent middle class and civil society organizations. In his historical account of the roots of dictatorship and democracy, Barrington Moore concludes that 'a vigorous and independent class of town dwellers has been an indispensable element in the growth of democracy' (Moore, 1966:418).

The third set of preconditions often brought forward in the attempt to determine the factors that favor and sustain democracy concerns the political culture – that is, the system of values and beliefs that define the context and meaning of political action. It is beyond doubt that feudalism and patrimonialism – such as shown by President Wahid – are not conducive to democracy. Conversely, democracy will prevail only in a society in which egalitarianism is the order of the day.

It seems that the norms of a democratic culture and civility have not yet become characteristics of the newly found democracy in Indonesia. A closer look at some recent examples of the transition to democracy in other countries confirms this view. In several countries in Latin America – not unlike Indonesia – the military continues to be a dominant player. In some of them, domestic conflict has resulted in a breakdown of authority and of rule of law accompanied by a high level of domestic violence. In Indonesia today, again not unlike some countries in Africa for instance, the corrupt practices of personal and charismatic rule remain strong in spite of democratic openings. In Eastern Europe, a civil society is only beginning to emerge, and the rule of law is challenged by the *nomenklatura* (the elite), who have retained a good deal of power. In short, a democratic culture is beginning to emerge in the new democracies, but it is arguable whether this culture has grown strong enough to constitute the domestic basis for peaceful resolution of conflicts between groups of citizens.

In addition to the above mentioned set of preconditions there are a number of related external factors; the economic, political, ideological and other elements that constitute the international context for the processes that take place in individual countries. The countries that are in transition to democracy are the most susceptible to external influence. As Sorensen points out, it is customary among modernization theorists to view this influence as beneficial to democracy. On the other hand, however, dependency theorists have drawn the opposite conclusion; that the inequalities and distortions of the economies and societies of the developing world, brought about by their dependent position in the world economic system, make democracy very difficult (Sorensen, 1993:27).

This external factor is becoming increasingly more dominant with the wave of globalization today. Individual countries that are in the transition to democracy are, to an increasing degree, being subjected to international forces over which they have little control. As Dahl maintains, it is true that this has always been the case. "Not just conflict but also trade, commerce, and finance have always spilled over state boundaries. Democratic states, therefore, have never been able to act autonomously, in disregard of the actions of outside forces over which they had little or no control" (Dahl, 1989:319).

Recent trends in the era of globalization are more than just replays of this unfortunate situation. In developing countries – and this is even more evident in Indonesia in this time of continued economic crisis – dependence on international structures has increased in the wake of the debt crisis, resulting in an expansion in the power over those countries by such international organizations as the International Monetary Fund (IMF) and the World Bank. The frustration of these countries at their increased dependency came out clearly in a speech by Julius Nyerere, President of Tanzania, as early as 1979 when he asked: "When did the IMF become an international Ministry of Finance? When did nations agree to surrender their power of decision making?" (Sorensen, 1993:21).

It is clear that nations facing democratization in the absence of all the above characteristics face yet another impediment. As can clearly be observed in the Indonesian case today, the democratic transition is now tending to take place in a climate of mobilization and impatience, if not outright violence. The benefits of gradualism and accommodation, which marked the Western experience in democracy, will thus be lost.

CONCLUSION

The transition from authoritarianism to authentic democracy is a very complex process. In Indonesia, the regimes of President Wahid and President Megawati Soekarnoputri have been freely elected but, according to Sorensen's categories (1993:40ff), they seem to be merely regimes of a "restricted democracy"; both regimes are more democratic than the previous one – that is the Soeharto regime – but are not yet fully democratic. Several phases of "democratic deepening" must be in place before an authentic democracy can be established; when democracy is seen by all major political actors as "the only game in town". Thus, in this stage, democratic institutions and practices become ingrained in the political culture.

In conclusion, as Juan Linz and Alfred Stepan have suggested, the transition to democracy or democratization is ultimately a matter of political crafting (cited in Di Palma, 1990:8). What they mean by "crafting" includes four aspects of democratization: first, the quality of the finished product (the particular democratic rules and institutions that are chosen among those available); second, the mode of decision making process leading to the selection of the rules and institutions (pacts and negotiations versus unilateral action); third, the type of "craftsmen" involved (the alliances and coalitions forged in the transition); and fourth, the timing imposed on the various tasks and stages of transition. It is these four aspects that ultimately influence the successful transition to democracy.

CHAPTER 4

THE MEGAWATI PRESIDENCY: THE CHALLENGE OF POLITICAL ISLAM

"To be sure, the legitimacy crisis of the nation-state in the world of Islam has not been brought on by religious fundamentalism. It is, rather, the other way around; the crisis of legitimacy derives from the failure of the nation-states to strike roots in an alien civilization, and fundamentalism, seeing its opportunity, is the political articulation of the crisis" (Tibi, 1998:8).

There have been concerns expressed by many Indonesians that the growing anti-US sentiments expressed in widespread, sometimes rowdy, street demonstrations in several cities in Indonesia could spell the end of the Megawati coalition government. In the aftermath of the terrorists' attacks on the World Trade Center New York and the Pentagon headquarters and the subsequent US and British military retaliation against Afghanistan, radical or hardline Muslim groups, have asserted themselves in a much more visible manner and accused President Megawati of being too lenient on the US. Her silence on the issue is perceived as a refusal to condemn the US military strikes in Afghanistan and has been viewed by Muslim hardliners as a reflection of anti-Islam sentiment or, at least, an unfriendly attitude to Islam and Muslims.

Certain individuals and Muslim groups have become increasingly critical of the Indonesian Government attitude and response to the US-Afghanistan crisis. The most visible among these Muslim hardliner groups are the Islamic Defense Front (*Front Pembela Islam* – FPI) and Communication Forum of the *Ahl al-Sunnah wa al-Jama'ah* (*Forum Komunikasi Ahlus-Sunnah wal-Jamaah* – FKAWJ) or more popularly known as "Lasykar Jihad" (Jihad Troops), and the Hizb al-Tahrir (Party of Liberation). Other Muslim groups and institutions, like the Indonesian Council of the Ulama (*Majelis Ulama Indonesia* – MUI) have, more recently, also become increasingly critical of the government. In addition, groups of Muslim students, who are generally members or affiliates of the Justice Party (*Partai Keadilan*), have staged the largest peaceful mass demonstrations thus far against the US military retaliation in Afghanistan.

The anti-American outburst has undoubtedly put a lot of pressure on President Megawati. Some observers believe that the current Muslim hardliners' expressions of anti-Americanism could result in serious political repercussions for the political future of President Megawati. How serious are those possible political repercussions?

This chapter attempts to discuss all these complex developments. One of the most important questions to answer is the viability of the government of President Megawati in the face of the growing tendency towards radical political and formal Islam among Indonesian Muslims.

THE HARDLINER MUSLIMS: RADICAL ATTITUDES

One of the most important challenges President Megawati faces is the continued rise of radical "political Islam" which appears to be one of the most visible political developments in post-Soeharto Indonesia. Recent widespread demonstrations contain not only anti-American sentiments, colored by religious feeling, but also some dissatisfaction towards the Indonesian Government, which in turn could affect the future of President Megawati.

The most visible challenge to President Megawati thus far comes from Muslim hardline groups like FPI, Lasykar Jihad, Hizb al-Tahrir, and many other smaller groups. These hardline groups originally consisted of those who were well-known for their refusal to accept President Megawati for reasons of gender. According to their literal interpretation of Islam, it is against Islamic teaching for a woman to hold a leadership position. Despite their refusal on religious grounds to acknowledge a woman's right to a leadership position, they have not been able to contest President Megawati's constitutional and political legitimacy.

The US confrontation with the Taliban and Osama bin Laden has only fueled these groups determination to reassert themselves more publicly. These groups began to express their strong anti-American sentiments when many high US officials stated that the terrorists who attacked the World Trade Center, New York, and the Pentagon headquarters, Washington DC, on September 11, were people with Muslim names who allegedly have had links with Osama bin Laden who was protected by the Taliban Government of Afghanistan. The American ultimatum and subsequent bombings of Afghanistan have only further radicalized these hardline Muslim groups.

Even though the Bush administration has maintained that its confrontation with the Taliban and Osama bin Laden is not an anti-Islam crusade, the Indonesian Muslim hardliners believe that the US has a plan to destroy Islam and Muslims. They argue that even though the US has failed to produce convincing evidence that Osama bin Laden and his organization, al-Qaida, were responsible for planning the attacks against US, it has proceeded with the bombing of Afghanistan. They believe that American military retaliation in Afghanistan was motivated by hostility and hatred against Islam, as evidenced, inter alia, by the use of the term "Operation Crusades" by President Bush. Later Bush changed the code name to "Operation Infinite Justice", which again created a lot of resentment among Muslims, since Muslims believe that it is only God who is infinite. Finally President Bush adopted the code name "Operation Enduring Justice", which is a more neutral term, having no religious connotation. Insensitivity on the part of President Bush and other high American officials has clearly contributed also to increased anti-American sentiment among Muslims.

Most Muslims have made it clear that terrorism and the terrorist attacks against the WTC and Pentagon that left some three thousand people dead must be condemned; such ruthless attacks run contrary not only to Islamic teachings, but also to universal humanity (*ukhuwwah al-insaniyyah*). At the same time, however, they appealed to the US and its Western allies to restrain themselves from attacking Afghanistan indiscriminately on the grounds of conducting a war against terrorism. They believed that military retaliation and any kind of violence would not put an end to terrorism but would only perpetuate the "cycle of violence" among those involved.

In contrast to this moderate position, the hardline groups have generally felt that the US and its Western allies have been unfair to Muslims or Islam as a whole. They believed that the US and Western world have used the WTC-Pentagon tragedy to express their hostility to, and disrespect for, Muslims and Islam. This attitude of Muslim hardliners has its origin in their belief in the so-called "conspiracy theory", according to which the US and Western world have a plot to destroy Islam and Muslims. This "conspiracy theory", in my observation, has strongly influenced the psychology of hardline Muslim groups. It is not difficult to find such a psychology among them; one can find a lot of material on the internet about the so-called Zionist-Western conspiracy against Islam and Muslims.

Deeply influenced by this kind of psychology, it is not surprising then that hardline Muslim groups have responded angrily to the US and its allies. Following President Bush's accusation of apparent links between the terrorists who attacked the WTC and Pentagon headquarters and al-Qaida or Osama bin Laden without producing strong proof, Indonesian Muslim hardliners issued threats to conduct "sweeping" operations against American expatriates and other Westerners in Indonesia. In fact, the Solo branch of the FPI had conducted a kind of search for foreigners in a number of hotels in that Central Java town. Even though they found no foreigners in these hotels and, therefore, did no harm to anyone, the political and psychological impacts of the "sweeping" have been enormous. News on the "sweeping" of foreigners in national and international media has created a lot of anxiety among Indonesians and foreigners alike.

Furthermore, hardliners took to the streets in Jakarta and some other major cities in Indonesia. They further appealed to Indonesians not only to boycott American products, but even demanded that the Indonesian Government cut diplomatic relations with the US. Sensing the imminent attack by the US against Afghanistan, they threatened to attack and occupy the American embassy in Jakarta and expel all American citizens residing and traveling in Indonesia. "We will not listen to any calls from anybody. If the US government does attack Afghanistan, we will immediately attack the US embassy and search for American citizens and expel them from Indonesia" said M. Siraj Alwi, operational commander of the FPI (*The Jakarta Post*, 2 October 2001).

With the continued escalation of the confrontation between the US and the Taliban government, Muslim hardline groups in Indonesia launched a nation-wide campaign for a *jihad* in defense of Afghanistan. To that end, they started to openly enlist Muslim volunteers to be trained and later sent to Afghanistan. In Jakarta, for instance, a *jihad* recruitment center was organized by the Indonesian Muslim Youth Movement (*Gerakan Pemuda Islam Indonesia* – GPII). It was reported that at least 1,800 volunteers, including several women, from Jakarta, West Java and Central Java had registered since the registration process began in the final week of September. The GPII stated that while waiting to leave for Afghanistan, volunteers would learn the latest developments of the situation in that country as well as the American attitude, and they could join the training program, which would include combat training and the use of firearms. The GPII further asserted that it has experienced instructors who had joined the Balkan war between the Bosnia-Herzegovina Muslims and the Christian Serbs from 1992 to 1994.

Jihad registration centers were also opened in other cities, like Makassar (South Sulawesi), Medan (North Sumatra), and Surabaya (East Java). Leaders who led Muslim gatherings in those centers again appealed to Muslims to express their solidarity with the Afghan Muslims in a concrete way. They called upon Indonesian Muslims to take up arms for a *jihad* against the US. According to their plan, the volunteers would be trained and later sent to Afghanistan together with the Muslim paramilitary groups such as the *Jundullah* (from the Arabic word *jund Allah*, or troops of God).

Even though one can expect some expression of solidarity – based on the principle of Islamic brotherhood (*ukhuwwah al-Islamiyyah*) – among Muslims with their co-religionists facing injustice and unfair treatment elsewhere in the Muslim world, it is clear that it is only now that the hardliners seem to have succeeded in grabbing the spotlight. There were a lot of expressions of Muslim solidarity during the time when the Soviet Union attacked Afghanistan in 1979, or when US and its allies attacked Iraq in 1990, and when the Serbs killed many Bosnian Muslims.

But the nature of Islamic solidarity in those cases is different to that of the on-going US-Taliban crisis. In the past there was no significant appeal for a *jihad* nor organized registrations for volunteers to go to Afghanistan, Iraq or later Bosnia. This clearly had much to do with the attitude of the Soeharto government, which provided only very limited room for the Muslim hardliners to express themselves publicly; and was willing to take very harsh measures against them. In contrast, after the fall of Soeharto in disgrace, and in the name of democracy or Islamic solidarity, any group – including Muslim hardliners – was able to assert themselves in a very forceful manner.

Despite their strong expressions of Islamic solidarity, it is important to point out that their solidarity and support for the Afghan Muslims does not necessarily mean that all of them also support the Taliban or Osama bin Laden. In fact many leaders of hardliner groups are very critical of both. Ja'far Umar Thalib, the national leader of the Lasykar Jihad, for instance, openly stated that Osama bin Laden has only a very limited knowledge of Islam and that he was surrounded only by opportunists who have made use of Islam for their own material ends. Furthermore, Ja'far Umar Thalib has suggested that the Taliban are the *Khariji* (seceders), who in the early history of Islam were extremists who abandoned the unity of the *ummah* (Muslim nation) for their own narrow ends. As a consequence of this view, the Taliban are not part of the *Ahl al-Sunnah wa al-Jama'ah* school of Islamic thought and law that is adhered to by the majority of Indonesian Muslims.

THE MODERATE MUSLIMS: MAINSTREAM VOICES

The increasing prominence of Muslim hardliners, one has to acknowledge, has significantly damaged the image of Indonesian Islam. Indonesian Islam has for many years been regarded as a tolerant and moderate Islam, or Islam "with a smiling face" (*Newsweek*, September 23, 1996). The fact that the hardliners were able to capture the public imagination has created a wrong impression that Indonesian Islam is in the transition to radicalization; in fact some observers have already talked about the "Talibanization" of Indonesian Islam.

This tendency to view the hardliners as representatives of Indonesian Islam is very unfortunate. Since, despite the growing prominence – at least in the mass-media – of the hardliners, meticulous observers will find that the mainstream of Indonesian Muslims remain moderate in their religious attitude as well as in their political behavior. Furthermore, it is hard to imagine that these mainstream Muslims would adopt the religious belief and practices, and the way, of the Afghan Taliban.

The moderate position of the mainstream Indonesian Muslims can be observed in the public responses of the two largest Muslim organizations in Indonesia, that is, the Nahdlatul Ulama (NU, "the Awakening of Ulama/ Muslim religious scholars"), and the Muhammadiyah ("followers of the Prophet Muhammad"). Each organization has claimed a membership of around thirty-five to forty million Muslims. These two largest Muslim organizations in Indonesia have publicly stated that they do not agree with, let alone support, the appeal to Indonesian Muslims to wage *jihad* in Afghanistan should the US attack the country. KH Hasyim Muzadi, elected as the successor to KH Abdurrahman Wahid (who had been elected as the fourth president of the RI) as the national leader of the NU, says the organization will not recruit its members as volunteers for a *jihad* in Afghanistan. He maintains that a *jihad* does not always mean holy war; efforts to develop Islam and the Muslim *ummah* are also called *jihad*. He further believes that the terrorist attacks in the US were a tragedy of humanity, not a tragedy of religion. He has, therefore, appealed for every society in the world not to transform the terrorist attacks into conflicts of religion.

A similar tone has also been expressed by the national chairman of Muhammadiyah, Syafii Maarif, who was elected to succeed Amien Rais, now the speaker of the Indonesian MPR (People's Consultative Assembly). Syafii Maarif, who is also a professor of history at the State University of Yogyakarta, says that Muhammadiyah will not get involved in radical actions. Syafii, therefore, criticizes statements about a *jihad* issued by the Council of Indonesian Ulama (Majelis Ulama Indonesia/MUI). He believes that the MUI's call for a *jihad* has been misunderstood by many Muslims, since they have their own way of interpreting that very word. He thinks that it will only raise Muslims' emotions and provoke radicalism. He therefore concludes that it is not wise to use *jihad* in that way at this time.

It is worth mentioning in passing that the MUI, a body consisting of representatives of various Muslim organizations, seemed to support the call for *jihad*. The MUI, after a meeting with the leaders of thirty-two Islamic organizations on 26 September, condemned the terrorist attacks on the

US. At the same time, however, the MUI called on Muslims to prepare a *jihad*, should the US and its allies attack Afghanistan to pursue Osama bin Laden. The General Secretary of the MUI, Din Syamsuddin, said that if the US attacked Afghanistan, the Muslim world should unite and wage a *jihad* against the US.

The MUI's statements were soon strongly criticized by many moderate Muslim leaders and organizations, including the NU and Muhammadiyah mentioned above. One example is Abdurrahman Wahid, former president of Indonesia and former national chairman of the NU, who points out that the idea of conducting *jihad* was definitely against his personal belief that a truthful struggle must be based solely on the principle of non-violence. As one might expect, he opposed the idea of "sweeping" Americans and other foreigners in Indonesia. Opposition to this idea was also expressed by Syafii Maarif. He called upon all Muslim groups to stop unlawful activities, such as conducting searches for foreigners, as it could worsen the image of Indonesia in the eyes of the international community.

Having faced such strong criticism, Din Syamsuddin clarified his position that *jihad fi sabillilah* (*jihad* in the way of God) means all efforts by Muslims in the various aspects of life for the glory of Islam; Muslims should undertake various efforts to improve their infrastructure – social, economic, education and also information. Such efforts are also part of fighting in the path of Allah. *Jihad* therefore means fighting in the path of God in a very broad sense, not in the form of war. Syamsuddin says that the MUI uses the term "*jihad*" in the statement because the Council wants to correct the misperception in various circles of Muslim and Western societies alike that *jihad* always connotes physical war.

While opposing the sending of a *jihad* force to Afghanistan, moderate Muslim leaders appeal to Indonesians to focus their attention on humanitarian concerns in Afghanistan rather than simply expressing their religious solidarity. They generally argue that it would show more solidarity if Indonesian Muslims dealt with the real problems facing the Afghan people. Syafii Maarif, says that Islamic organizations in Indonesia could show their support for the Afghan people through collecting donations, without any regard to whether the US attacks Afghanistan or not. He maintains that our solidarity should be addressed to those who are suffering by sending them food, medicine, nurses and doctors. This kind of aid is more important than *jihad* forces.

A similar appeal is also voiced by Salahuddin Wahid, a member of the national executive of the NU. He calls for Indonesians to show their solidarity by sending food and clothes, and not by registering to become part of a *jihad force*. He further believes that Islamic groups in Indonesia have the capability of sending persons to Afghanistan. In his opinion, to go there, we need money and we should also have skills to fight in a war zone. The presence of Indonesians in Afghanistan in fact may cause problems for the Afghan.

Again, it is important to point out that all these leaders of moderate mainstream Indonesian Muslims have also, from the very beginning of the US-Afghanistan crisis, appealed to the US to refrain from attacking Afghanistan on the ground of punishing Osama bin Laden or the Taliban government. They believe that military operations will not solve terrorism, and, in fact, would victimize innocent Afghan civilians. When the US and its allies did attack Afghanistan, they demanded that the US end its military operation as soon as possible.

The US military operations in Afghanistan have created new tension in Indonesia. On the one hand, hardliners appeal to the Indonesian Government to break off diplomatic relations with the US. On the other hand, moderate Muslim leaders of the NU and Muhammadiyah believe that Indonesia has to maintain good relations with the US and its allies to help resuscitate the Indonesian economy.

There is little doubt that the US military operations in Afghanistan have brought new pressure on President Megawati and her government. Moderate Muslim leaders urged the government to explain its stance on the US military operations in Afghanistan to both hardline groups in Indonesia and the US and its allies to avoid misunderstanding. Hasyim Muzadi, says that the government should explain to hardline groups what it can do and cannot do in responding to the US attacks based on the national interest. Similarly, Muhammadiyah national chairman, Syafii Maarif urges the Megawati Government to explain the difficult position it found itself in to the US and other Western countries. He further says that President Megawati was facing a dilemma in deciding how to respond to the US attacks. He believes that Indonesia is in a very difficult situation; on the one hand Indonesia needs aid from the International Monetary Fund, the World Bank and donor countries, but on the other hand, Indonesia cannot come to terms with the US military operations in Afghanistan.

PRESIDENT MEGAWATI: SPEAKS LITTLE BUT FIRMER

Even though Muslim hardliners opposed the election of Megawati to the presidency to replace Abdurrahman Wahid – as argued above – in the end they had to accept the political reality. Realizing that their opposition to President Megawati was not supported by mainstream Muslim parties and organizations, the hardline groups seemed to lose their momentum and an issue to publicly fight for. The furor in the aftermath of the terrorist attacks on the WTC and Pentagon and subsequent US military operations in Afghanistan have provided them with new vigor. How has President Megawati dealt with all of these pressures, both domestically and internationally?

Unlike most opinion that believes President Megawati has been slow to respond appropriately to the crisis, I would argue that she has been firm in her attitudes. She has, of course, spoken too little on the US-Afghanistan crisis, but I believe that she has in her mind a kind of vision on how to respond to the continued crisis.

I would argue that President Megawati has outlined the Indonesian Government response to the crisis from the very beginning. During her visit to the US only one week after the WTC and Pentagon tragedy, President Megawati made it clear to President Bush that Indonesia would help the US in its fight against international terrorism. At the same time, however, President Megawati also urged the US government to restrain itself and to not make any hasty decision to launch a military retaliation.

This attitude changed when the US and its allies did launch military operations in Afghanistan. In her speech at the commemoration of the Ascension Day of the Prophet of Muhammad in the Istiqlal Grand Mosque in Jakarta in the middle of October, President Megawati reiterated that Indonesia does not wish to see any country commit violence against another, even if they were responding to acts of violence committed against them. She maintained that violence should not be answered with violence. Whoever commits terror must be punished, but it is unacceptable that someone, a group or even a government – arguing that they are hunting down perpetrators of the terror – attack people or another country for whatever reason.

Even though she made no mention of any specific country in her speech, the message is clearly directed at the US which had already launched military strikes against Afghanistan a week before. Before long, US officials responded, expressing the dissatisfaction of the US with President Megawati. This was followed by statements from the Australian Prime Minister, John Howard, that strongly criticized President Megawati's changing attitude. Later, high Indonesian officials stated that Indonesia remains committed to the fight against terrorism, although it could not condone violent military actions in the war.

On the other hand, Megawati's statements were warmly welcomed by various parties in the country. While the hardliners judged that the remarks were not strong enough, moderate Muslim leaders, like Syafii Maarif said that the government has taken a step ahead in responding to the crisis. They urged the government to follow up this stronger attitude with concrete action.

The stronger Indonesian position in the crisis was further enunciated by the appeal of Minister of Foreign Affairs, Hasan Wirayuda, to the US to end its military operations in Afghanistan before the commencement of Ramadhan in the middle of November. He stated that the fasting month of Ramadhan is very important for Muslims to reflect and express solidarity and he, therefore, thinks that there will be an explosive reaction if military actions are still being conducted in Afghanistan. Prolonged military conflict in Afghanistan will have the effect of destabilizing countries with large Muslim populations like Indonesia, Pakistan and Malaysia.

With the change in its position regarding the US-Afghanistan crisis, Indonesia has a firmer policy compared with the position of the Organization of Islamic Conference (OIC). OIC member countries have not criticized the US-led strikes on Afghanistan. They have only expressed their concern that the military operations do not harm innocent civilians. Vice President Hamzah Haz has, therefore, called on the OIC to take a new stance similar to that of Indonesia's position, namely an end to US military operations before the month of Ramadhan starts. The firmer line in Indonesian foreign policy in this latest case is a shift from the usual "ambiguous" Indonesian foreign policies relating to Muslims and Islam (Azra, 2001).

President Megawati has, of course, been criticized from many quarters for remaining silent and not taking a stronger position while anti-US mass protests have erupted daily in several Indonesian cities. After a meeting with leaders of the Indonesian parliament two days before making the above strong statements, however, President Megawati broke her silence. She promised that the Indonesian Government would review its "soft" stance on the US attacks on Afghanistan.

The change of government attitude was also backed by Vice President Hamzah Haz. While he initially seemed to encourage anti-US demonstrations and give "a green light" to Indonesian Muslims to wage a *jihad* in Afghanistan, he later repeatedly called on Muslim hardliners to stop the anti-US rallies in the country. He appealed time and time again for the rallies to stop. As Vice President and being from a Muslim-based party, he said that he understood the feelings of Muslims, but it concerned him when a rally turns violent. Vice President Hamzah Haz believes that if the rallies continued, Indonesia was going to face more economic hardship and if the country could not escape from the economic crisis, then Indonesia would collapse.

Furthermore, Hamzah Haz stated that the continuing rallies would hurt the image of Islam; and Indonesian Muslims should show the world that Muslims in this country have a peaceful way to uphold the truth. He maintained that the government had taken into account the interests and feelings of Muslims in this country; and that President Megawati has conveyed a message to the US to consider the voice of Islam in the Afghan crisis.

The firmer position of the Indonesian Government – as announced by President Megawati – can also be seen in the handling of the Muslim hardliners by various agencies of the government. President Megawati has indeed given a hint that the government would take firmer action against Muslim hardliners. Speaking after her return from Japan, she pointed out that she objected to the "sweeping" of foreigners. She said that the government would clamp down on hardliners if they carried out their threats.

Further indications of the government's firmer attitude towards Muslim hardliners has also been given by Coordinating Minister of Political and Security Affairs, Susilo Bambang Yudhoyono. Several days after Megawati's above statements, Yudhoyono said that the government would issue a strict ban against Indonesians planning to go to Afghanistan for a *jihad* against the US. He further stated that the Indonesian Government has an obligation to protect its citizens. And the act of physically taking part in a foreign war is not acceptable. The Indonesian immigration office then warned those would-be *jihad* fighters in Afghanistan that the government would revoke their citizenship.

Furthermore, Yudhoyono warned hardliner groups not to carry out their threats to harm Americans and other foreigners. The government further announced that it would take stern action against people who burned the flags or symbols of other nations, or effigies of their heads of state. For that reason, the Indonesian security agencies would not hesitate to disperse or stop demonstrations that had the potential to erupt into anarchy.

This stern action that was foreshadowed of the security agencies soon materialized when some hardliner groups, such as FPI, FPI-Surakarta, Jundullah and the Hizbullah Front, staged an anti-US rally in front of the Parliament building on the holiday of the Prophet Muhammad's Ascension. Protesting the US attacks against Afghanistan, and demanding that the government sever diplomatic relations with the US, the hardliners were confronted by the police. The police ordered them to disperse because – according to the Law – it is prohibited to demonstrate on a holiday, and that Monday was a national holiday. Ignoring the police warning, the clash started after the police fired warning shots; hundreds of police officers then began to fire tear gas, water and blanks at the demonstrators, whereupon they fled to the FPI headquarters on Jalan Petamburan, Tanah Abang. After the incident some five hundred police officers were deployed in the area surrounding the FPI headquarters. The possibility of violence between the two parties was finally avoided only with the intervention of the Minister of Religious Affairs who promised to mediate between them.

The firmer policy of the police does not stop there. The police not only arrested a number of FPI members, but also questioned the leader of FPI, Habib Muhammad Riziq Shihab. The Habib was charged with insulting police and instigating mass hatred; he was also charged with violating the law that bans demonstrations on national holidays.

CONCLUSION

In my view, it is again clear that a hardline version of political Islam has very little prospect in Indonesia. By the same token, it is very doubtful that the hardline Muslim groups will be able to pose a real threat to President Megawati's government.

The reasons are clear. Firstly, hardliner groups are only splinter groups among the vast majority of mainstream Muslims. One should not exaggerate the influence of these hardliners. The nature of Indonesian Islam which is basically tolerant, peaceful and "smiling" will prevent these groups from exerting significant influence. If Indonesia succeeds in re-establishing political stability and economic recovery, Muslims' social, economic and political disorientation will diminish – or at least decrease – and, in the end, will limit the tendency among them to subscribe to radical ideas and practices.

Secondly, the majority of moderate Muslims, on the other hand, continue to support Megawati; some for practical reasons that Megawati should be given a fair chance to lead the nation out of the crisis. Although there is some dissatisfaction among these moderate Muslims with President Megawati's slow political responses, they have refrained from criticizing her strongly, since this will only create an opening for the hardliners to question her legitimacy and ability to lead the country. This is obvious in Amien Rais' attitude and response to President Megawati's policies. Having been known for his strong criticism of Indonesian presidents from Soeharto to Habibie and Wahid, it is now obvious that he is restraining himself from criticizing President Megawati publicly.

Not least in importance is Hamzah Haz's changing attitude. In the case of the US-Afghanistan crisis, he has been criticized for his vague and conflicting statements. In fact, he has been regarded as having split with Megawati. This observation, I would argue, has some truth; but this is not the whole story. We have to acknowledge that there is some suspicion among certain circles towards Hamzah Haz. He is the national leader of the *Partai Persatuan Pembangunan* (PPP/United Development Party) which, as discussed above, is known for its support for the reintroduction of the "Jakarta Charter", an entry point for the implementation of the *shari'ah* (Islamic law) in Indonesia.

Considering his latest attitude, I would suggest that he is making some adjustments and compromises, not only to the reality of Indonesian politics, but also to President Megawati.

In conclusion, I believe President Megawati will survive the challenges posed by Muslim hardliner groups. At the same time, however, she could be kept busy by their continued threatening activities, which, in the end, could affect President Megawati's ability to lead Indonesia into political stability and economic recovery.

CHAPTER 5

COMMUNAL RIOTS IN INDONESIA'S RECENT HISTORY

The fall from grace of President Soeharto in May 1998 in the aftermath of the monetary, economic and political crises has shaken and threatened Indonesian national unity. The emergency installation of incumbent Vice President B.J. Habibie to replace President Soeharto, Indonesian strong man for more than three decades, did to some extent create further division within Indonesian society. Certain political groups in some quarters questioned the legitimacy of Habibie who was sworn in as the new President not in front of the MPR, but in the State Palace. Indeed some people who argue that Soeharto should have declared his resignation in the MPR Assembly considered the self-declared resignation of Soeharto illegal. Thus, with a shaky start, Habibie began his relatively short tenure as the third President of the Republic of Indonesia.

It is beyond doubt that the unusual succession to the presidency was a culmination of the turbulent social, economic and political changes that Indonesia faced in the second half of the 1990s. Since 1995 there have been signs of widespread social and political discontent, not only among the lower classes of the population, but also among the middle classes. It seems that this discontent had its roots, at least in the initial phases, in the widespread economic injustices and deprivation that occurred even though at the time, Indonesia continued to enjoy an "economic boom". In a later phase, this economic discontent merged with the political deprivation that most Indonesians had suffered since the 1970s. The monetary and economic crises that swept most of South East Asia towards the end of 1997 created the momentum for all these feelings of discontent to be expressed more clearly.

This chapter attempts to discuss the communal riots that occurred in Indonesia during the second half of the 1990s. During this period the scale of the riots seems to have increased significantly in both number and in the areas which were (and still are) affected. In addition, there is also strong evidence to suggest that certain communal riots have been part of a much larger separatist movement in certain provinces wanting to gain independence from the Republic of Indonesia. Does this mean that Indonesia is facing disintegration? Will Indonesia have to face a similar "Balkanization" scenario to that of the former Soviet Union or Eastern Europe?

COMMUNAL RIOTS: SEVERAL CASES

Indonesia, which contains vastly different ethnic groups, religions and social systems, seems to have become more and more fragile in the 1990s, This is evident from the fact that communal riots have taken place more often, with increasingly larger numbers of people involved. All of this became more apparent before the general election of 1997 when a number of riots took place in several areas in Indonesia. It is not possible, however, for us to discuss all cases of communal riots in Indonesia given the very large number involved. For our purpose here, therefore, I will only discuss several major cases that will help us to better understand not only the causes, motives and patterns of the riots, but also the political implications of the riots for the future of Indonesian nationalism and the nation state.

EAST TIMOR

There is no doubt that communal riots in East Timor were the ones that have attracted the most international attention. In fact, the riots were only part of the much larger East Timor question that has gripped the imagination of such international bodies as the United Nations, Human Rights Watch and others. Furthermore, from the perspective of many East Timorese, the riots have been an inalienable part of their struggle for separation from Indonesia and, finally, towards independence.

One of the largest riots in East Timor was the Santa Cruz incident. This incident was triggered by the Indonesian military (ABRI) shooting East Timorese civilians who were marching to a public cemetery in order to pay their condolences to Sebastio Gomes, a young man who had been killed by Indonesian soldiers during their attack on the Motael Church, which the ABRI believed was one of the havens for anti-Indonesian East Timorese. The Santa Cruz incident, which left hundreds of East Timorese dead, brought Indonesia international condemnation. Worse still, the Santa Cruz massacre was a very crucial setback for Indonesia's cause in East Timor. Before the Santa Cruz massacre, Indonesia had almost won its case, that is, wider international recognition of Indonesian authority over the area. The incident provided momentum not only for anti-Indonesian forces in East Timor, but also for the UN, Portugal, and others to launch an international campaign against Indonesian rule in East Timor.

Even though the Indonesian military was in full control of the situation in East Timor, it was also clear that the embers of conflict remained. It is not surprising that another large-scale communal riot later erupted in Comoro Market, Dili, in the middle of November 1994. The trigger for the riots was the killing of an East Timorese trader by Buginese migrant traders who originally came from South Sulawesi. The killing soon triggered wide-scale riots and violence against virtually all migrant traders, especially the Buginese who had, since the early 1980s, dominated the East Timorese economy. Pasar Comoro, a center for Buginese trading, was burned down, and a great number of traders (estimated at more than 150,000), were forced to take refuge at police and military stations and other government buildings.

If these two above mentioned cases were economically and politically motivated, then the communal violence that erupted in early September 1995 in Viqueque and Maliana was religious in nature. Religious coloring was obvious in both of these cases. In the case of the Maliana riots, it was reported that Sanusi Abu Bakar, a Muslim, had acted in a manner considered blasphemous to Catholicism. In Viqueque, the cause was a mixed marriage between a Protestant man and Catholic woman. The marriage, which had not been condoned by the Catholic Church, finally led to communal and religious violence, not only in the burning of Protestant churches, markets, schools and other buildings, but also attacks on virtually all non-Catholic people. Communal riots with a strong religious fervor once again took place on the 21 February 1997 in Ambeno. A non-Catholic person was reportedly blasphemous to a Catholic pastor. Before long, masses ran amuck, burning houses and other buildings belonging to non-Catholics, and non-Catholic people had to be taken to safe places.

The fall of Soeharto in May 1998 only fueled further social and political unrest in East Timor. With the decline of the military grip on power in most of Indonesia – including in East Timor – the East Timorese believed that this was the time to build momentum in their bid for separation from Indonesia. President B.J. Habibie, without serious consultation with the MPR or the Parliament (DPR), finally decided to hold a referendum offering two options to the East Timorese people: greater autonomy within the Republic of Indonesia, or independence. In the referendum, which was held under UN auspices, the East Timorese, as expected, overwhelmingly chose the second option.

With the referendum result, mass violence loomed larger in East Timor since the pro-Indonesia militias, believing that the referendum had been manipulated by the United Nations Assistance Mission for East Timor (UNAMET), declared that they would fight to the last. This very alarming situation only led to further international interference in East Timor with the formation and arrival of the International Force for East Timor (Interfet) under the leadership of Australia, which had shown a great deal of hostility to Indonesia during the whole process. With the arrival of Interfet, East Timorese independence had been guaranteed, and in early November, the United Nations Transition Administration in East Timor (UNTAET) officially took over the administration of East Timor from Indonesia.

The East Timor case of "separatism" is indeed a special case in the rise of "local nationalism" in Indonesia. Despite the fact that Indonesia had failed to win international recognition of East Timor's integration into Indonesia in 1975, many Indonesians believed that this area was an integral part of Indonesia. The separation and independence of East Timor could, therefore, only inspire other provinces with tendencies of political separatism such as

Aceh, Irian Jaya, Riau and others to follow suit. Indeed, there are convincing signs that separatist movements have increasingly gained momentum in these provinces over the last two years.

It is important to point out that almost all Indonesians have now finally, albeit with regret, accepted the separation and independence of East Timor. At the same time, however, they also believe that the East Timorese case was in stark contrast to that of some other provinces that are now voicing their intention to separate from the Republic. All other provinces concerned not only were integral parts of the area administered by the Dutch colonial government, but also have been unified within the Republic of Indonesia since the proclamation of Indonesian independence on 17 August 1945. Accepting and treating the other provinces in the same way as that of East Timor will, therefore, only mean the end of the Indonesian nation-state.

ACEH

The Aceh case does have certain similarities with the East Timor case for separation and independence, particularly in the aftermath of President Soeharto's fall from grace. With the significant decline in Jakarta's central authority, together with the rapid plummeting in popularity of the Indonesian Army, Acehnese local "nationalism" is apparently attracting more Acehnese supporters. Further, the political gestures and accommodation made by subsequent presidents have failed to appease many Acehnese with the result that the Gerakan Aceh Merdeka (GAM), or Free Aceh Movement appears to continue to gain a greater following. With the escalation of Acehnese pressures on Jakarta, which now leaves very limited options, one wonders how the then newly elected President Megawati Soekarnoputri will solve the Aceh case.

One has to be very careful before putting the Aceh case in the same pigeonhole as the East Timor case. Aceh is an integral part of the Republic of Indonesia, partly as a result of Dutch colonialism, which unified virtually the entire archipelago under a single administration. In contrast, East Timor became a province of Indonesia only after military annexation in the early 1970s. A further significant difference is the fact that the Acehnese are Muslim while the East Timorese are Catholic. In other words, the Aceh case to a certain degree represents a "rebellion" against the central government of Indonesia, which is at least predominantly Muslim. In this regard, one may argue that the Acehnese case does not involve religious sentiments as in the case of East Timor.

Furthermore, the Aceh case seems also to represent the unfinished formation and forging of Indonesian nationalism. Aceh has long been acclaimed as among the first regions in Indonesia that fully supported Indonesian independence and declared itself an integral part of the newly established Republic of Indonesia in 1945. In fact, the Acehnese collected money and gold for the central government so that Jakarta was able to purchase an aircraft named *Seulawah*, the name of a mountain in Aceh. Despite this support, the central government, since the time of Soekarno, Indonesia's first President, has apparently neglected Aceh.

It is no surprise, therefore, that the "honeymoon" period between Aceh and Jakarta did not last long. The Jakarta government implemented some policies that were unacceptable to the people of Aceh. Jakarta, in fact, did not deliver on its promises such as the recognition and implementation of a special status for Aceh. As a result, political and social discontent was soon widespread in Aceh, which led to the rise of the secessionist movements, better known as the Darul Islam movement (1953-1954). The movement was even stronger when the charismatic Acehnese *ulama* Daud Beureuh joined it. Even though the Indonesian government was able to restore law and order in Aceh, the seeds of Acehnese separatism continued to grow under the leadership of Hasan Tiro who, in New York in 1954, initially proclaimed the "Islamic Republic of Indonesia" but this move was of no interest to many Indonesians. On 4 December 1977, Hasan Tiro proclaimed "Aceh Merdeka", the independent Aceh.

Since then, Acehnese history has been a history of military repression and political and economic injustice. Economic development, which was accelerated by Soeharto in Aceh through a process of industrialization, only created further social discontent. Aceh received few benefits from its own economic bonanza, especially in petroleum and gas. As a result, social and political unrest increasingly worsened. This led to Soeharto's regime to impose the "Aceh Military Zone" (*Daerah Operasi Militer* – DOM), which was finally suspended by President Habibie in 1998.

The suspension of the Aceh Military Zone has meant not only the withdrawal of Indonesian combat troops from Aceh, but also the disclosure of widespread military atrocities and human rights abuses in many parts of Aceh. It is very difficult to get an exact number of the victims of the period of DOM. According to the NGO Forum of Aceh, they have found fifteen mass graves, which are estimated to contain some 1,240 human skulls or skeletons. There are also estimates that at least 1,321 people were killed, 1,958 went missing, 3,430 were tortured, and more than 209 women were raped or sexually abused during this period (Al Chaidar 1999).

With these findings, it is clear that the Aceh case is becoming difficult to resolve. The disclosure of widespread atrocities by the military during the DOM period has added fuel to the Acehnese appeal to Jakarta to bring all the military personnel involved in the atrocities to justice. It is also evident though that President Habibie and military commander General Wiranto were reluctant to do so and when Abdurrahman Wahid and Megawati Soekarnoputri took over the presidency, they inherited a more complicated Aceh case.

It is important to point out that since the time of the Habibie presidency, Jakarta has attempted in a variety of ways to listen to the Acehnese grievances and accommodate their aspirations. Firstly, President Habibie offered his condolences and regrets to the victims of the DOM, and asked forgiveness for all past ill treatment of the Acehnese. He also introduced a number of development projects to be implemented in the shortest time possible. Later, the DPR passed a bill that recognizes Aceh province as having special status. The bill, which was soon approved as law by President Habibie, allowed for greater local autonomy for instance in the ability of the Aceh provincial government to implement Islamic law -instead of national law- throughout Aceh. In addition, in accordance with the newly passed laws on the sharing of local revenues, Aceh will get the lion's share of its revenues from petroleum, gas and other resources. Finally, the general session of the MPR in October 1999 issued a special decree granting wide autonomy to Aceh together with Irian Jaya.

All of these accommodations and concessions by Jakarta, however, seem to have failed to appease many Acehnese. President Abdurrahman Wahid, who was expected to find quick solutions to what were rapidly becoming more complicated problems, was instead regarded by many Acehnese as well as by the speakers of the MPR and DPR (Amien Rais and Akbar Tandjung respectively) as having been too slow to take the necessary actions. President Abdurrahman Wahid, better known as Gus Dur, publicly assigned himself the task of solving the Acehnese question, and Vice President Megawati of solving the Ambon case. The President later appeared to be more interested in foreign travels to several Asian countries, the US and the Middle East. Not only that, but Abdurrahman Wahid created further controversy by stating that the Indonesian military had not been involved in atrocities and other human rights abuses in Aceh. After a great deal of harsh criticism from many quarters, former President Gus Dur appeared to change his attitude toward Aceh, and offered some "persuasive" means for resolving the Aceh case.

At the same time, however, political action continually gained momentum in Aceh. The Acehnese, for instance, held huge rallies on 8 November 2000 in Banda Aceh, the provincial capital, which were reportedly attended by more than one million Acehnese from all over the province. As one might expect, they appealed to the central government to accept a "referendum" as the only means of settling their case peacefully. For them, there are only two options to be decided in a proposed referendum: wider autonomy within the Republic of Indonesia, or independence. This kind of proposed referendum is certainly similar to that held in East Timor.

Hopes for a referendum appeared to run high among the Acehnese when President Wahid, during a press conference while traveling in South Asia, stated that he accepted the proposed referendum. He stated that if the East Timorese had been given the chance to hold a referendum, then why not the Acehnese? He considered it unfair not to give the same chance to the Acehnese. However, Gus Dur later clarified what he meant by "referendum". According to him, he would accept a referendum which would basically consist of three options: first, much wider autonomy; second, implementation of Islamic law; and finally, a much fairer share in the province revenues. So, according to Wahid, any referendum would not include the option to become independent. It remains unclear if all the options proposed by former President Gus Dur were acceptable to many Acehnese.

Thus, it is difficult to predict the future of Aceh even during Megawati's presidency. For the Republic, allowing Aceh to hold a referendum with an option to become independent could lead to the final separation of Aceh from the Republic. Learning from the East Timor experience, almost everybody in Indonesia has every reason to believe that the majority of Acehnese would choose to become independent from Indonesia if a referendum were held. If this happened, it would set a harmful precedent that could inspire other provinces with similar aspirations for separatism to galvanize their efforts to obtain their own independence. In other words, an independent Aceh will certainly create a "domino effect" in other provinces that have separatist agendas, such as Irian Jaya, Riau, East Kalimantan, etc. Not only this, but certain countries in Southeast Asia such as the Philippines with the Moro separatist problem, or Thailand with its Patani question, may also be affected. It is, therefore, important to note that all ASEAN countries as well as Japan, China, Korea, the US, Australia and others have made it clear that Aceh is under the sovereignty of Indonesia. They agree that Aceh must remain an integral part of the Republic. At the same time, however, they express the wish to see Indonesia find a peaceful means to resolve the case.

AMBON

The Ambon communal violence, which worsened and spread to other parts of the province of Maluku, is perhaps most often quoted as a clear case of religious conflict and violence in Indonesia today. This observation is, at least on the surface, perhaps true to some extent. Communal conflict and violence in Ambon and other places in Maluku such as Halmahera and Ternate, involves the Muslim community on the one hand, and the Protestant community on the other. The large scale violence which has and continues to take place between the two religious groups resulted not only in the killing of a large number of people (both Muslims and Christians), but also in the burning of mosques, churches, houses, markets and other public buildings and facilities. According to a report (on 27 November 1999), the violence that occurred in the eleven preceding months left 693 people dead and almost two thousand injured, and countless numbers of buildings destroyed. The scale of the violence is certainly worsening, and there are no clear signs of an end in sight.

It is no secret, of course, that Muslims and Christians in Maluku have long been involved in a sort of race to gain the upper hand in religion, economics and politics. According to more reliable sources, Islam came to Maluku in the fifteenth century, and by the turn of that century, the Ternate Sultanate had been established. The Portuguese who came to Maluku in 1513 not only to trade, but also to spread Christianity soon challenged the Sultans of Ternate. Conflict and wars soon erupted between the two opposing sides, however the Portuguese surrendered in 1575 after a long siege of their fort in Ternate by Sultan Baabullah. Before long, the European forces were again coming to Maluku. This time the Dutch, who initially came in 1599, began to take control of one area after another in Maluku. Later, with their firm grip on control, Dutch missionaries were also in a strong position to spread Christianity in Maluku.

After Indonesia gained independence on 17 August 1945, groups of Moluccan Christians, who used to possess political and military privileges during colonial times, proclaimed the independence of the South Moluccan Republic (in April 1950). This separatism, despite the fact that it created prolonged political problems for both the Republic of Indonesia and the Netherlands, failed to realize its political ambitions.

This brief historical account seems to justify the argument that the still ongoing communal riots and violence in Ambon and elsewhere in Maluku are religious in nature. I would argue that religion indeed plays a certain role in this communal conflict, but this role came only later. In other words, there are other important factors that have worked to create hostilities and conflicts between the two religious communities. When clashes were (and are) taking place between religious groups (Muslims and Christians) religion has been used to rally and legitimize violent acts on behalf of each respective religion.

As I argued elsewhere, the Ambon or Maluku communal riots have their roots in the contest for economic resources and the increasingly disproportionate distribution of political power in the local bureaucracy between Muslims (consisting of indigenous Maluku people and migrants better known as the BBM [Buginese, Butonese, Makassarese], all from South Sulawesi) and indigenous Christians over the last two decades at least. The New Order government of President Soeharto failed to address these latent problems. Instead, the regime tried to hide the problems under the carpet mainly through the all too familiar security approach. In the framework of this approach, no one has been allowed to discuss the problems openly and thus find feasible and viable solutions for these problems, all of which involved issues of SARA (*Suku, Agama, Ras, Antar-golongan*, or ethnicity, religion, race, inter-group), which were considered by the regime to be very sensitive and divisive issues.

As has been mentioned above, during the Soeharto era, the demographic composition of the Maluku province changed rapidly. According to some reports, up until the 1970s, the indigenous Christians constituted a slim majority of the total population. Since the early 1980s, however, with the improved economy and better means of transportation, the BBM people from South Sulawesi came steadily in large numbers and settled in various areas of Maluku, particularly in Ambon. With their arrival, the Muslims in Maluku increasingly outnumbered the Christians. This development not only affected the demographic composition, but also resulted in increasing changes in the fields of economics and politics. Before long, BBM migrants dominated the Maluku economy as economic opportunities opened for them and the indigenous Christians showed more interest in being civil servants than traders. The resentment of the indigenous Christian population was twofold since almost all the BBM migrants were Muslims.

Communal relations rapidly worsened when the Muslims became increasingly politically active. To take one obvious example, the last two governors of Maluku province have been Muslims. This seemly unstoppable Muslim political mobility challenged the Christians who used to dominate the local bureaucracy, and undoubtedly was an important factor in the rapid growth of ethnic and religious hostilities. All these demographic, economic and political changes strained the already fragile fabric of Maluku society, waiting only for the right time to explode.

Like the cases of East Timor and Aceh, therefore, the sudden fall of Soeharto and the shaky authority of President Habibie soon rekindled the embers of the conflict and tension within Ambon and Maluku society. Triggered by a trivial matter, a quarrel between a Christian youth and Muslims over the fare of a city public bus, large scale riots erupted in Ambon on 19 January 1999, the very night before the Muslims were to celebrate *Idul*

Fitri, the celebration which marks the end of the fasting month of Ramadhan. Since that time, intermittent clashes and violence between Christian and Muslim groups has continued, leaving large numbers of people dead and countless homes, markets and other buildings completely destroyed. Clashes and riots, which initially erupted in Ambon, the capital city of Maluku province, continue to spread to other parts of the Maluku province, giving the strong impression that the communal riots are far from being resolved by the central government which has its hands full with other pressing national problems.

One of the most important factors contributing to the prolonged nature of the communal riots has been the indecisiveness of the police and military. They have thus far failed to put an end to the continuing conflicts. At the same time, there is a lot of evidence that Indonesian security forces are entangled in the violence. Some members are taking partisan positions by defending either the Christian or Muslim groups. Worse still, they use their armaments to confront groups of people who do not belong to their religion. This is why the military commander in Jakarta has replaced most of the security forces in Maluku with those recruited from other places in Indonesia although this policy, by and large, has also failed.

The election of Abdurrahman Wahid brought new hopes for a peaceful settlement of the Ambon case. President Wahid, a few days after his inauguration, assigned Vice President Megawati to resolve the case through dialogue and other peaceful means. The situation in Ambon and Maluku remained unsettled with continuing outbursts of violence taking place. Although she is now president, Megawati seems to be very indecisive and has not yet implemented any specific policy or action to stop the killing, burning and self-destruction in Maluku.

Lastly, I would argue that, thus far, the Ambon case seems to have little to do with separatism. Suspicion and accusations have, of course, come from certain camps that the RMS continues to play a certain role in the riots in order to revive their old ambition of establishing a South Moluccan Republic. In my opinion, there is no convincing evidence of involvement by the RMS. It is true that unless the Indonesian Government takes quick and decisive action to resolve this issue, there will be no immediate end to the conflict.

WEST KALIMANTAN

The West Kalimantan case is certainly different from the East Timor and Aceh cases, and has little similarity to the case in Ambon. If the East Timor and Aceh cases contain strong "local nationalism" or separatist sentiments, the West Kalimantan case has been strongly colored by deep-rooted ethnic conflict between the indigenous Dayak (who were later supported by the West Kalimantan Malay), and the migrant Madurese. Religious factors are clearly not important in this conflict for the three ethnic groups involved in the communal riots are not aligned along religious lines. The first group consists of the Dayak, who are mainly Christians, and the Malays who are Muslims. The second group is the Madurese who, like the Malays, are Muslims. Thus, the motivating factors of the communal riots in West Kalimantan are not religious, but largely ethnic.

One should be very cautious, however, before jumping to the conclusion that the West Kalimantan communal riots are genuinely motivated by ethnicity alone. Ethnic factors, in fact, only emerged later when the conflict intensified. Ethnic motives seem to have been merely a rallying point to justify conflict and violence between the two groups. Stereotyping of each ethnic group by the other has been created, perpetuated and used as a justification for attacks against one another.

Taking all this into consideration, the West Kalimantan case clearly has nothing to do with the rise of local nationalism and separation. The case is largely one of economic deprivation, which is associated with ethnicity. The West Kalimantan communal riots took place mostly in the Sambas and Pontianak areas at the end of 1996, and continued into early 1997. The scale of the riots was unprecedented. It is reported that more than 1,720 people were killed in the Sanggau Ledo (Sambas) riots alone, and more people were killed in the aftermath of the Sanggau Ledo riots when they spread to other areas in West Kalimantan, particularly in Pontianak, the capital city of the province. Furthermore, countless houses and buildings owned by the Madurese were completely destroyed, and thousands of Madurese were displaced and had to be removed permanently from the Sambas and Pontianak areas. Many of them are still housed in temporary refugee camps. This is indeed a pitiful case of human suffering. Most of the Madurese refugees are not able to return to

Madura since many of them were born in West Kalimantan and no longer have relatives and property in their original homeland.

Despite this large-scale human suffering, the communal riots between the Dayaks and Madurese are not new. Over the last forty-seven years, there have been at least eleven recorded incidents of communal riots, although on a much lesser scale of human and material losses. This means that, on average, one clash has occurred every five years. Communal conflicts and riots have, therefore, been a latent element in inter-ethnic relations in West Kalimantan.

How do we explain the West Kalimantan case? The answer is that there is no single explanation. The explanation of the case lies not only in various factors in West Kalimantan itself, but also in the policies of the Central Government in Jakarta. At the provincial level, there is no doubt that communal conflict and violence have their roots in the strained relationship between the indigenous Dayak in particular and the migrant Madurese. As mentioned earlier, the conflict between the two ethnic groups has resulted in intermittent conflict and clashes over the last fifty years. In this context, the bloody clashes of 1997-1998 are not new, but are, in fact, a recurrent and unsolved problem.

The cultural differences between the two ethnic groups seem to be the most important factor behind the strained relations between them. In West Kalimantan the Madurese are generally perceived as aggressive, stubborn and cunning, who do not respect the local people's culture, customs and sensitivity. The Madurese also allegedly take their clurit (a Madurese keris or sword) wherever they go. This stereotype of the Madurese is, of course, not new as the Madurese have been stereotyped in the same way since the Dutch colonial period. The persistence of the stereotype indicates two possibilities only: first, that the stereotype is indeed true and is part and parcel of the Madurese character; or second, that the Madurese have not changed their nature even after taking up residence outside their original homeland, as in West Kalimantan.

On the other hand, the Dayak have also been stereotyped by many outsiders, including by the Javanese and perhaps also by the Madurese. The Dayaks have been mostly regarded as uncivilized people whose main preoccupation is hunting for human scalps. This seemingly mutual stereotyping and the daily attitudes and habits of the Madurese observed by the Dayaks – and also the Malays – in West Kalimantan, have created not only a clash of culture, but also hostility and hatred between them. As in the case of Muslim and Christian relations in Ambon, the strained relations between the Dayaks and the Madurese were never allowed to be discussed openly under Soeharto, as they were considered to be SARA issues.

Even though economic factors have also been mentioned as one of the most important factors contributing to the communal violence between the two ethnic groups, it does not seem to be entirely true. It is true that the Madurese are very aggressive in their economic ventures, but most of them are very poor, living as small vendors and becak (pedicab) drivers. In fact, those who play a more visible role in the West Kalimantan economy such as the Chinese, Malays and Buginese, have never been targets of Dayak hostility and hatred. There appears to be no recorded communal riots between the Dayak and the Chinese.

For the time being, the communal riots between the Dayak and the Madurese seem to have calmed down. It is clear, however, that the case is still far from being resolved and possible further conflict and violence is anticipated. Formal and informal leaders both in West Kalimantan and at the national level have not yet contemplated any serious discussions and policies to resolve the issue.

CONCLUSION

There is strong evidence that Indonesian nationalism is in decline. At the same time, parochialism and nationalism in certain provinces is on the rise. In the post-Soeharto period, these sentiments have become more vocal and determined *vis-à-vis* the central government in terms of seeking greater autonomy, or even independence from the Republic of Indonesia (such as in East Timor, Aceh, Irian Jaya, Riau and East Kalimantan).

Since the fall of Soeharto, Indonesian politics has undoubtedly been in disarray. President Habibie did a good job in providing much greater room for freedom of political expression by allowing the establishment of a large number of political parties as well by suspending restrictions imposed on the press and media by the Soeharto regime. One has to acknowledge that

Habibie, Wahid and Megawati have all failed to address the growing tendency of separatism. In his relatively short tenure – fifteen months only – Habibie raced against time to introduce two important laws: the law of provincial autonomy and the law of revenue sharing between the provincial and national governments. With the continued rise in parochial and nationalist sentiment, it is now clear to the central government that these two laws fall short of fulfilling the political aspirations of the belligerent provinces. Given the political eclecticism of President Wahid, one really wonders how he could have put an end to local separatism and rejuvenated Indonesian nationalism.

The five principles outlined in *Pancasila* are no doubt the backbone of Indonesian nationalism and the nation-state. It is fair to say, however, that there has been a significant erosion among many Indonesians of the belief in *Pancasila*. This erosion has a lot to do with the fact that the Soeharto regime made use of the *Pancasila* for its own purposes by claiming exclusive rights to its interpretation. Worse still, the New Order regime carried out the indoctrination of *Pancasila* according to Soeharto's interpretation, and forced all organizations to accept the *Pancasila* as the sole basis of their organization.

Despite the erosion of belief in the *Pancasila*, many Indonesians are also in agreement that there is nothing wrong with the *Pancasila* itself. The *Pancasila*, in their opinion, has been able to function as one of the most important unifying factors of post-colonial Indonesia. The problem was the Soeharto regime's hegemony over the *Pancasila* and the use of *Pancasila* for its own purposes. Another huge task facing President Megawati is, therefore, the realization and rejuvenation of the *Pancasila*.

In addition to this, in order to revive Indonesian nationalism, President Megawati needs to reassess the orientation and strategy of Indonesian economic development. It is clear that one of the most important factors in the rise of local nationalism is economic inequality and injustice. Unless President Megawati institutes viable and sustainable policies to implement a more balanced, fair and just economic program, Indonesian nationalism will certainly continue to face very deep trouble.

PART TWO

INDONESIA, ISLAM, AND THE INTERNATIONAL ORDER

CHAPTER 6

ISLAM IN INDONESIAN FOREIGN POLICY

In the last two decades, the Islamic world has witnessed something of an Islamic revival. Indonesian Muslims to a certain extent are likewise affected by the euphoria of Islamic revivalism; and there is much evidence to suggest that Islam, like other religions in Indonesia, is also experiencing a revival. As a result, since the end of the 1980s, Muslims have frequently succeeded in influencing the making of government domestic policy for the interests of Islam and Muslims. For this reason, it is interesting to consider how Muslims' increasing pressure on the government has affected the course of Indonesia's foreign policy, so far as Islamic issues are concerned. This paper attempts to delineate the "role" or, more appropriately, the position of Islam in Indonesia's foreign policy by taking into consideration several cases, involving Islam directly or indirectly.

Indonesia is the most populous Muslim nation in the world. Despite the fact that Muslims constitute a majority of Indonesia's total population, Indonesia is not an Islamic state, nor, for that matter, a secular one. It is a *Pancasila* state which places religions – including Islam – in an important position. This can be seen, for instance, in the national ideology of *Pancasila* ("Five Principles"), which adopts "belief in One Supreme God" as its very first principle. Furthermore, in the cabinet, there is also the Ministry of Religious Affairs which is responsible for developing and maintaining a healthy and dynamic national religious environment. Finally, and not least in importance, religions are considered one of the most important ethical bases of national development, and this has been accelerated by the New Order government in the last two decades at least.

Muslims have overwhelmingly accepted *Pancasila* as the final ideological basis of the Indonesian state. So, it seems, there is little question about national ideology and the form of the Indonesian state. Questions most commonly arise on the extent to which Islam (or, more precisely, Muslims) becomes a factor in both domestic and foreign policies; and how Muslims influence Indonesia's foreign policy. This point seems to be significant for, as Hasjim Djalal argues, foreign policy is a reflection of domestic policy; in many cases domestic politics even dictates foreign policy; or as Jusuf Wanandi points out, the borders between internal affairs and international developments have become blurred. (Djalal, 1996: 34; Wanandi, 1989: 356, Abdulgani, 1989: 322).

But, so far as Indonesia's domestic politics is concerned, it appears that Islam is not regarded as a significant factor that can influence foreign policy. Both Djalal, a former diplomat and leading scholar on Indonesian foreign policy, and Wanandi, an expert in international relations, exclude Islam as a domestic factor which influences Indonesia's foreign policy. Instead, according to Djalal, there are several other domestic factors that influence Indonesia's foreign policy. (Djalal, 1996: 35-6).

The first factor is national development, particularly in the social and economic fields. Djalal argues further that the foreign policy of Indonesia will continue to be "development oriented" in the sense that it will continue to support the development efforts of Indonesia. In this regard, Indonesia's foreign policy is aimed at maintaining and developing a regional or international environment for Indonesia that would promote regional peace and stability, social and economic growth and a cooperative relationship among foreign states. The efforts to promote international peace and cooperation will, therefore, continue to gain Indonesian attention.

The second domestic factor is the issue of national unity. This factor is closely related to the fact that Indonesia is a plural state not only in terms of ethnicities, cultures, languages and religions, but also in terms of the relative stages of economic development among Indonesia's twenty-seven provinces.

Problems could arise from each of these; and they may affect national unity and political stability, which could make it difficult to pursue an effective foreign policy. It is a mission of foreign policy to, therefore, support and promote national unity, stability and development in Indonesia.

The third factor is the enforcement of justice and law. Djalal argues that the growing interest among Indonesian citizens in the issue of justice and law enforcement could affect the credibility of the government, thereby making it difficult to pursue an effective foreign policy. The debate on the laxity of justice and law enforcement may, in turn, affect the direction and essence of Indonesia's economic development strategies and, subsequently, the implementation of foreign policy as well, since foreign policy is itself oriented to economic development. (Djalal, 1996: 41-43).

The fourth factor concerns the issues of democratization and human rights. According to Djalal, while Indonesia maintains a certain kind of democracy based on its own experience and cultural background, the democratization process is continually pursued in order to give it more "substance" and "form". Indonesia takes a good lesson from the case of the former Soviet Union where a hasty and abrupt democratization process became uncontrollable and unmanageable and, in the end, brought about the disintegration of the whole system. Yet, without the proper substance and form, a slow democratization process could also create problems. Equally, human rights issues have been a global concern and, therefore, it is difficult for Indonesia to avoid such issues. Thus, the issues of democratization and human rights, particularly in East Timor and Irian Jaya will continue to influence the implementation of Indonesia's foreign policy in the future. Any retrogression in the process of democratization and promotion of human rights in Indonesia will make it more difficult for foreign policy makers to maneuver.(Djalal, 1996: 43-4; Wanandi, 1989: 351-2).

INDONESIA, MIDDLE EASTERN COUNTRIES AND ISLAM

Thus, as is clear from some of the arguments outlined above, the Indonesian Government is believed to have disregarded Islam as an important factor in the development of its foreign policy. Despite the fact that Indonesia generally remains on good terms with Muslim states in the Middle East, Indonesia has tended not to associate itself with Islam. This could surprise some people considering the fact that Indonesian independence on 17 August 1945 was firstly recognized by some Muslim countries in the Middle East, such as Egypt and Saudi Arabia, and that Indonesia has such a large Muslim population.

It is therefore important to clarify that if Indonesia has extended support to certain Middle Eastern countries or groups of Muslim people, then that support was basically not on the grounds of religion [Islam]. Rather, it has been on the basis that Indonesia supports those who struggle for independence and justice in order, as is stated in the Preamble of Indonesia's 1945 Constitution, to create a just international order.

One case in point, for instance, is Indonesia's support for the Palestinian struggle. Indonesia continually supports the Palestinians in their struggle against Israel on the principle, outlined in the Indonesian National Constitution of 1945, that the Palestinian people, like other peoples, are entitled to independence, free from injustice and suppression. In other words, Indonesia's support for the Palestinian cause is not based on the principle of Islamic solidarity, but on humanity. As a result, Islam is almost absent in formal Indonesian foreign policy.

Even though Muslims in the archipelago have had a long and rich history of religio-intellectual relations with their co-religionists in the Middle East, (Azra, 1992; von der Mehden, 1992; and Abaza, 1994). Indonesia's diplomatic relations with Middle Eastern countries have not always been warm. From the time of Indonesian independence to the 1950's, Indonesia's foreign policy, by and large, was oriented to establishing a close political relationship. The reason for such a policy is clear: Indonesia was in need of continuing support to preserve its newly-gained independence. At the same time, Indonesia and Middle Eastern countries had similar interests in their opposition to colonialism.

The close relations between the two sides were celebrated with the Asian-African Conference which was held in Bandung in 1955. The conference was attended by twenty-nine countries, including such Middle Eastern countries as Egypt, Iraq, Iran, Turkey, Jordan, Libya, Lebanon, Saudi Arabia, Syria and North Yemen. The Bandung Spirit led the General Assembly of the United Nations in 1960 to pass the well-known resolution known as the "Declaration on the Granting of Independence to Colonial Countries and Peoples", which was later and better known as the "Resolution of Decolonization" (Kusumaatmadja, 1983). In the implementation of the resolution, Indonesia was appointed as a member of the Committee on Decolonization. Thereafter, the decolonization process proceeded rapidly. By 1955, only eleven Middle Eastern countries had gained their independence; there are now some twenty-five Middle Eastern countries that are independent. (Dipoyudo, 1985: 479).

The conference succeeded not only in strengthening relations between Indonesia and Middle Eastern countries in particular, but also in enhancing Indonesia's reputation for its major role in the decolonization process of the so-called third world countries, including those in the Middle East. Furthermore, Indonesia also lent its support to Egypt when it nationalized the Suez Canal in 1956. Indonesia declared that Egypt had inalienable rights to nationalize the Canal in accordance with the Universal Company of the Suez Canal (Deplu RI, 1971: 251-252). In addition, in November 1956, Indonesia, together with other Asian-African countries, put forward a resolution that was accepted by the UN General Assembly on the withdrawal of British, French and Israeli forces from Egyptian soil. President Soekarno himself further cemented Indonesia's close relationship with the Middle East through his visits to Egypt and Saudi Arabia in May 1956, and to Iraq in April 1960 (Pender, 1975: 98-9). In return for this Indonesian support, Middle Eastern countries gave their support to Indonesia, particularly to Indonesia's struggle to win control of West Papua (now Irian Jaya province).

Indonesia's relations with Middle Eastern countries, however, changed significantly during Soekarno's "guided democracy" era in the early 1960s. During this period the makers of Indonesia's foreign policy abandoned the independent and active principle which they had adhered to thus far. President Soekarno, instead, created a new demarcation line against what he called the "old established forces" (Oldefos) championed by Western countries, which was led by the US. From then until the demise of Soekarno following the Indonesian Communist Party's abortive coup d'etat on 30 September 1965, Indonesia's foreign policy became more and more radical (Abdulgani, 1985: 324-5).

With this change in its foreign policy, Indonesia's relations with Arab countries soured. Indonesia was disappointed with most of the Middle Eastern countries which showed no solidarity with Soekarno's gestures. Indonesia had refused to allow Israel's athletes to participate in the Asian Games IV held in Jakarta in 1962 but Middle Eastern countries did not support Indonesia when the latter withdrew from the Olympic Games in Tokyo in 1964. Similarly, Middle Eastern countries were not supportive of Soekarno's *konfrontasi* policy against Malaysia. Even though Indonesia opposed the Malaysian presence at the Non-Aligned Summit in Cairo (1964), Arab countries accepted it in the Conference as an observer (Roesnadi, 1979: 250).

The rise of the New Order government under Soeharto in the aftermath of the abortive communist coup d'etat in 1965 did not significantly improve Indonesia's relations with Middle Eastern countries. Even though Soeharto abandoned Soekarno's high profile in foreign policy, it was not until the second half of the 1970s that Indonesia made serious attempts to improve its relations with Middle Eastern countries. In fact, some Arab countries questioned Indonesia's position, for example, in the case of the Arab-Israeli conflict. Arab countries felt that Indonesia did not show its full support for the Arab countries in their war against Israel in 1967 (Roesnadi, 1979: 252).

Driven to a large extent by economic concerns, Indonesia began to seriously improve its relations with Middle Eastern countries in the second half of the 1970s. Indonesian leaders realized that Indonesia had gained very little of Arab petro-dollars compared with the large amount of financial aid and investment made in other countries by the rich Arab states. Worse still, when the emerging industrial countries such as Japan, South Korea, Taiwan and Singapore were competing for, and winning access to, the Middle Eastern market for their products, Indonesia was unable to increase its share in Middle Eastern trade, despite the visits of Indonesian special trade missions in the two years after 1973 to a number of Middle Eastern countries.

For these reasons President Soeharto visited Iran (June 1975) and a number of Arab countries such as Egypt, Saudi Arabia, Kuwait, Syria, Bahrain, and United Arab Emirates (October 1977). These visits not only ameliorated Indonesia's diplomatic relations with the Middle East, but also encouraged closer economic ties between them. In June 1978 President Soeharto ordered the establishment of the "Coordinating Team for Export Activities to the Middle East" within the Department of Trade and Cooperatives. Indonesia also took part in trade fairs in Cairo, Izmir, Damascus, Baghdad, Sharjah and Jeddah. In addition, Indonesia held a sole trade exhibition in Jeddah and carried out market surveys in Bahrain, Kuwait and Algeria (von der Mehden, 1992: 26-7). Economic concerns were also prominent in the visit (14 to 16 November 1996) of former President Soeharto to the Middle East, to be exact, to Jordan. The issue of how to boost economic cooperation dominated the talks between President Soeharto and King Hussain of Jordan. They also appealed to Israel to be serious in its peace efforts in the Middle East (*Jakarta Post*, 13 November 1996).

It is thus clear that religious affinities alone between the two regions have played a less significant role than economic and trade considerations. Indonesia had to carry out serious and concerted efforts to gain greater economic benefits from their Middle Eastern counterparts. To this end, Indonesia had to make some readjustment and reorientation in its foreign policy, and this has been done apparently without involving Islam formally or explicitly.

Apart from economic motives, one should also take into account some significant developments in Indonesian domestic politics that have influenced the course of Indonesia's foreign policy. The most crucial development began at around the time of Muslims' acceptance of *Pancasila* as the sole ideological basis of all political and social organizations in 1985. The acceptance proved to have ended a relatively long period of mutual suspicion between Muslim groups and the Indonesian government. From then on, there has been mutual rapprochement or, as some observers call it, a "honeymoon" between the Muslim *ummah* and the government. One of the most important results of the rapprochement was the establishment of the All-Indonesian Muslim Intellectual Association (ICMI) in December 1990. With President Soeharto's approval, the Minister of Research and Technology, B.J. Habibie was elected as the Chairman of ICMI.

President Soeharto himself in the post-1985 period shows some signs of greater "Islamicness". In 1990, for instance, he visited Samarkand in Central Asia, where he performed prayers in the historic Bukhara mosque. Bukhara is mostly known in Indonesia and elsewhere in the Muslim world as the birthplace of Imam al-Bukhari, one of the most prominent *hadith* scholars in Islamic history. The President's visit, therefore, had special meaning for many Indonesian Muslims. Soeharto visited Bukhara once again in 1995 (*Pelita*, 4 October, 1995).

The most momentous of all events marking Soeharto's new orientation to Islam was arguably his performing of the *hajj* pilgrimage to Mecca in 1991. Accompanied by his wife (who died in 1996) and his daughters and sons, Soeharto's pilgrimage aroused a great deal of Muslim sentiment both in Indonesia and abroad; many Indonesian Muslims believed that Soeharto was (and is) now one of them. The symbolic meaning of Soeharto's greater Islamicness was even strengthened with his acceptance of his new first name given by King Fahd of Saudi Arabia, that is, "Muhammad" (thus, his complete name now is Haji Muhammad Soeharto) and of his wife's first name, that is, "Fatimah" (thus her complete name is Hajjah Siti Fatimah Hartinah Soeharto).

These events led to much speculation among political observers. The question often posed is whether or not Soeharto's pilgrimage was politically motivated. Most Muslims believed that his pilgrimage was genuine, that it was undertaken in order to fulfill the Islamic obligation for every Muslim man and woman to perform the *hajj* pilgrimage at least once in his/her life-time. Many foreign observers, however, asserted that his pilgrimage was politically motivated. Michael Leiffer in his article in *The International Herald Tribune* (21 June 1991), for instance, asserted that Soeharto's pilgrimage has to do with his attempts to maintain the *status quo* of his rule. Another observer, Margaret Scott in *The New York Times Magazine* (2 June 1991) made the assertion that with his pilgrimage, Soeharto was playing "Islamic cards" (Thaba, 1996: 322). For a complete account of Soeharto's pilgrimage, see, Perjalanan Ibadah Haji Pak Harto, Jakarta: Departemen Agama R.I., 1993.

Despite these assertions, Soeharto, accompanied by his wife and children, once again visited Mecca in 1995 on his way back to Indonesia from the NAM Summit Meeting XI held in Colombia. According to the Minister of State Secretariat, Moerdiono, the President performed the *umrah* ("lesser *hajj*") in order to thank God in conjunction with the fiftieth anniversary of Indonesian independence (*Pelita*, 31 October, 1 November 1995; *Media Indonesia*, 31 October, 1995).

The last example of Soeharto's attempts to win the hearts of Indonesian Muslims that is worth mentioning here is his visit to war-stricken Sarajevo in April, 1995. This visit has been celebrated by Indonesian Muslims as a sign of strong universal Islamic solidarity; it was a brave action on the part of the President for his plane had been targeted by snipers in Sarajevo. In order to commemorate this historic visit, the Indonesian National Committee for Bosnian Muslim Solidarity decided to build the Haji Muhammad Soeharto Mosque in Sarajevo. Preparations for the construction of the mosque are now under way (*Kompas*, 10 April, 15 August, 9 November, 1996; *Jakarta Post*, 9 November, 1996; *Pelita*, 19 August, 1996).

Is there any impact of Soeharto's new Islamicness on Indonesia's foreign policy? There is no easy answer to this question. Based on what we are going to argue by way of several cases below, it is fair to say that there is probably no direct relation between Soeharto's new attention to Islam and foreign policy. The conduct of Indonesia's foreign policy basically remains in accord with the pre-existing official principle of keeping Islam at bay in Jakarta's international relations. There is little doubt, however, that at the same time Jakarta has associated itself with Islam and the Muslim world more closely.

POLICY OF AMBIGUITY

Even though Islam, as argued above, has not formally been a factor in Indonesian foreign policy, tone should take a very cautious attitude for, in one way or another, the Indonesian Government seems to take careful consideration when issues relating to Islam and Muslims appear at the forefront. It is correct that, on the one hand, Jakarta seems to consistently play down the Islamic factor in its foreign policy. On the other hand, however, there are some cases where the interests of Islam seem to have been given serious consideration by the Indonesian Government. Thus, as far as the Islamic factor is concerned, there is some kind of ambiguity in Indonesian Government foreign policy. Leifer has summed this up in the following words:

> "Indonesian governments, especially from the advent of the New Order inaugurated by General Soeharto, have taken great care not to allow foreign policy to be dictated by Islamic considerations...Islam, however, is not without influence on Indonesia's foreign policy but that influence has been expressed much more in the form of constraint than in positive motivation" (Leifer, 1983: 144).

Leifer's conclusion might still be relevant to some extent in assessing the Islamic factor in contemporary Indonesian foreign policy. I would argue, however, that since the late 1980s, there has been some subtle shift in Indonesian foreign policy. As indicated above, Indonesia since the late 1970s has shown some sign of paying more attention to foreign policy; Indonesia plays a more active role in international affairs; Indonesia, for instance, has played a greater role in the Non-Aligned Movement (NAM) than several years ago. Indonesia also played a crucial role in negotiations regarding the MORO problem in the Philippines. Thus, after a decade of inwardly-looking policy focusing on national economic development in the late 1960s and 1970s, the Soeharto Government by the end of the 1980s became more and more assertive in its foreign policy, becoming an important actor in international politics.

This change, as has been shown above, was motivated to a large extent by economic concerns. In order to boost its economic development, Indonesia needed a constant flow of foreign investment as well as markets for its non-oil products. At the same time, Indonesia was facing the issue of East Timor. These in turn led Indonesia to forge closer relationships with foreign countries, including Islamic countries, especially in the Middle East. To this end President Soeharto visited some Middle Eastern countries in June 1975 and in October 1977. During these visits, Soeharto stepped up the economic relationship by seeking credits and capital investment. In addition, he made efforts to obtain their support concerning the East Timor issue (*Antara*, 20 October, 1977/B). In the process, Indonesia seems to have given more space for the Islamic factor to exert its influence; a space that seems to have widened when Soeharto showed a greater leaning towards Islam. Nevertheless, the old pattern of ambiguity towards the Islamic factor remains observable, as we will see in several cases below.

Iranian Revolution & Libya Connection: Even though the Indonesian Government had attempted to forge closer economic ties with some Middle Eastern countries, as was mentioned briefly above, Indonesia adopted a very cautious policy towards some hard-line Middle Eastern countries, especially Iran and Libya. During the late 1970s and 1980s, in the aftermath of Khomeini's Iranian Revolution, Indonesian authorities were very suspicious of what they called the "Iranian Connection" or "Libyan connection". Iran or

Libya had often been accused by certain high-ranking Indonesian officials of giving financial aid and even military training to certain radical groups in Sumatra and Java. For example, Indonesian military authorities accused an organization called the "Indonesian Islamic Revolution Board" of seeking Iranian support to overthrow the government. There have also been charges that "Muslim radicals" in Indonesia have sought to implement an Islamic state in the pattern of Iran (Indonesia Reports, October 1986: 5-7; Indonesia Reports 13, November 1985: 36; and Indonesia Reports 16, June 1986: 45; von der Mehden, 1990).

In addition, the government was also very suspicious of some Indonesians returning from their travels or studies in certain Middle East countries. In the mid 1980's the Indonesian Government formally barred its citizens from studying in thirty-two countries. Of those states, twenty-one were communist, four (Israel, South Africa, Taiwan and Portugal) were those with which Indonesia had no diplomatic relations for politically sensitive reasons, and six were Muslim countries defined as "extreme" which included Libya, Iran, Iraq, Syria, Lebanon and Algeria (Al-Nahdah, 5, No. 3, 1985: 50). It is not hard to understand why Indonesian officials suspected that students returning from Libya or Iran, in particular, would spread radical ideologies on Indonesian soil and many of them were put under military surveillance. As a result, many of these Libyan or Iranian graduates returned to Indonesia through third countries where they "suppressed" evidence of their stay in Libya or Iran by applying for new passports at the Indonesian Embassy in that country.

This cautious policy toward Iran and Libya appears to have been relaxed significantly towards the end of the 1980s. The issue of an Iranian or Libyan connection in Indonesia was conspicuously absent in the Indonesian media by the 1990s. Indonesian officials also stopped accusing certain individuals of having Iranian or Libyan connections. Instead, Indonesia was now active in the efforts to lift economic and air travel sanctions imposed by the UN on Libya. In response to Libya's appeal to him as the chairman of the NAM, towards the end of 1993 President Soeharto sent the Indonesian ambassador for the NAM to negotiate with the UN and US, asking them to lift sanctions and normalize relations with Libya (Pelita and Jakarta Post, 24 September, 1993).

The Indonesian Government also began to show a warmer attitude towards Iran; by putting religious issues aside, Jakarta once again attempted to establish a firmer economic relationship. This can be seen, for example, from the high priority given to the visit by Iranian President Ali Akbar Hashemi Rafsanjani to Jakarta in the middle of October 1994. In his talks with Rafsanjani, President Soeharto revealed Indonesia's plan to invest in Iran, particularly in textiles, mineral water and palm oil. Both presidents agreed to bolster trade between the two states, and to form a joint team for this purpose. Rafsanjani was also warmly welcomed by Muslims in general; he was surrounded by large crowds when he did his Jum'ah prayers in the Istiqlal Mosque, Jakarta (*Jakarta Post*, 15 October 1994; *Kompas*, 14, 15 October, 1994).

Iraq Case: The attack by the US and its allies on Iraq in the middle of January 1991 had brought a strong reaction from Muslims and Islamic organizations in Indonesia. Muslim youth staged demonstrations in various cities to protest US military actions against Iraq which had earlier occupied Kuwait. The two largest Muslim organizations in Indonesia, Muhammadiyah and Nahdlatul Ulama (NU), strongly deplored the American military action in Iraq. The Muhammadiyah, after a meeting with President Soeharto, appealed for a peaceful settlement of the conflict. The Muhammadiyah also urged the Indonesian Government to play a more active role in seeking a peaceful settlement of the conflict (*Kompas, Suara Pembaruan*, 22 January, 1991; *Jakarta Post, Kompas*, 29, 30 January, 1991).

What was the reaction of the Indonesian Government to these Muslim organizations? Indonesia's official position in this case was "neutralism". The Indonesian Foreign Ministry supported the UN resolution opposing Iraqi aggression and allowing the UN Security Council to use force in order to liberate Kuwait from Iraqi aggression. Jakarta, however, did not accept the Saudi proposal to join the multinational military forces (*Far Eastern Economic Review*, 24 January 1991).

Furthermore, government officials, by and large, played down the Islamic factor in this instance; they apparently feared that if they recognized the Islamic factor, then they could provide an opportunity for Muslims to dictate Indonesia's foreign policy, for instance, by formally condemning the US and its Western allies. At the same time, however, Indonesia was also concerned with conflicts and divisiveness among Middle Eastern Muslim countries.

In this respect, Jakarta always emphasized that no religious elements were involved in those conflicts.

This can also be clearly seen in the statement of the Minister of Religious Affairs, Munawir Sjadzali, who pointed out that the Gulf War was not a religious war. He appealed to the Indonesian people to believe that it was not a war between religions (*Kompas*, 26 January 1991). This statement was confirmed by President Soeharto himself when he stated that the Gulf War was not a religious conflict but a political one; he reiterated at the same time Indonesia's official "neutral position" that Iraq should leave Kuwait so that a peaceful settlement could be achieved (*Jakarta Post*, 2, 13 February, 1991). In line with this neutral policy, Indonesian army leaders discouraged the idea of some followers of the Qadiriyyah *tarekat* in Kediri, East Java, to go to Iraq in order "to save" the tomb of Shaikh 'Abd al-Qadir al-Jilani, the founder of the Muslim brotherhood, in Baghdad (*Editor*, 19 January, 1991).

Thus, as in the cases of Iran and Libya mentioned earlier, the Indonesian Government also put religious issues aside in the controversies surrounding Iraq's case. Instead, Indonesia stressed the humanitarian and economic issues involved. Based on humanitarian grounds, President Soeharto once again appealed to the UN to respect Iraq for implementing UN resolutions (*Jakarta Post*, 13 May, 1995). Economic motives were strongly present when the Iraqi Vice-President, Taha Yasin Ramadan, visited Indonesia in the middle of May 1995. After thanking Indonesia for its continued support to lift the UN economic embargo on Iraq, Ramadan proposed that the two states form a joint economic committee to bolster Indonesian-Iraqi trade (*Media Indonesia*, 18 May, 1995).

Palestinian Question: From the time of independence, Indonesia has officially supported the Palestinian cause, including the unconditional withdrawal of Israel from the Occupied Territories and the fulfillment of the rights of the Palestinian people to have an independent state. As President Soeharto said; "Our attitude has always been clear from the beginning, that is, we stand on the side of the Arab peoples and that of the people of Palestine who are fighting for their just rights against the arrogant Israel" (Leifer, 156; Dipoyudo, 1981: 475-85).

As von der Mehden suggested, however, this public rhetoric has not been able to hide Indonesia's "real" foreign policy toward the Palestinian cause.

In his opinion, since the days of Soekarno, Jakarta has tended to present its criticism of Israel in anti-imperialist rather than in Islamic terms. For his part, Soeharto has also tended to avoid religious factors in defining Jakarta's position (von der Mehden: 48).

Thus, despite its continuing support for the people of Palestine, Indonesian Government is once again ambiguous and very cautious towards the idea of "the Palestinian state" and its leaders. For instance, PLO leader Yasser Arafat did not visit Jakarta for the first time until July 1984. During his visit, the Soeharto Government promised that the PLO could set up a bureau in Jakarta. In deference to Indonesia's Palestinian policy, Arafat was careful enough to emphasize that his organization was not an Islamic movement but was pluralist in its religious composition. Despite Arafat's assurance, Indonesia was only willing to give diplomatic support to the PLO in the UN and was worried about the PLO having an office on Indonesian soil (*New Straits Times*, 27 July 1984).

Thus, Indonesia for a relatively long period did not actually approve the establishment of a Palestinian embassy in Jakarta. It is not surprising, therefore, that Zuhdi Labib Tarzi, Palestinian Ambassador to the UN, raised this issue once again when he visited Indonesia on 27 January 1989. He hoped that in the near future, the Indonesian Government would give its approval for the opening of a Palestinian embassy in Jakarta (*Kompas*, 28 January, 1989). Nevertheless, it took two years (until 1991) before a Palestinian embassy opened in Jakarta.

When Israel and Palestine signed a peace pact in September 1993, controversy soon erupted in Indonesia. Most Muslim leaders and organizations condemned Arafat for, in their opinion, being fooled by the Israeli Government. At the same time, they appealed to the Indonesian Government not to open diplomatic relations with Israel on the grounds that it would be a violation of the Indonesian National Constitution of 1945 which, among other things, opposes any kind of colonialism (*Jakarta Post*, 20 September 1993).

Responding to this development, Indonesian Minister of Foreign Affairs, Ali Alatas, stated that Indonesia would not recognize the state of Israel as long as the Jewish state had not solved its problems with the Arab countries. Alatas added that talk about the recognition of Israel was premature because political developments in the Middle East after the signing of the Israel-PLO Pact were still unclear. He was of the opinion that the implementation of the Pact would be very difficult. Alatas also explained his meeting with the Israeli Foreign Minister, Shimon Peres, which led to speculation that Indonesia would soon open diplomatic relations with Israel. According to Alatas, it was an "accidental meeting" which took place at an international conference in Vienna, Austria; in conformity with the alphabetical order of the names of their countries, they sat side by side. On that occasion, Peres asked him when Indonesia would recognize Israel; and Alatas answered, "shortly after the problems between Israel and Arab countries have been settled" (*Republika*, 20 September 1993).

In the meantime, Indonesia's support of the peace initiative was again voiced by President Soeharto. On 24 September 1993, Yasser Arafat, accompanied by his wife, Suha Arafat, and a delegation, arrived in Jakarta from Beijing, for a one day visit. In his meeting with Arafat, President Soeharto in his role as Chairman of the NAM stated that he welcomed the agreement. Soeharto expected that it would become the first step towards a comprehensive settlement of the Middle Eastern problems, particularly through establishment of a sovereign state for the Palestinian people on their own land. Moreover, the President said that Indonesia was ready to offer real support to the struggle of the Palestinian people for the implementation of the pact (*Pelita*, 25 September 1993; *Republika*, 25, 26 September, 1993).

Arafat's visit was followed by an unofficial visit by the Prime Minister of Israel, Yitzhak Rabin, on 15 October 1993. Rabin, who met President Soeharto in his capacity as the Chairman of the NAM, appealed for Indonesia's support of the peace process that was taking place in the Middle East. To avoid any potential controversy surrounding the Rabin visit, President Soeharto dismissed any possibility of Indonesia opening diplomatic relations with Israel. Thus, Soeharto's position was successful in silencing any criticism of him over Rabin's visit (*Kompas*, 16 October 1993; *Republika*, 16 October 1993).

Controversy erupted, however, when some Indonesian Muslim leaders who seemed to be very enthusiastic about the prospect of a peaceful settlement of the Palestine question visited Jerusalem and Israel in January 1994. They were Abdurrahman Wahid, chief leader of the Nahdlatul Ulama (NU); Habib Chirzin, a leader of Muhammadiyah; and Djohan Effendi, a leading Muslim intellectual. They were condemned by various sectors of Muslim society who opposed any gesture to Israel; and Effendi was finally dismissed from his office at the State Secretariat (*Kompas*, 3 March 1994; *Media Indonesia* 4 March, 1994). Until this day, Indonesia remains faithful to its policy not to open diplomatic relations with Israel (*Jakarta Post*, January 30, 1997).

Bosnian Crisis: In the case of Bosnia, Indonesia also attempted to adopt a policy of "neutrality". This was implemented in two ways. Firstly, by emphasizing that the conflict in Bosnia had nothing to do with religion. In other words, the Serbian Orthodox Christian genocide of Bosnian Muslims was not motivated by religious conflict. Secondly, by emphasizing Indonesian "neutrality" and appealing to international organizations such as the UN and the Non-Aligned Movement (NAM) to play a greater role. These policies, however, could not be strictly maintained by the Indonesian Government; in fact it had to take into consideration Indonesian Muslims' strong show of solidarity for their Bosnian co-religionists as well as to the Muslim world at large.

As I argued elsewhere, the Bosnian crisis was one of the largest displays of Muslim solidarity in contemporary Indonesia. It appears that the response of Indonesian Muslims to the Bosnian crisis has been far more passionate than to the Palestinian plight. One might wonder why Indonesian Muslims express such passionate solidarity with the Bosnian Muslims. Religious feeling is of course the main factor; but this soon becomes entangled with political reasons, particularly in connection with the Western political double-standard and with Indonesia's ambiguous official attitude to the crisis (Azra, 1995).

It is, therefore, easy to understand why the Indonesian Minister of Foreign Affairs, Ali Alatas, left for Istanbul to attend the extraordinary meeting of the Organization of the Islamic Conference (OIC) on 17 June 1992. The meeting, which was held to discuss the situation in Bosnia-Herzegovina, had been organized by the OIC because the war continued in spite of a series of cease-fire announcements. The Conference appealed to all sides in Bosnia to start negotiations in order to reach a political settlement (*Berita Buana*, 16 June 1992).

Two Indonesian cabinet ministers reacted to the flood of Indonesian Muslims' feeling of solidarity with the Bosnian Muslims and of appeals to the Indonesian Government to take a firmer stand. Indonesian Minister of Religious Affairs, Munawir Sjadzali, again emphasized that the oppression in Bosnia had nothing to do with religion; but it was a humanitarian and political problem. Nevertheless, he pointed out that the government would seek ways to provide assistance to the Bosnian people; apparently not on the grounds that the Bosnians were Muslims, but simply because they were human beings who had been oppressed by the Serbians.

Meanwhile Minister of Foreign Affairs, Ali Alatas, asserted that the Indonesian Government had, from the beginning, taken a clear and firm stand on the conflict in Bosnia. According to Alatas, Indonesia had recognized the existence of Bosnia-Herzegovina together with Croatia and Slovenia as independent states on 20 May 1992. In addition, Indonesia had also voiced its concern and criticism in the meeting of OIC in June 1992 and supported the UN initiatives to put an end to the conflict (*Jakarta Post* and *Kompas*, 20 August, 1992).

In reality, to what extent can Indonesia put its recognition of Bosnia into practice? In this respect, one would again see Indonesia's ambiguity. Indonesian Muslims, for instance, had been very insistent that, in accordance with Indonesia's policy to recognize Bosnia, it should break its diplomatic relations with "Yugoslavia" which was in fact dominated by Serbia. Responding to this, Alatas argued that as future Chairman of the Non-Alignment Movement (NAM), Indonesia should also seek a consensus for a solution of the conflict, the more so because Yugoslavia was the actual president of the NAM and the presidency should be transferred to Indonesia in a smooth way. Indonesia could not, therefore, give up its diplomatic relations with Yugoslavia.

This position was once again reiterated by the Director General of International Organizations of the Ministry of Foreign Affairs, Hadi Wayarabi. Responding to appeals by the Muslim community that Indonesia should break off its diplomatic relations with Yugoslavia, he pointed out that in order not to worsen the problem, the Indonesian Government would not take such a step. In the meantime, Bosnia-Herzegovina had applied for the status of observer at the up coming conference of the Non-Aligned Movement (NAM) in Jakarta. Wayarabi said that the application would be discussed at the beginning of the conference (*Pelita*, 24 August, 1992).

The Bosnian application for membership in NAM was later put aside in the discussion at the NAM Conference in Jakarta while "Yugoslavia" retained its membership. The Bosnian case was raised once again by President Soeharto in the opening ceremony of the Tenth Summit Conference of NAM, held in Jakarta from 1-6 September 1992. Soeharto stated in his speech that quick and resolute action was needed to end the Bosnian tragedy and uphold the sovereignty, territorial integrity and cultural heritage of Bosnia-Herzegovina. For that reason, he urged the UN Security Council to give the UN Secretary General the necessary authority and support in order to be able to restore peace in that region. He also urged NAM to play a more active role in the peaceful settlement of the issue (*Jakarta Post*, 2 September, 1992).

Thus, instead of involving itself directly in the peace process, Indonesia passed the buck to international organizations. At the same time, Indonesia showed a token of solidarity to the Bosnian people on the grounds of humanitarianism. On 2 October 1993, the Indonesian Ministry of Foreign Affairs announced that the Indonesian Government would give an amount of US\$ 100,000 in cash for humanitarian aid to the people of Bosnia-Herzegovina. The aid would be channeled through the UNHCR (*Kompas*, 23 October, 1992).

In accordance with the principle of using international organizations – in this case, NAM – on 24 June 1993, President Soeharto ordered the co-ordinating bureau of NAM in New York to urge the UN to end the arms embargo on the former Yugoslavia. Soeharto also revealed his plan to send a diplomat to Europe on his behalf as the NAM Chairman. According to Nana Sutresna, the executive assistant to the Chairman of NAM, NAM would press the world community to lift the arms embargo on Bosnia, so that Bosnian Muslims could defend themselves against the well-armed Serbian forces. NAM also demanded that the UN, especially its Security Council, take a more resolute stand against the Serbian forces to force them to end their violence in Bosnia. In addition, Sutresna criticized the efforts of the U.S. and its allies to introduce "safe havens" in Bosnia, which could be interpreted as a justification of the Serbian use of aggression to gain territory (*Jakarta Post*, 25 June 1993).

Such policies clearly failed to appease Indonesian Muslims. Confronting a flood of criticism that the Indonesian Government had done very little to halt Serbian atrocities in Bosnia, the Minister of Foreign Affairs, Ali Alatas, said that the Indonesian Government was well aware of what was going on in Bosnia. He stated that President Soeharto himself was very concerned about the Bosnian tragedy. As Chairman of NAM, the President had sent Ahmad Tahir, ambassador-at-large to NAM, to Geneva to obtain information about the situation in Bosnia before making further policy. The President agreed that Indonesia should take more concrete steps to deal with the problem, but there were limits to what Indonesia could do.

What Alatas further revealed gave further clues to Indonesia's ambiguity in its foreign policy. According to Alatas, OIC members had suggested that Indonesia send its troops outside the UN framework, but Indonesia declined this suggestion. The reason was that Indonesia would maintain its long-held principle that military aggression could not be confronted with similar aggression. It was reported during a meeting in Pakistan that seven members of the OIC had pledged to send more than seventeen thousand troops to join with the UN peace-keeping forces in Bosnia. Indonesia, which took part in that meeting, was not among these seven (*Jakarta Post*, 15 July 1993). Later, after a meeting with President Soeharto, Alatas said that Indonesia was considering dispatching its troops to Bosnia. This plan had not yet been finalized as talks on the subject were still going on between his ministry, the Minister of Defence and Security, Edi Sudrajat, and the commander-in-chief of the Armed Forces, Gen. Faisal Tanjung (*Jakarta Post*, 16 July 1993).

In the end, the Indonesian Government decided to only send some military officers and observers rather than combat units. After a meeting with several ministers, the Co-ordinating Minister for Politics and Security, Soesilo Soedarman, said that Indonesia was unable to send its troops because it would take an extraordinary degree of preparation to organize, train and equip Indonesian military units in order to be well-prepared militarily in Bosnia. He also pointed out another important problem in that the terrain in Bosnia was very different from that in Indonesia or Cambodia where Indonesian troops were participating in a UN peace-keeping force (*Jakarta Post*, 30 July 1993).

OIC and Other Muslim International Organizations: Indonesia, as stated above, had never played a prominent role, nor occupied an important position in international Islamic organizations. This was an official position of the

Indonesian Government, not simply the result of other Muslim countries underestimating Indonesia and its large Muslim population. Indonesia simply did not want to identify itself closely with international Islamic organizations.

This attitude can be clearly seen in the establishment of the Organization of Islamic Conference (OIC). Indonesia did not officially participate in the conference of Muslim heads of government in Rabat (1969), which addressed the question of the burning of the Aqsa Mosque and other issues. Neither did it participate in the Jeddah Conference (1970) where Muslim foreign ministers agreed to set up a permanent secretariat that led to the establishment of OIC. Indonesia did send a delegation to the Jeddah meeting in March 1972 which promulgated the charter of the OIC but Indonesia declined to sign the charter nor seek formal membership of the OIC (Leifer, 152-3; von der Mehden, 59-61).

This position resulted in controversy in Indonesia. On the one hand, Muslim leaders regretted the Indonesian Government taking such a position. On the other hand, non-Muslims, particularly the Catholic-dominated Center for Strategic and International Studies (CSIS) applauded Indonesia's position. Minister of Foreign Affairs, Adam Malik, by the end of 1972 issued a press statement to the effect that the government was not yet prepared to sign the Islamic Charter because the Republic was not an Islamic state (*Monthly Review*, Nov-Dec 1972: 7). This was elaborated further by an official of the Ministry of Foreign Affairs who stated that Indonesia did want to have an Islamic orientation in its foreign policy. He questioned what Indonesia would gain by joining OIC formally and fully. To him, for practical purposes it did not really matter whether or not Indonesia was a signatory of the Islamic Charter. It was a non-issue (Hein, 1986: 242-3).

This issue was not yet resolved however. Mochtar Kusumaatmadja, Indonesian Minister of Foreign Affairs after Adam Malik, was also continuously confronted with this issue. In the end he stated that "Indonesian membership in the ICO [OIC] is an indication that our foreign policy cannot ignore the reality that 88 per cent of our population belongs to the Muslim religion" (Hein, 141). Furthermore, Kusumaatmadja maintained that the involvement of Indonesia in the OIC was also partly motivated by Jakarta's policy to prevent this organization from becoming a pan-Arab organization with its traditional Islamic leaning. Indonesia instead encouraged the OIC to become a mainstream movement among developing countries (Kusumaatmadja, 1994: 165).

The very same explanation was given by some Indonesian Muslim members of parliament when a number of their counterparts in the OIC proposed in 1996 to form an organization of Islamic parliaments which would represent every Muslim state. The Indonesian MPs argued that Indonesia was not an Islamic state so it was not appropriate for Indonesia to be officially involved in such a parliament of Muslim states. They proposed, instead, that an association of Muslim members could be formed; thus, they would represent themselves, not their respective state (*Media Indonesia*, 2 November 1996).

Partly because of the resurgence of Islam in Indonesia in the ensuing years, however, the Republic has been getting closer to the OIC. Indonesia signed the General Agreement on Economic, Technical and Commercial Cooperation among Member Countries of the Islamic Conference, and hosted the OIC's Islamic Chamber of Commerce in 1983. Indonesia has always been represented in the Secretariat of Islamic Countries and Islamic Development Bank (IDB). The IDB itself has invested US$ 50,000,000 in Indonesia since 1974. This is a rather small amount compared to the IDB investments in Turkey and Syria (Tempo, 10 September 1988). The Indonesian rapprochement to the OIC and its affiliated institutions has led Hamid al-Gabid (the OIC General Secretary) to praise Indonesia. After the Jeddah Conference in April 1989, he paid a visit to Indonesia as an official guest of the Ministry of Foreign Affairs. He praised Indonesia for its genuine membership and regular payment of contributions to the OIC (*Berita Buana*, 23 May 1989, *Suara Pembaruan*, 25 May 1989).

The new Indonesian leaning towards closer relations with the OIC and other international Islamic organizations was strengthened further when President Soeharto for the first time attended the Sixth Summit Conference of the OIC, which was held in Dakar from the 9-12 December 1991. That Indonesia sought closer relations with the Islamic world as a whole could be seen in Soeharto's official address in the Summit. He, among others, welcomed the Saudi Arabian proposal to hold an international conference on society and Muslim minorities in Mecca. He also said that Indonesia was ready to share its successful experience in agricultural development, especially in food production, with other Muslim countries. At the same time Soeharto was also willing to share information about Indonesia's successful family planning program with other Muslim countries. He therefore reminded the Conference of the "Aceh Declaration", formulated in the international conference on Islam and population policy, which was held in Lhokseumawe, Aceh, in February 1990. He hoped that the Summit would recommend that OIC member countries use the guidebook on family planning management which had been produced by a "Workshop on Family Planning according to Islamic Orientation and Guidance" as a follow up of the Aceh Conference. In addition, he re-stated at the Summit Indonesia's willingness to develop the Center for Telecommunication Training in Bandung as a training facility for the OIC member states (*Pelita*, 11, 12, 18 December 1991). The President's gesture was quickly acted upon by high-ranking Indonesian officials. Undoubtedly, the most prominent among them was the Minister of Research and Technology, B.J. Habibie, who was elected with the President's approval as the Chairman of the All Indonesian Muslim Intellectuals Association (ICMI) in late 1990.

In the middle of April 1992, Habibie visited Saudi Arabia and Egypt, where he met King Fahd and President Husni Mubarak. In his meeting with high-ranking Saudi Arabian officials, Habibie was able to secure IDB co-operation with the Indonesian Government to organize a seminar on the marketing of products of Indonesian strategic industries to member countries of the OIC to be held in Jakarta in November 1992. He also revealed that Indonesia would hold an exhibition of these products in Jeddah in October 1992, which, at the request of the Egyptian President, would be continued in Cairo at the end of October. Habibie said that Indonesia produced airplanes, ships, heavy equipment and the means of telecommunication which were ready to be marketed in the OIC countries. Minister Habibie, who also acted as the Chairman of the ICMI, on various occasions introduced this organization and revealed the ICMI plan to build an Islamic Center in Jakarta, including a mosque with sermons in foreign languages as well as a library with collections of scientific books from all over the world. After hearing about this plan, Saudi Minister of Foreign Affairs, Prince Sa'ud and the president of IDB, Ahmad Muhammad Ali, promised to support the development of the Islamic center (*Berita Buana*, 14 April, 1992).

CONCLUSION

Indonesia, as one might observe, feels the need to maintain good relations with Middle Eastern [Muslim] countries partly for historical and political reasons; it was Middle Eastern countries, namely Egypt and Saudi Arabia which were among the first to recognize Indonesian independence. Most of them were also strong supporters of Indonesia's rule in East Timor. Another motivating factor is economics. With the growth of its economy, Jakarta regards Middle Eastern countries as potential markets for Indonesian products.

At the same time, however, the Indonesian Government is very cautious about religious (or Islamic factors) in its relations with Middle Eastern countries. Admitting the Islamic factor in its foreign policy would mean that the Indonesian Government surrenders to Muslim pressures. This could, in turn, create certain domestic political repercussions.

CHAPTER 7

THE BOSNIAN CRISIS AND THE INDONESIAN RESPONSE

There is little doubt that the Bosnian crisis is responsible for one of the largest displays of Muslim solidarity in contemporary Indonesia, the multicultural Southeast Asian country where Islam spread rapidly in the fifteenth century – and which today has the world's largest Islamic population. The response of Indonesian Muslims to the Bosnian crisis has been far more passionate than it was to the Palestinian plight. In an *Antara* news bulletin on 8 September 1992, Lukman Harun, Chairman of the Committee for Islamic Solidarity, founded several decades ago to support the Palestinian cause, points out that the response of Indonesian Muslims to the Bosnian crisis has been the most passionate in Indonesian history. This indicates that Muslim solidarity (*ukhuwwah Islamiyyah*) is still deeply embedded among Muslims in this part of the Islamic world.

Indonesia has long been regarded by many foreign observers as a region peripheral to "centers of the Islamic world in the Middle East." I would argue, this is only true in terms of geographic location, but not in terms of religiosity or religious solidarity. Therefore, its Muslim population has often been involved in various affairs that appealed to the *ukhuwwah Islamiyyah*. Most were political, but they soon mixed with deep religious feelings, which were heavily colored by what some scholars call "pan-Islamic" sentiment.

One might wonder why Indonesian Muslims express such passionate solidarity with the Bosnian Muslims. Religious feeling is, of course, the main factor; but this soon becomes entangled with political reasons, particularly in connection with their anti-Western political and military stance and with Indonesia's official attitude to the crisis.

One kind of response by Indonesian Muslims to the Bosnian crisis can be classified as rhetorical. Almost all leaders of Muslim organizations in Indonesia have expressed strong resentment at the role of the United Nations. When the crisis began to fill the headlines of the mass media, Lukman Harun, soon called for both UN and US intervention for a peaceful solution in the former Yugoslavia. According to Harun in the *Berita Buana* daily, 20 May 1992, the UN must take more courageous and stern action against the Serbs.

Lukman Harun maintained, moreover, that the Bosnian case is a clear example of Western hypocrisy. In his opinion, the UN, the US and the Western world in general applied a double standard in dealing with different Muslim nations or states. On the one hand, when Iraq invaded Kuwait in 1991, they urged the UN to pass a resolution to suppress the Iraqi aggression by international military forces. On the other hand, when the Serbs slaughtered the Bosnian Muslims, they were reluctant to take similar action. In *Pelita* daily, 15 August 1992, Harun deplored the attitude of UN Secretary General Boutros Boutros-Ghali, who took no serious action in defense of the interest of the Muslims.

The same appeal was also voiced by Muhammad Dja'far Siddiq, a leader of the United Development Party, a Muslim-oriented political party in Indonesia's parliament (DPR). On behalf of the party, he regretted the failure of the UN to take necessary action against the Serbs. The party also appealed to the Organization of the Islamic Conference (OIC) to take appropriate action to stop the genocide of Bosnian Muslims (*Suara Pembaharuan*, 13 August 1992; *Jakarta Post*, 14 August 1992).

Again, the condemnation of the Serbs was made by the Council of Indonesian *Ulama* (MUI) and the Indonesian Council of Islamic Dakwah (DDII). Signed by their respective chairmen, K.H. Hasan Basri and H. Yunan Nasution, both leading organizations condemned the Serbs for their slaughter of Bosnian Muslims. They also strongly urged the UN Security

Council to take concrete steps to halt the "ethnic cleansing" and to uphold the sovereignty of Bosnia-Herzegovina (*Pelita*, 18 August 1992).

On the same day, four large youth organizations – the Association of Muslim University Students (HMI), the Muhammadiyah Youth (*Pemuda Muhammadiyah*), the Kosgoro Student Movement (*Mahasiswa Kosgoro*), and the Indonesian Muslim Youth Movement (*Pemuda Muslim Indonesia*) – declared that what was happening in Bosnia-Herzegovina was a violation of the right to freedom and a threat to world peace. They stated that as part of the Indonesian nation and the world community, they had the obligation and responsibility to defend the rights and survival of the Bosnian people (*Pelita*; *Kompas*; *Jawa Pos* (18-19 August 1992).

Criticism of the UN, the US and the Western world in general came from almost all quarters of Indonesian Muslim organizations and leaders. This criticism snowballed and, in turn, was directed towards the Indonesian Government, which had shown a great deal of reservation with regard to the Bosnian crisis. Thus, on 19 August 1992, the Central Board of the Ansor Youth Movement issued a statement criticizing the Serbs as well as the Indonesian Government. It demanded that the Indonesian Government play a more active role in efforts to settle the conflict in Bosnia in accordance with one of the fundamental objectives of Indonesian foreign policy; that is to contribute to the creation of lasting world peace (*Pelita*, 20 August 1992).

In addition to the rhetoric, about thirty students who belonged to the Islamic Communication Forum of Jakarta came to the headquarters of the Indonesian Ministry of Foreign Affairs. They strongly urged the government to take a firmer and bolder stance in condemning the Serbs; to play an active role in stopping genocide in Bosnia by demanding that the UN Security Council take immediate military action; to bring the Bosnian crisis to the agenda of the coming Summit Conference of the Non-Aligned Countries; to reject the presence of the Yugoslavian delegation at the Summit; and to break off bilateral relations with Yugoslavia (*Pelita*, 20 August 1992). The same demand was also put forward by four other Muslim organizations. They demanded, among others, that the Bosnian crisis be put on the meeting table of the Summit Conference of the Non-Aligned Countries (*Pelita*, 21 August 1992).

Responding to continuing criticism and the demands on the Indonesian Government, two cabinet ministers issued an official statement. Minister of Foreign Affairs, Ali Alatas pointed out that from the beginning of the crisis, the Indonesian Government had taken a clear and firm stand; it had recognized the existence of Bosnia-Herzegovina together with Croatia and Slovenia as independent states. Furthermore, the Indonesian Government had voiced its concern and criticism in the regular meeting of the OIC in June 1992 that supported UN initiatives to put an end to the crisis. Alatas added, however, that as the future Chairman of the Non-Aligned Movement (NAM), Indonesia would also seek a consensus for a peaceful solution to the conflict, the more so because Yugoslavia was the incumbent president of the Movement, and the presidency should be transferred to Indonesia smoothly. For this reason, Indonesia would not renounce its diplomatic relations with Yugoslavia (*Jakarta Post, Kompas, and Pelita*, 20 August 1992).

In the same vein, Minister of Religious Affairs Munawir Sjadzali maintained that the Indonesian Government's stance on the Bosnian crisis had been very clear. He even argued that the Bosnian crisis had no religious background but was instead a humanitarian and political problem. "It is true that the majority of Bosnia's population is Muslim, but this does not mean that the so-called ethnic cleansing is religiously motivated". (*Kompas*, 20 August 1992). Nevertheless, he stated that the government would seek ways to provide assistance to the Bosnian people. Four days later, however, Sjadzali appealed to all Indonesian Muslims to assist their fellow Muslims in Bosnia (*Bisnis Indonesia*, 24 August 1992).

It is apparent that Muslim leaders and organizations were disappointed by the statements of these ministers. Thus on 29 November a number of Muslim organizations, united in a newly established Forum of Islamic Solidarity, sent a letter of concern directly to President Soeharto. In the letter, the Forum appealed to the government to break off its diplomatic relationship with Yugoslavia (Serbia and Montenegro) and to expel all Yugoslavians (Serbs) who were living in Indonesia. It also urged the Indonesian Government to step up diplomatic efforts in order to safeguard Bosnia-Herzegovina. Finally, the Forum appealed to the government to press the UN to lift the arms embargo in Bosnia so that the Bosnians could defend themselves (*Kompas*, 30 November 1992).

As if responding to the continuing waves of appeals, President Soeharto set the tone in his inaugural address in the opening ceremony of the NAM Summit meeting held in Jakarta 1-6 September 1992. Soeharto said that speedy and resolute action was needed to end the Bosnian tragedy and uphold the sovereignty, territorial integrity and cultural heritage of Bosnia-Herzegovina. He urged the UN Security Council to give the UN Secretary-General the necessary authority and support to restore peace in Bosnia. He further appealed to NAM to play a more active role in the settlement of the crisis (*Jakarta Post*, 2 September 1992).

Even though the Summit meeting was marred by heated debates over whether the Yugoslavian delegation should be expelled from the meeting, the final document of the conference called for the full respect of the sovereignty, independence and territorial integrity of Bosnia-Herzegovina. It also supported the proposals of the London Conference on Bosnia and urged all conflicting parties to resolve their problems peacefully, in line with the conclusions of this conference and to fully respect the UN Charter (*Jakarta Post* and *Kompas* , 7 September 1992).

In his capacity as the NAM Chairman, on 24 June 1993, President Soeharto ordered the coordinating bureau of the NAM in New York to urge the UN to end the arms embargo on the former Yugoslavia. He also revealed his plan to send a special envoy to Europe (*Jakarta Post*, 5 June 1992). As Minister of Foreign Affairs Ali Alatas pointed out, Indonesia's president was very concerned about the Bosnian crisis. Fulfilling his promise, Soeharto sent Ahmad Tahir, ambassador-at-large to the NAM, to Geneva to assess the latest situation in Bosnia in order to formulate a proper Indonesian foreign policy. Meanwhile President Soeharto agreed that Indonesia should take concrete steps to deal with the crisis. According to Alatas, the OIC members suggested that Indonesia send troops outside the framework of UN coordination, but Indonesia maintained its foreign policy, that aggression could not be met with an aggressive response. After a meeting with President Soeharto, however, Alatas said that Indonesia was now considering the dispatch of troops to Bosnia (*Jakarta Post*, 15 July 1993).

As one might expect, this stand of Soeharto's, as conveyed through Alatas, created euphoria among many Indonesian Muslims. Some members of the Indonesian Parliament (DPR) expressed their gratitude. Dja'far Siddiq of the United Development Faction in the DPR said that the dispatch of troops would give the Indonesian Armed Forces important international standing and would further enhance Indonesia's relations with the East European countries and with other predominantly Muslim countries. Aisyah Amini, a member of parliament of the same faction, also endorsed the plan to send troops in the framework of either the UN or the OIC. Endorsement also came from K.H. Hasan Basri, the Chairman of the Council of Indonesian *Ulama* (*Jakarta Post*, 17 July 1993).

President Soeharto's overtures were soon seized upon by Muslim youth, stimulating new waves of mass demonstrations to support him. Since August 1992, they had been holding demonstrations against Serbian atrocities in various cities including Semarang, Malang, Yogyakarta, Surabaya, Bandung and Jakarta. In Jakarta, the UN office and the embassies of (the former) Yugoslavia, the United States and Britain were also targeted by demonstrators. On 21 July 1993, some five hundred Muslim students from several universities and senior high schools staged a demonstration at the DPR building. The students joined a newly formed organization called Youth in Support of the Sending of Troops and Volunteers to Bosnia, and urged the government to send Indonesian troops to Bosnia immediately. They even offered themselves for training by the Indonesian Armed Forces before being sent to the war-torn country (*Pelita*, 22 July 1993).

Three days later, in Bogor, a mass demonstration was held by students from the Communication Forum of Muslim Students. As in previous demonstrations, they supported the dispatch of Indonesian troops to Bosnia. They also criticized the United States and Britain for their refusal to lift the arms embargo and threatened to boycott all products of these two countries (*Republika*, 26 July 1993).

Despite this growing pressure, at the end of July, the Indonesian government decided to send some military observers rather than combat units. Coordinating Minister of Politics and Security Soesilo Soedarman said that the reason for Indonesia's failure to send troops to Bosnia was that it would take an extraordinary amount of preparation to organize, train and equip mobile units. Not least in importance, the situation in Bosnia was also very different from that in Indonesia (*Jakarta Post*; *Pelita*, 30 July 1993).

This announcement was very disappointing to many, including some Muslim leaders who openly expressed their disappointment. Some three thousand people gathered in the grounds of the Azhar mosque in Jakarta to protest the government decision not to send troops to Bosnia. More and more protests and demonstrations were staged in various cities expressing regret over the government's stance (*Kompas*; *Pelita* 31 July and 3 August; *Republika* 2 September 1993).

In addition, several organizations established during this period opened registration for Muslims who wished to volunteer for a "holy war," to fight in war-torn Bosnia-Herzegovina. The leading entity in this effort was the Committee for Muslim Solidarity (KISDI), which claimed that nearly 100,000 Muslims throughout Indonesia, men and women, young and old, registered as volunteers ready to be sent to Bosnia. This presented quite a problem for the government and the Armed Forces, which had been urged to give them some form of military training. The volunteers who registered generally maintained that their only motivation was to show Islamic solidarity toward their brethren in other parts of the globe (*Jakarta Post*, 7 March 1994).

Although the government allowed for such a move, General Faisal Tanjung, Chief Commander of the Armed Forces said that it was not possible for the Armed Forces to train the volunteers or for the government to allow them to leave for Bosnia. At the same time, Minister of Foreign Affairs, Ali Alatas, agreed to KISDI and other organizations continuing to register volunteers, in order not to disappoint them. He pointed out, however, that what Bosnia really needed was arms, not volunteers who were unfamiliar with the local situation in Bosnia (*Republika*, 7 March 1994).

Meanwhile, at the end of October 1993, the Indonesian Armed Forces sent twenty-four military officers to Bosnia as observers for the UN Protection Force (UNPROFOR). Later, a battalion of over two hundred Army medics and a smaller team of civilian officers were also sent to Bosnia. In October 1994, the Commander-in-Chief of the Indonesian Armed Forces, General Faisal Tanjung, visited Zagreb where he met with an Indonesian contingent stationed in the region (*Jakarta Post*, 16, 21, 22 October 1994; *Republika* 27, 28 September 1994).

In addition to the responses described above, Indonesian Muslims expressed their solidarity with Bosnian Muslims in some other forms. For instance, during 1992 and 1993 almost all Muslim leaders and preachers, in mass gatherings and in their sermons in the mosques, appealed to Muslims to perform the *qunut nazilah*, a special prayer for co-religionists who are struck by disaster. The Council of Indonesian *Ulama* even went so far as to instruct Muslims to perform the *qunut nazilah* at every obligatory salah (prayer).

Not least dramatic was the effort to raise funds for Bosnian Muslims. For example, on the occasion of a mass gathering attended by thousands in the Grand Mosque al-Azhar, in Jakarta, on 16 August 1992, an amount equal to US$8,500, two rings, and one gold bracelet were spontaneously donated to help the Bosnian Muslims. On the same occasion some two hundred people declared themselves prepared to become foster parents for Bosnian orphaned children. Some orphanages were also willing to assist (*Pelita*, 18, 21 August 1992).

A more serious effort to raise funds has been carried out since early September of 1992. In a meeting in the Istiqlal Mosque, sixty-five representatives of Islamic organizations agreed to undertake a massive fundraising campaign for the Bosnian people. The Chairman of the Council of Indonesian *Ulama*, K.H. Hasan Basri, called on all mosques to channel all the alms collected every Friday to a special committee established to coordinate the help for Bosnia.

On 2 September 1992, at a meeting in the Le Meridien Hotel of Jakarta, the Council of Indonesian *Ulama* and about one hundred noted Indonesian businessmen agreed to establish the National Committee for Solidarity with the Bosnian Muslims. During the announcement of its establishment, the Committee collected about US$500,000 from the businessmen in attendance. Later, in a meeting with the Minister of Religious Affairs, it was revealed that the Committee had already collected US$1.5 million (*Kompas*; *Pelita* 3 September 1992; *Jakarta Post*, 12 October 1992). By May 1994, almost US$2.5 million had been raised nationwide. The fund was partly channeled through a delegate of the Bosnian Government who visited Indonesia, and the remainder was taken directly to Bosnia by special envoys of the Committee (*Kompas*, 26 May 1994).

Why are Indonesian Muslims so passionate about helping the Bosnian Muslims? There are at least two reasons behind the various responses described briefly above. First, until the Bosnian crisis, most Indonesian

Muslims had not realized that there were significant numbers of Muslims in Eastern Europe. Realizing that the Bosnian Muslims had a long history of struggle maintaining their Islamic identity in Christian Europe, Indonesian Muslims fervently believed that they should do something to help their co-religionists. Second, their passionate responses are colored by a deep resentment about what they regard as a Western "double-standard"; they even believe that the ethnic cleansing in Bosnia is part of a hidden ploy among Western powers to destroy Islam and Muslims.

Not least in importance, the displays of Indonesian Muslim solidarity to the Bosnian crisis also signal a growing Muslim political force in Indonesia clamoring for greater roles in the domestic political scene. In the last few years, Muslim groups have become more and more political. Rallies and demonstrations have been familiar means for Muslim groups to express their aspirations. In November 1993, for example, Muslim groups were successful in "forcing" the government to abolish the state-sponsored lottery. Some Western diplomats in Jakarta were then reported to have expressed concern about the revitalized Muslim movement, with its growing demands, particularly those in conjunction with the Bosnian crisis.

CHAPTER 8

INDONESIAN ISLAM
IN A GLOBAL CONTEXT

Indonesia is the most populous Muslim nation of the world. Despite the fact that Muslims constitute the largest single proportion of the Indonesian population, Indonesia is not an Islamic state, nor a secular one. Indonesia is a *Pancasila* state which places religions – including Islam – in an important position. This can be seen, for instance, in the national ideology of *Pancasila* (Five Principles/Pillars), which adopts "belief in One Supreme God" as its very first principle. Muslims have overwhelmingly accepted *Pancasila* as the final ideological basis of the Indonesian state. So, it seems, there is little debate about the national ideology and the form of the Indonesian state.

Questions most commonly arise on the extent to which Islam (or the Muslims) becomes a factor in both domestic and foreign policies; and how Muslims influence Indonesia's foreign policy in order, let's say, to play a greater role in the Islamic world. Basically, the Indonesian Government has traditionally or conventionally disregarded Islam as an important factor in its foreign policy. Despite the fact that Indonesia generally remains on good terms with Muslim states in the Middle East, Indonesia has tended not to associate itself with Islam. It is, therefore, important to make it clear that if Indonesia has extended support to certain Middle Eastern countries or groups of Muslim people – such as the Palestinians – then that support is basically not on the grounds of Islamic solidarity. Rather, it is on the basis that Indonesia supports those who struggle for independence and justice in order, as stated in the Preamble of Indonesia's 1945 Constitution, to create a just international order.

Based on such tendencies, it is futile to expect that Indonesia would, and could, play a greater role in the Islamic world. In fact, Indonesia has never played a prominent role nor occupied an important position in international Islamic organizations, such as the Organization of Islamic Conference (OIC). This has been (and still is today) an official position of the Indonesian government, not simply the result of other Arab Muslim countries underestimating Indonesia with its overwhelming Muslim population. Indonesia simply does not want to identify itself closely with international Islamic organizations; while at the same time realizes the need to maintain good relations with Middle Eastern [Muslim] countries.

The fact that Indonesia has no agenda to pursue a greater role in the Islamic world has a lot to do with the nature of Islam in Indonesia. Indonesian Islam has a number of distinctive characteristics vis-à-vis Middle Eastern Islam. Indonesian Islam, by and large, is a moderate, accommodating kind of Islam, and the least Arabicized Islam. For this reason, the American anthropologist Clifford Geertz loves to refer to Islam in Java as the "religion of Java" which he adopts as the title of his acclaimed book published in 1964. The term "religion of Java" refers to Islam in Java – as in many other places in Indonesia – that has been mixed and amalgamated with old and pre-Islamic beliefs and socio-cultural traditions. Indonesian Islam is, therefore, much less rigid compared to Middle Eastern Islam. For that reason, *Newsweek* magazine not long time ago called Indonesian Islam "Islam with a smiling face"; Islam which in many ways is compatible with modernity, democracy, and plurality (*Newsweek*, 23 September 1996).

With its distinctive characteristics, it is not surprising, therefore, that Indonesia, according to a report entitled "Freedom in the World 2002: The Democracy Gap" is one of the bright spots of democracy together with the other less-dominantly Arabicized Muslim countries such as Bangladesh, Nigeria and Iran. Freedom House found that while there is an obvious democracy deficit in the Islamic Arab world – which is called the Arabic core – democratic ferment is considerable in countries which have predominant or significant Muslim populations such as Albania, Bangladesh, Djibouti, the Gambia, Indonesia, Mali, Niger, Nigeria, Senegal, Sierra Leone and Turkey.

The formation of these distinctive characteristics of Indonesian Islam has a lot to do with at least two factors; firstly, the peaceful spread of Islam, which TW Arnold in his classic book, *The Preaching of Islam*, called "penetration pacifique". (London 1913) The spread of Islam was not through the use of force – from Arabia, for instance – but rather by way of slow penetration through centuries involving accommodation of local belief and cultures. This process can also called be called the "indigenization" or "vernacularization" of Islam. Secondly, the structure of Indonesian society which is very different from Middle Eastern society. To take one example, while Islamic Middle Eastern society is a male-dominated society where women are confined to the domestic sphere, Islamic Indonesian society is basically more loosely structured, where women enjoy much greater freedom.

The election of Vice President Megawati Soekarnoputri to replace the embattled President Abdurrahman Wahid on 23 July 2001, represents freedom that women enjoy in Islamic Indonesia. President Megawati gained uncontested support not only from the Peoples' Assembly (*Majelis Permu syawaratan Rakyat* – MPR) but also from the majority of Indonesian Muslims. It is important to make it clear that large mainstream Muslim organizations such as the Nahdlatul Ulama (NU) and Muhammadiyah – which claim a membership of forty and thirty-five million followers respectively – did not object on religious grounds to the election of a woman, Megawati, as the president. Other large regional Muslim organizations in western and eastern Indonesia took a similar attitude on this particular question. Similar positions have also been taken by Islamic or Muslim-based parties like the PPP (*Partai Persatuan Pembangunan*, or United Development Party), PBB (*Partai Bulan Bintang*, Moon and Crescent Party), PK (*Partai Keadilan*, Justice Party), PKB (*Partai Kebangkitan Bangsa*, National Awakening Party), and PAN (*Partai Amanat Nasional*, National Mandate Party). The PPP which had staunchly opposed Megawati on religious grounds in the pre- and post-general election of 1999, later accepted her as president; and in fact the national chairman of PPP, Hamzah Haz, was elected during the special session of MPR on 24 July 2001, as Vice President, so creating a leadership duo that consists of a secular nationalist represented by Megawati and a religious nationalist represented by Hamzah Haz.

There was only a limited number of hardliner Muslim groups who opposed the ascendancy of Megawati on the grounds that – in their literal understanding of Islam – it is not permissible, according to Islamic law, for a woman to hold the highest leadership position in a Muslim society and state. These groups, losing momentum with the impeachment of President Wahid, came to the forefront in a more visible, vocal and militant manner in the aftermath of the terrorists' attacks on the WTC New York and the Pentagon in Washington DC. Even though these groups, like the Front Pembela Islam (FPI, Islamic Defenders Front), Lasykar Jihad, Hizb al-Tahrir (Party of Liberation) and Majelis Mujahidin Indonesia (MMI, Indonesian Council of Jihad Fighters), exert only a limited influence among Indonesian Muslims as a whole, they would try to make use of any possible issue related to Islam and Muslims for their own purposes including, inter alia, to undermine President Megawati's authority. President Megawati, however, will survive the challenge of radical political Islam given the sustained support of mainstream Muslims.

The existence of hardliner, militant, radical, or even "fundamentalist" Muslims within Indonesian Islam that have been so overt recently is actually not new. They are even regarded as having kidnapped the center stage of Indonesian Islam in the aftermath of the WTC and Pentagon terrorist attacks. There were radical groups during the period of both Presidents Soekarno and Soeharto that attempted to establish an Islamic state in Indonesia, replacing *Pancasila* as the common ideological platform that had been accepted by virtually all Muslim nationalist leaders as well as secular nationalist leaders. These groups had been known as the DI/TII (Dar al-Islam/*Tentara Islam Indonesia*, or Islamic State/the Army of Islam in Indonesia) in the 1950s. Later, during the Soeharto period, there had been radical groups like the NII (*Negara Islam Indonesia*, Islamic State of Indonesia) and "Komando Jihad" (Jihad Command) groups that, again, attempted to establish an Islamic state in Indonesia. It is important to point out that some of these radical groups during the Soeharto period were believed to have been engineered by certain army generals in order to discredit Islam. Despite that, all attempts of these radical groups failed, not only because of the Indonesian army's harsh and repressive measures, but also because they failed to gain support from mainstream Muslims.

The fall of President Soeharto from his long-held power of more than three decades which has been followed by political liberalization, has brought momentum for the rise of Muslim radical groups. Many of them are new groups that were previously unknown, such as the *Front Komunikasi Ahlu-Sunnah Wal-Jama'ah* (FKASWJ) with its better known paramilitary group, the Lasykar Jihad (Jihad Troops), the *Front Pembela Islam* (Islamic Defense Group), the *Majelis Mujahidin Indonesia* (Indonesian Council of Jihad Fighters), the Jamaah al-Ikhwan al-Muslimin Indonesia (JAMI), and some other smaller groups. There is no accurate account of the origin and establishment of these groups, which have made their appearance since the *interregnum* of President B.J. Habibie. There are reports that their leadership circles have been close to certain army generals; therefore some observers assert that their rise has been sponsored, or at least helped, by certain elements of the Indonesian military. Despite this, what is conspicuously clear is that these groups tend to be led by leaders of Arab – particularly Yemeni – origin; the leader of FPI is Habib Rizq Shihab, of the Lasykar Jihad is Ja'far Umar Thalib; the MMI is led by Abu Bakar Baasyir and the leader of Ikhwan al-Muslimin Indonesia is Habib Husen al-Habsyi. Even though each of these groups claims a large membership, it is clear that their membership and influence are very limited.

Religiously speaking, these groups tend to adopt a literal interpretation and understanding of Islam. They, furthermore, insist that Muslims should practice only what they call the "pure" and "pristine" Islam as practised by the Prophet Muhammad and his Companions (*Sahabah*, or the *Salaf*). By this definition, they can be included among the Salafi movements. Based on their literal understanding of Islam and Salafi's activism, they attacked discotheques, bars and other places they considered to be "places of vice". It is also within this kind of Islamic worldview that they understand the concept of *jihad* as "holy war" against those they considered as enemies of Islam and Muslims. The fact is that the meaning of "*jihad*" is "exerting oneself to the utmost" in any kind of Muslim activities. "*Jihad*" as "war" is only allowed as the last resort to defend Islam and Muslims from hostile enemies.

In addition to the above-mentioned groups, there are older groups that have been in existence since the Soeharto time, but escaped the regime's harsh measures because they made some adjustments not only politically vis-à-vis the regime, but also religiously vis-à-vis the mainstream Muslims. The most important of such groups is the Hizb al-Tahrir (Party of Liberation), which was originally established in Lebanon by Shaykh Taqi al-Din al-Nabhani, and firstly introduced to Indonesia in 1972. The main objectives of the Hizb al-Tahrir are to perpetuate what they regarded as the true Islamic way of life globally and, most importantly, to re-establish the *khilafah* (caliphate), a universal Islamic political entity, which is believed to have been the most suitable and effective political system by which to achieve Muslim unity. To achieve these goals, the Hizb al-Tahrir seems to have little difficulty in resorting to radicalism. This is why it soon became one of the most popular movements among disenchanted students and young people, not only in the Middle East, but also among Muslim students pursuing their degrees in Western countries. After the fall of Soeharto the Indonesian Hizb al-Tahrir became more visible, assertive, and vocal in pursuit of their ideals; it is also very active in mass demonstrations against the US in the aftermath of the WTC and Pentagon tragedy and the subsequent US military operations in Afghanistan. Despite its being more visible today, as its leader told me, the membership of the Hizb al-Tahrir has not increased significantly.

There is little doubt that all of these radical groups have, in one way or another, certain connections at either the theological or organizational levels or both with particular groups in the Middle East or elsewhere in the Muslim world. It has already been stated that the newer groups have a leadership that is of Middle Eastern origin and tend to be Middle-Eastern oriented in their ideology and movement. On the other hand, an older group such as the Indonesian Hizb al-Tahrir did, in fact, genuinely originate in the Middle East. It is difficult, however, to ascertain their possible connection with Osama bin Laden or al-Qaida. The leaders of FPI, Lasykar Jihad and JAMI have denied any connection with Osama bin Laden or al-Qaida. In fact many leaders of these groups are very critical of Osama bin Laden whom they accuse of being "*Khariji*" (*Khawarij* or the seceders), that is those Muslims who seceded from the *ummah* (Muslim nation).

The MMI, centered in a village in Surakarta, Central Java, has been accused of having connections with the al-Qaida. The group led by Abu Bakar Baasyir, a religious teacher who is also the head of the *Pesantren* al-Mukmin, is known to have close links with the Malaysian Militant Muslim Group (Kumpulan Muslim Militan Malaysia – KMMM). In the late 1980s Baasyir went to Malaysia to escape Soeharto's repressive measures because of his illegal activities against the Indonesian Government. He returned to Indonesia only after the fall of Soeharto while maintaining, it seems, contacts with his Malaysian counterparts. He was later also associated with the Jamaah Islamiyah which is believed by authorities to have cells operating in Malaysia, Singapore and Indonesia. Some of these groups have allegedly been linked with al-Qaida after the arrest of Fathur Rahman al-Ghozi by Philippines police. Abu Bakar Ba'asyir, who has been questioned by Indonesian police, denied the allegation that he is the leader of the al-Qaida-linked Jamaah Islamiyah network. Indonesian authorities and police have maintained that both al-Ghozi and Baasyir have no links to al-Qaida but they promise to investigate further. A much deeper investigation involving governments of ASEAN is, therefore, needed in order to clarify the matter. It is time to follow up, in a concrete way, a series of discussions on the issue of terrorism that was held by leaders and officials of ASEAN. These discussions, initiated during President Megawati's recent tour of ASEAN member states raised a high level of awareness among ASEAN members that a plan to defeat terrorists who have global connections and reach must be put into action.

The increased radicalism of the groups mentioned above undoubtedly has a lot to do with the government's failure to enforce the law and solve a number of acute social ills such as continued ethno-religious conflicts, a marked increase in crime, rampant corruption at every level of society, more widespread drug abuse, and the like. The abrupt decline of central government authority together with the demoralization of the police force have become *the raison d'etre* for these groups to take the law into their own hands. One important key to solving the rise of radicalism is, therefore, restoring government authority and strengthening law enforcement agencies.

With the apparent continuing rise of radical groups, the two largest mainstream Muslim organizations – the NU and Muhammadiyah – have voiced their objection to radical means. But their voices appear to have either been not strong enough, or have tended to be overlooked by the mass media, which is more interested in the voices and action of radical groups. Since November 2001, however, the two organizations have begun to give more serious attention to the impact of Muslim hardliners upon the image of Indonesian Islam. They admit that the image of Indonesian Islam in particular has worsened following the massive demonstrations against the US in the aftermath of the US military operation in Afghanistan. Leaders of both organizations have, therefore, agreed that they will again project a calm image of Islam that protects people of other religions. The national leaders of the NU and Muhammadiyah, Hasyim Muzadi and Ahmad Syafii Maarif respectively, state that the image of Islam has been politicized by certain radical groups for vested interests; such radicalism demonstrated by the groups represents political influences and not the Islamic way of thinking. Both organizations will, therefore, carry out a series of activities to tackle extremism through open dialogues, joint-programs and the like. Both have also appealed to the Indonesian Government to take harsh measures against groups that transgress the law. Syafii warns that should the law enforcers be afraid to take stern measures against radical groups, they could pave the way for increased radicalism.

With the stronger position that has been taken by the mainstream Muslim organizations, it is admittedly very hard to imagine that Indonesia would become a hotbed of "Talibanism". This is, of course, not dismissing at all the possibility of the existence of radicalism in Indonesian Islam; it is clear that like any other religion, radicalism of one kind or another, for one reason or another, would continue to exist among Muslims, including in Indonesia. With the stronger position held by mainstream Muslim organizations, the influence of radical groups can be contained and will be very limited and, therefore, will fail to have any significant impact that could change the peaceful nature of Indonesian Islam.

President Megawati is expected to rebuild Indonesian political stability as well as lead the country to economic recovery. The expectation seemed to be fulfilled by the Megawati presidency up until the September 11 tragedy and the subsequent US military operation in Afghanistan. Massive demonstrations and the threat of foreigner sweeping by the Muslim hardliners have hurt Indonesian political stability as well as economic recovery. The slow response of President Megawati has only worsened the Indonesian political and economic situation. President Megawati's tougher policy towards hardliner Muslims has helped the government to restore its credibility. The key here is that the Indonesian Government should consolidate its policy at both domestic and international level in order to make it possible for President Megawati to silence skepticism and criticism originating from the government's indecisiveness and slow response.

The US and Western countries should adopt a very cautious policy to handle Muslim radicalism in Indonesia. Americans should not overemphasize the threat of such radical groups, since it could give them the publicity that they seek. As is clear from above, there is little sympathy among the majority of Indonesian Muslims to radicalism expressed by some of their co-religionists. American overreaction at the same time could further foment uneasiness towards the US among the mainstream Muslims. Thus, American overreaction on this question could alienate moderate Muslims; this is really what the radicals are looking for; that is to bring the moderates into their fold. Furthermore, it could again provide momentum for the radicals to challenge the Megawati presidency, creating Indonesian political instability.

Further strengthening and empowerment of democratic elements within mainstream Indonesian Islam is one of the ways to address radicalism. It is the responsibility of all of us to enhance Indonesia's nascent democracy; and given Islam's numerical majority, this could be done through mainstream Islamic institutions and organizations that have committed themselves to the ideals and building of Islamic civility, democracy, plurality, tolerance and peaceful co-existence among various groups as well as respect for human rights. To take an example, sponsored by the Asia Foundation, the State Institute/University for Islamic Studies (IAIN/UIN) Jakarta has launched a new course in 2000 on "Civic Education" for its new students and student leaders. Through the "Civic Education" course, students are introduced to the idea and practice of Islamic civility in relation to democracy, plurality and other related subjects. The program is now at the initial phase of nationwide implementation by involving thirteen other IAINs and thirty-three Islamic colleges (STAINs). We hope that through this, and other similar, programs, Indonesia as a bright spot of democracy is able to promote democracy as the "only game in town".

CHAPTER 9

ISLAM AND
THE WEST REVISITED

S ome recent developments in international affairs have worsened relations between Muslims and the West. In the wake of the terrorist attacks on the World Trade Center, New York, and the Pentagon headquarters, Washington DC, on 11 September 2001, and the US' subsequent military operations in Afghanistan, much of the Muslim world felt that they have become the target of the US-led war against terrorism. The US war in Iraq further aggravated their resentment and bitterness towards America.

In its hasty efforts to find the terrorists who were responsible for the attacks, the US administration immediately pointed its finger at Osama bin Laden, and the Taliban, and listed a number of "Muslim groups" in the UN's list of terrorist groups. In certain cases, the listing of certain Muslim groups has been counterproductive, since it is mostly based – it seems – on prejudice and prejudgment. One example is the recent inclusion in the UN list of the "Haramayn Foundation" that is affiliated with leaders of the Islamic Justice and Welfare Party (PKS or *Partai Keadilan Sejahtera*) in Indonesia. The US Ambassador to Indonesia later had to publicly apologize after it was found that this particular foundation has nothing to do with a terrorist group with a similar name in Saudi Arabia.

The American-led attack on Iraq has – for whatever reason – undoubtedly created a lot of outcry and anger in the Muslim world and in other parts of the world. On 14 May 2003, the English-language newspaper *The Jakarta Post*, editorialized that it is heartening that opposition to the war is widespread, and is not confined to only one section of the community. Muslims in Indonesia have joined hands with people of other faiths in denouncing US military aggression in Iraq. The war has been seen as not solely an attack on Muslims and, therefore, on Islam, but as an attack against all religions and the values they represent. *The Jakarta Post* concludes that the war is rightly seen as an attack against humanity and therefore against the values of just about all religions that preach peace. "You do not have to be a Muslim to feel horrified at the sight of Iraqis living under the terror of constant US bombings, or of Iraqis fleeing the war in fear", writes the *The Jakarta Post*.

Further reflecting an unfavorable view of America during the war against Iraq, *Kompas*, the Indonesian daily newspaper with the largest circulation which is known for its considered attitude, editorialized under the title "America fails morally" (14 May 2003): "the US and allies victory over Saddam Hussein could not ease our deep disappointment regarding the US government…Isn't it right that the US and its allies should be held responsible for the chaotic situation in Iraq?" Don't we remember that when the Indonesian military (TNI) was deemed to have failed to uphold law and maintain order in East Timor, America and Australia shouted the loudest, accusing TNI officers of negligence. The result is that many TNI officers were, and are being, tried for crimes against humanity. *Kompas*, owned by Catholic interests, further writes: "We just need to remind the world that a double standard must be avoided in such a similar case. Law and human rights are universal. The coalition forces should be held accountable for the chaos and violence in Baghdad and its surrounding towns. From the military and economic points of view, the coalition force has won the war in Iraq, but – morally – they have lost". *Kompas* concluded that "the war was a reflection of the moral degeneration of the US".

An official view of the Indonesian Government states that the US attack on Iraq is a kind of aggression. Branding the US campaign in Iraq an act of aggression, Indonesia urged the UN to call an emergency meeting to force the US to stop the war as soon as possible. The statement further said that the Government and people of Indonesia strongly deplore the unilateral action taken by the Government of USA and its allies, who have decided to go to war against Iraq. Indonesia deeply regrets that the multilateral process through the UN Security Council has been sidelined. Indonesia is of the view that the use of military force against Iraq based on unilateral decision constitutes an act of aggression, which is in contravention of international law. This unilateral military action has also threatened the world order. The Indonesian Government stance undoubtedly echoed public sentiment in the country, with interfaith leaders, political parties and other community leaders having publicly opposed the attack.

In the wake of the terrorist attacks in the US on September 11, 2001, and the US' military operations in Afghanistan and Iraq – many Muslims believe the world has witnessed yet another tragedy with even far greater consequences. The subsequent US military campaign in Afghanistan was successful in ousting the Taliban regime, but failed to find Osama bin Laden. And, less than two years later, the US, supported by Britain and Australia, attacked Iraq without the UN's authorization. Despite the Bush administration's claim that President Saddam Hussein was a dictator who cheated the UN arms inspectors, most Muslims believed that this was an unjustified and illegal war. With the US failure to find Saddam Hussein, many Muslims believe that the US has actually pursued another agenda.

At the public level, the situation also seems to be getting worse. Goaded by the patriotic press, much of the US public has been afflicted by some kind of mass hysteria and renewed "Islamo-phobia". In certain parts of the Western world, mosques and Muslim community centers were attacked, and Muslims were (and are) singled out in "ethnic profiling" by the police and other government agencies. Responding to these actions, Muslims in various countries conducted mass rallies and demonstrations against the US and its allies and anti-American sentiment is on the rise in many Muslim countries. A new episode of Islam's harsh encounter with the West seems to have been taking place.

Thus, there is a strong impression among Muslims that the US-led war in Afghanistan and the war against terrorism was a war against Islam and Muslims; this impression grew stronger when President George W. Bush gave his military operation in Afghanistan the code name "crusade" and later "infinite justice". Even though President Bush, and British Prime Minister Tony Blair, attempted to make it clear that the war was not against Islam by visiting mosques and Islamic centers and having meetings with Muslim leaders to stress that their military operations in Afghanistan are not against Islam, the perception persists among many Muslims that the West continues to show its hostility towards Islam and Muslims.

The US' unilateral military action in Iraq against President Saddam Hussein has only reconfirmed Muslims' perception of the renewed hostility to Islam and Muslims and, furthermore, strengthened the belief among some Muslims in the so-called "conspiracy theory" that the US administration, together with certain governments of the Western world, has a plot to destroy Islam and Muslims. The failure of the US and the British to find the Weapons of Mass Destruction (WMD) in Iraq has damaged US credibility, not only among Muslims but also among many other people.

Worse still, much of the Western media continues to report sensationalized accounts that, in the final analysis, only reiterate the idea that the Muslim world is in a state of perpetual chaos and corruption, unable to govern itself except through the use of force or via Western supervision and aid. This provides momentum for a more pronounced demonization of Islam and Muslims in much of the Western world, causing more problematic historical relations between the Western world and the world of Islam today.

CONFLICT AND ACCOMMODATION

Looking at the totality of recent developments, it is clear that Western perception of Islam and the Muslim world has not changed very much; on the contrary, it is worse now than when Islam first became known to the Western world – or more precisely the Europeans – with the establishment of the first contacts between them and the Muslims as early as the seventh century. In the first one hundred years of Islam, the extent of Islam's territorial expansion reached its maximum level. Byzantium and Spain confronted the Muslims across the battlefields of Eastern and Western Europe.

There is no doubt that the expansion of Islam was painful for Europe because much of European territory was lost to Muslim forces. The "Crusade" was the European answer to the spread of Islam. Beginning in the early eleventh century, the earliest crusaders under the Frankist knights made attempts to arrest the development of "Muhammadanism". The Crusade, as the word implies, was a struggle to save Christian Europe by warding off the "barbaric" Muslims. The series of bloody encounters, which took place in the numerous Crusades that followed, constituted a major part of European history. Even though the Europeans had reconquered the Iberian Peninsula from the Muslims in 1492, they faced a new strong force of Muslims, that is, the Ottomans who had made their way into Southeastern Europe.

Despite these harsh encounters and contacts, and despite the Muslims allowing the European Christians to remain in the conquered territory, European understanding of Islam was basically minimal. In fact, the Europeans launched continued propaganda to tarnish the image of Islam; this religion was held in contempt, it was condemned as false, and the Prophet Muhammad was depicted as "anti-Christ". This attitude went on for centuries. It was only since the second half of the twentieth century that this kind of perception of Islam and the Prophet Muhammad was somewhat corrected. Other than this, misperceptions and distortions of the image of Islam and the Muslims remain strong among much of the Western public.

Throughout the history of its relationship with Islam and the Muslims, Europe's understanding and appreciation of Islam and Muslims was generally negative. There had been, however, some Christian notables who tried to learn about Islam and to change the attitude of the Christians for the better towards Islam and Muslims. One of the most prominent among them was Peter the Venerable, the Abbot of Cluny, who initiated the first Latin translation of the Qur'an, Muslim legends, history and an explanation of Islamic teachings. These works contributed significantly to a better understanding of Islam and Muslims in Europe.

During the Renaissance, a number of prominent Europeans further tried to acquire a better understanding of Islam. After the Turkish defeat of Byzantium, John of Segovia pointed to the need to cope with Islam and the Muslims in other ways besides wars and conversion. He initiated a new translation of the Qur'an in cooperation with Muslim jurists. He also proposed an international conference to exchange opinion between Muslims and Christians.

In addition, during the Renaissance, Arabic and Islamic studies were initiated in many institutions, which led to a more realistic and accurate view of Islam and the Muslims; this is the origin of "Orientalism". Unfortunately,

Orientalism had been practiced not only for academic purposes, but also for colonialism and evangelization. Since the early 1970s, Orientalism has been severely criticized for retaining certain biases and distorted images of Islam and Muslims (cf. Said 1978). As a result, a new approach to Islamic and Muslim studies has evolved, and the term Orientalism and "Orientalists", have tended to become "dirty" words; the term "Islamic studies" and "Islamicists" have been increasingly adopted instead.

It is also now widely recognized that various aspects of Islamic civilization have contributed greatly to the rise of Europe and the West as a whole. The Muslims during the heyday of Islamic civilization not only preserved Greek learning, but also made a considerable original contribution to the knowledge of nature with their research and experiments. Various kinds of knowledge and sciences that had been developed by Muslim scientists were later transmitted to Europe. The Muslims, therefore, with their intellectual supremacy in scientific discovery, and in the physical and natural sciences, prepared the ground for the European Renaissance. It is now increasingly recognized that Western civilization owed its origins not only to the Greek, but also to the Judeo-Christian-Muslim traditions.

REFORMS OF THE MUSLIM WORLD

The Muslims, on the other hand, have not made any significant progress. While Europe continued to progress in science and technology, the Muslim world fell prey to European colonialism and imperialism. By the late nineteenth century, virtually the whole of the Islamic world was under European domination. The liberation of the Muslim world from Western colonialism came about only after World War II. Despite their political freedom, many Muslims, however, still suffer from some kind of defensive, apologetic and reactionary psychology. This kind of psyche leads some Muslims to be suspicious of anything Western and, worse still, to isolationism.

Even though half a century has elapsed since a great number of Muslim nations began to gain their independence, most of them – if not all – are still heavily dependent on Western political and economic support. Many of them have become "clientele" of Western powers who – for their own political interests – lend their support to even the most undemocratic and dictatorial Muslim regimes. These regimes, in turn, often show their strong hostility towards Islamic movements and use violence against them that, in the end, creates a vicious circle of violence.

The consequence of political instability is clear. Many regimes in Muslim countries have been preoccupied by security problems, rather than economic development. As a result, until today, there is no single Muslim country that can be classified as developed; much of the Muslim world today remains in a state of backwardness. Poverty, ignorance and instability have become such a common feature in Muslim nations that it is assumed this is a natural consequence of subscribing to the teachings of Islam. The Muslims themselves have done very little to help themselves; they have weakened themselves more and more by their constant feuding among themselves. With the defensive and apologetic psychology mentioned earlier, many Muslims tend to blame others – in this case the West – for their continued misery and predicament.

A number of reforms have been initiated and launched in most Muslim countries since the early twentieth century. These include reforms in the theological, legal, social, cultural, economic, educational and political fields. Reforms in Islamic theology and law have been successful to a great degree. Modern theology that put a strong emphasis on freewill and freedom of action is now the predominant theological school among most Muslims. Meanwhile, reforms of Islamic law have also been continuing; reinterpretation and new interpretation of Islamic legal doctrines have been introduced. A limited number of Muslims, frustrated by the failure of their respective governments to enforce law and order to resolve social ills such as rampant corruption, the rapid spread of narcotics and other crimes, have increasingly proposed the introduction of Islamic law.

The reforms in social and cultural fields are closely related to economic and educational reforms. As mentioned earlier, most Muslim countries have failed in their economic reforms. Economic development in most Muslim countries has been very slow. Even though certain Muslim countries are rich in natural resources, they fail to extract the greatest benefits from them. The wealth from natural resources has been lost as the result of rampant corruption, mismanagement or extravagant life-styles. The wealth has not been used wisely for strategic purposes such as education and poverty alleviation.

Educational reforms have also been very slow in most Muslim countries. Many of them have introduced modern education systems, which include science and technology but they have failed to accelerate educational reforms because of the very limited budget that has been spent on education. In addition, in certain Muslim countries, traditional Muslim educational institutions (such as *madrasah, pesantren, pondok* and the like) mostly remain isolated from mainstream modern education. In Pakistan and Afghanistan at least, *madrasah* remain outside the mainstream education system, while in Indonesia, *madrasah* have been included in the national educational system. Despite this, in terms of finance and human resources, these *madrasahs* are in poor condition. There is, therefore, a lot to be done in order to bring them into the mainstream of education.

There is little doubt that political reforms are the most crucial for many Muslim countries. Many Muslim countries – as mentioned above – are undemocratic; there is an obvious democracy deficit in the so-called core area of the Islamic world in the Middle East. In contrast, there are some bright spots of democracy in the least Arabicized Muslim countries such as Indonesia, Malaysia and Nigeria. Democracy needs to be consolidated and deepened in these countries in order for them to not only be a model of a success story of democracy in Muslim countries, but also of the compatibility between Islam and democracy. The West can help them in this regard by at least respecting democratic processes, and by not implementing counterproductive policies such as supporting undemocratic regimes or resorting to militarism in the name of establishing democracy as has been taking place in Iraq.

TOWARD GREATER UNDERSTANDING

It is clear that, apart from conflict and hostility between Islam and the West, there has been much accommodation. In fact, Muslims and Christians had lived in peaceful co-existence for centuries. There is a great deal of exchange between the two civilizations. Islamic civilization in the medieval period had contributed significantly to the renaissance of Europe and the Western world as a whole. One should, therefore, not be misled by the so-called theory of the "clash of civilizations" as notoriously proposed by Samuel Huntington (1996).

In regards to unfortunate international developments in recent years, the two worlds should conduct concerted efforts to re-enhance a greater understanding between them. One of the most important ways is to develop inter-civilizational dialogue. Dialogue is now not simply a matter of choice, but a necessity for the two civilizations and cultures in order to be able to live in harmony and peace. Fair, frank, honest, and thoughtful dialogue between Western and Islamic civilizations will, undoubtedly, be very helpful and beneficial, not only in reducing tension and conflict today, but also in finding the best solutions to some of the grave problems that the world faces such as poverty, environmental destruction, etc. Successful and beneficial dialogue can be achieved only when those involved are on a par, based on freedom and freewill of each side. In dialogue, no idea and privilege should be imposed on the other side; one side should respect the national, cultural and religious identities of the other. Only in such a case, can dialogue be the preliminary step leading to peace, security and justice.

This leads us to the necessity for each side to uphold the principles of multiculturalism. There should be greater application of the "politics of recognition" between Islam and the West. The politics of monoculturalism – imposed by either side – certainly seems likely to fail, but will exacerbate tension among people of the world. A similar scenario looms in the case of the politics of unilateralism. No side can, for any reason, take the law into its own hands; all sides must learn to respect multilateral bodies, particularly the United Nations (UN), to find peaceful solutions for conflict. In this regard, it is also important to reform the UN to reflect a better balance between states, to end the domination of the great powers. Under-privileged countries should have a greater say in this body. The reform of the UN in such a way will enhance the credibility and accountability of the UN in the eyes of all people around the globe.

CHAPTER 10

INDONESIA'S ROLE IN THE MUSLIM WORLD AND INTERNATIONAL AFFAIRS

The visit of Indonesian President Susilo Bambang Yudhoyono to Cairo on the eve of 'Id al-Fitr in November 2004 to offer condolences to the deceased Palestinian President Yasser Arafat seems to have certain symbolic meanings. At the first instance, it shows that Indonesia remains committed to supporting the struggle of the Palestinian people. Since the time of independence (17 August 1945), Indonesia has declared to take side with the Palestinian people in their struggle to gain their rights and independence.

Implicitly, the visit also indicates that Indonesia is still a good friend of the Muslim Middle East; this is particularly true since President Bambang Yudhoyono was accompanied in his visit by prominent Muslim leaders, like Hidayat Nurwahid (also Speaker of the MPR), Din Syamsuddin (Council of Indonesian Ulama/MUI), Hasyim Muzadi (national leader of NU), and Amin Abdullah (leader of Muhammadiyah); the three organizations are often considered as representatives of Indonesian Islam.

With this kind of delegation, the President sent a wrong message: that the struggle of the Palestinian is the struggle of Islam. Despite the rise of Hamas and *intifada* in the last decade, the Palestinian struggle is clearly not the same with the struggle of Islam. The fact is that the struggle is basically secular nationalist in nature without particular reference to Islam or any other religion. He should have included leaders of other religions, particularly of Catholicism and Protestantism among his delegate. This is particularly important, since the Palestinian people also include a significant element of Christians who also fought for their holy sites in Palestine that are occupied or controlled by Israel (cf Azra 2000:7).

NEW ORIENTATION?

But what is more important for the purpose of this chapter is whether the visit is a sign that Indonesian foreign policy would re-orient itself to the Islamic world; whether Indonesia would take a greater role in the Middle East affairs, particularly in the Palestinian question and Iraqi problem, as has been mandated by the preamble of the 1945 Indonesian constitution. Accordingly, Indonesia should play an active role in the creation of a just and peaceful international order. Indonesia, for that reason, should oppose any kind of colonialism, imperialism, and aggression.

Another important question is whether the visit of President Yudhoyono and his subsequent participations in the APEC Summit Meeting in Santiago, Chile, and ASEAN Summit Meeting in Vientiane, Laos are the signs of Indonesia's more assertive role in the international diplomacy. There has been a great deal of hope among Indonesians that Indonesia could play a greater and more assertive role in the international affairs and regain respect from the international communities.

There is little doubt that the role and position of Indonesian in international affairs and diplomacy has decreased significantly since the fall of President Soeharto in 1998. Since then, I would suggest that Indonesia is the "sleeping giant" of Southeast Asia. This is not because Indonesia has adopted low profile diplomacy at the international level, but mostly because it has lost it élan. This is of course mainly due to the internal crises Indonesia has been facing since the sudden fall of President Soeharto. Following the monetary and economic crises, for instance, the number of staff at many Indonesian embassies has been reduced quite significantly. This arguably might have affected the effectiveness of the embassies to perform their diplomatic function.

More importantly, however, domestic political uncertainty and instability have been mainly responsible for the decreased role in the international diplomacy. Three presidents – BJ Habibie, Abdurrahman Wahid and Megawati Soekarnoputri – who ruled Indonesia after the fall of Soeharto had apparently no clear foreign policies, or else they were occupied with a great deal of serious domestic problems that needed to be urgently resolved.

Furthermore, for many Indonesians, President Habibie – during his *interregnum* – had been responsible for the fiasco of Indonesian international posture, when he allowed East Timor to conduct referendum that led to violence; this became an official and formal *raison d'etre* for international institutions, like the UN, and foreign countries, especially Australia, to intervene. In the end Indonesia has to let East Timor to declare its independence under the protection of the UN.

When Abdurrahman Wahid was elected President by the Peoples' Consultative Assembly (MPR) in 1999, it appears that he intended to revive Indonesia's role in the international diplomacy. For this purpose he traveled to many foreign countries; but rather than producing clear results of his visits in certain foreign countries, he used his visits also to issue controversial domestic policies. Therefore, it is debatable whether his frequent visits were taken seriously by foreign countries he had visited.

At the same time he also created public controversy when he announced to open trade and economic relations with Israel. As one might expect, he was opposed bitterly by many Muslim groups that forced him to abandon the plan. But damage had been done, and he was considered insensitive to Muslims' feeling in his foreign as well as in domestic policies.

There is even unclear foreign policy during the period of President Megawati Soekarnoputri who replaced President Wahid whom had been impeached by the MPR for mismanagement, controversial policies, and erratic attitude. Known for her indecisive attitude, President Megawati chose to be passive rather than active not only in foreign affairs, but also even in the domestic ones.

The September 11, 2001 events in the US, however, put President Megawati Soekarnoputri in a very awkward position. Only a few days after the fateful events, President Megawati met President Bush to offer her condolences; the move and her further attitude to the US were regarded by Muslim hardliner groups in Indonesia that she had surrendered to the US pressures.

The election of Susilo Bambang Yudhoyono on September 20, 2004 direct presidential election brought a lot of hopes from Indonesian people and many leaders of foreign countries that Indonesia would regain political stability. Many Indonesian have been tired of the decline of their country's role in international affairs. Political and economic stability would of course allow Indonesia play an important role in international affairs. A weak and instable Indonesia would be a disadvantage for the world; Indonesia is at least expected by the world to be a mediating and stabilizing force in the ASEAN and Pacific regions.

CONVENTIONAL POLICY

It seems, again, that President Yudhoyono wishes that Indonesia could play a greater role in the international affairs. Whether he would be able to do that would depend much on domestic political developments. As Djalal and Wanandi argue, domestic affairs greatly influence Indonesia's foreign policy (Djalal 1996; Wanandi 1989). Thus, if President Yohoyono is able to consolidate his government and has a good cooperation with the Parliament (DPR) – in which his party occupies only a minority position – then he would have a good chance to assert a more active role of Indonesian in the international diplomacy.

Next year (2005) Indonesia will commemorate 50 years of the famous Bandung Conference that has been regarded as the corner stone of the Non-Aligned Movement (NAM); preparation is underway to celebrate the Conference. Indonesia under the leadership of President Soeharto was of course the leader of the NAM in the early 1990s. The commemoration of the Bandung Conference as well as the reminiscents of Indonesia's leading role in the NAM could be a momentum for a more assertive Indonesia's foreign policy under President Yudhoyono.

But the question now is whether Indonesia would abandon or to make some adjustment of the long-held "policy of ambiguity" particularly towards the Muslim world. There is a number of cases in which Indonesia's foreign policy showed a strong tendency towards the policy of ambiguity (cf Azra 2000:12ff). On the one hand, the Indonesian government seems to take careful consideration when issues relating to Islam and Muslims appear at the forefront of international events. But, on the other hand, Indonesia seems to consistently play down the Islamic factor in its foreign policy.

Leifer concludes that Indonesian governments, especially from the advent of the New Order inaugurated by General Soeharto, have taken great care not to allow foreign policy to be dictated by Islamic consideration. He admits, however, that Islam is not without influence on Indonesia's foreign policy, but that influence has been expressed much more in the form of constraints than in positive motivation (Leifer 1983:144).

Despite the "policy of ambiguity" towards the Islamic factor, from the late 1970s to the end of Soeharto period, Indonesia had shown some signs of more active role in international diplomacy and affairs. Indonesia, for instance, took a greater role in the NAM; played a crucial role in negotiations regarding the Bangsamoro problem in the Philippines; and established stronger relations with certain countries of the Middle East. This change to a large extent was motivated by economic interests. Thus, after a decade of inward oriented policy of national economic development in the late 1960 and 1970s, the Soeharto government became more assertive in its foreign policy, becoming an important actor in international politics.

But as indicated above, the Indonesian posture in international politics declined considerably following the fall of President Soeharto; again, Indonesia has been occupied mainly by internal problems from politics, economics, social to cultural.

Apart from these internal crises and problems, there is little doubt that the Islamic factor becomes more apparent in domestic politics that, in turn, influence Indonesia's foreign policy. The so-called "Islamic revival" that has been taking place since the last decade of the Soeharto period seems to gain new momentum in the post-Soeharto reforms period (*masa reformasi*). The reappeareance of political Islam, represented by many Islamic parties, has brought about new emphasis on the importance of Islamic factor in both domestic and foreign policy.

An even stronger pressure is brought by a number of hardline groups that become more pronounced in the post-Soeharto period. These groups, known for their anti-American sentiment, appeal to Indonesian governments to pay more attention to and to take a more active role in the Middle Eastern problems, that is, the Palestinian question, and the American aggression in Iraq. They bitterly criticized President Wahid for comtemplating a plan to open trade and economic relations with Israel, and shunned President Megawati Soekarnoputri for having "surrendered" to the pressures of President George W Bush in his war against terrorism. They by and large have been idle since the arrests of a number of perpetrators of Bali, Marriot and Kuningan bombings; but they could reactivate themselves and challenge President Yudhoyono.

CONCLUSION

Despite some signs shown by President Yudhoyono of possible more active and assertive foreign policy, it is also clear that he will concentrate mainly on domestic affairs. For that purpose, he appealed to his cabinet ministers not to travel abroad unless very necessary and urgent. He has of course broken his promise not traveling abroad by going to Cairo, Santiago, and Viantiane.

Therefore, it is difficult to expect that President Yudhoyono admininistration has a strong aspiration to play a greater role in the Muslim world and other international affairs. Despite some efforts in the past by President Soeharto to get closer to a number of Arab countries, Indonesia has never played a prominent role nor occupied an important position in international Islamic organizations such as the Organization of Islamic Conference (OIC). This has been the official position of the Indonesian government that seems to be adopted also by President Yudhoyono.

There is a lot of hopes among Indonesian Muslims as well as foreign scholars, such as the late Fazlur Rahman, John Esposito and others that Indonesia could be a model for other Muslim countries in its political system and modernization. The hopes in fact find a stronger basis with the success of Indonesia in the consolidation of democracy, as has been shown particularly in the peaceful legislature and presidential elections of 2004. Indonesia, in this perspective, should be more active as a model of the compatibility of Islam and democracy.

But, again, the hopes seem to be very difficult to materialize. This is not only because Indonesia continues to adopt a policy of ambiguity, but also because Arab Muslim countries tend to underestimate the importance of Indonesian Islam and the country's huge Muslim population. Indonesian

Islam is considered not 'real Islam' as opposed to Middle Eastern Islam; and Indonesian Muslims are regarded not 'Islamic' enough. A number or prominent scholars, such Nikki Keddie, Fazlur Rahman, Esposito and others through their comparative studies have shown the fallacies of that kind of perception and bias.

Thus, there is long way for Indonesia in order to be able to play a greater role in the Muslim world and international affairs. For the purpose, Indonesia firstly needs to improve domectic conditions particularly politics and economy. If that can be done, then Indonesia could reorient its foreign policy, playing a more pro-active role in the Muslim world and international affairs.

CHAPTER 11

THE HISTORICAL ROOTS
OF MUSLIM CRISIS

"... Despite the immense destruction inflicted on the Iraqi people at the hands of the Crusader Jewish alliance, and in spite of the appalling number of dead, exceeding a million, the Americans ... nevertheless, are trying once more to repeat this dreadful slaughter. It seems that the long blockade following after a fierce war, the dismemberment and the destruction are not enough for them. So they come again today to destroy what remains of this people and to humiliate their Muslim neighbors" (Osama bin Laden, cited in Lewis 2003: xxv-vi).

This statement by bin Laden was issued before the American, British and Australian attack on Iraq. In fact, it was published on 23 February 1998, in *al-Quds al-'Arabi*, an Arabic newspaper published in London. The text of the statement cited fully in Bernard Lewis' most recent book, *The Crisis of Islam; Holy War and Unholy Terror* (2003), is, in retrospect, a kind of prophesy with respect to last month's war against Iraq.

The statement, furthermore, maintains the perception of many during the American war in Iraq. It asserts that, while the purposes of the Americans in these wars are religious and economic, they also serve the petty state of the Jews. The wars are diverting attention from their occupation of Jerusalem and their killing of Muslims in the city. Moreover, according to the statement, there is no better proof of this than their eagerness to destroy Iraq, the strongest of the neighboring Arab states, and their attempt to dismember all the states of the region into petty states. The division of the states in the Middle East would, in turn, ensure the survival of Israel and the continuation of the calamitous Crusader occupation of the lands of Arabia.

WHAT ISLAM MEANS

There is little doubt that the writings of Bernard Lewis have gained greater prominence as a result of the increased conflict between the West and Islam since the late 1980s. In fact, it is Lewis who coined the oft-used phrase "the clash of civilizations", not Samuel Huntington. The eventual violent clash is reflected in the September 11 attacks on the US and, since then, Lewis, Emeritus Professor of Near Eastern studies at Princeton University, has been even more prolific. In a relatively short period after September 11, he produced two important books; *What Went Wrong?: Western Impact and Middle Eastern Response* (2002) and *The Crisis of Islam.* (2003)

In terms of substance, the two books are, in fact, closely related to each other. In the first book, Lewis basically examines the historical roots of resentment among Muslims that have arisen because of their encounters with modern Europe; these resentments in the world today are increasingly being expressed in acts of terrorism. He discusses the historical origins of political Islam which have inspired the rise of militant Muslims – both individuals and groups. The second book also deals with the historical roots of the Muslim rage throughout history, but in particular, he charts the key events of the twentieth century leading up to the violent confrontations between certain radical groups of Muslims and the US today. Among these key events are the creation of the state of Israel, the cold war, Ayatollah Khomeini's Islamic revolution, the Soviet defeat in Afghanistan and the September 11 attacks on the US.

Bernard Lewis has been a target of Edward Said's harsh criticism in his masterpiece *Orientalism* (1978) for being biased and prejudiced against Islam and Muslims because of his Jewish background, among other reasons. Said even maintains that Lewis – as an outsider of Islam and the Arabs – has no moral right to study Islam and its society. Lewis is, of course, insistent that the study of Islam is not solely the privilege of insiders but also of outsiders like him. It seems that Lewis is trying to be more objective and more balanced in the views outlined in his two books. It is a pity though that the title of his second book is very misleading; what he is discussing in the book is, in fact, not the crisis of Islam, but rather the crisis among Muslims.

Lewis attempts to define Islam but what he means by Islam is, once again, Islam as it has been represented and actualized by Muslims throughout their history. What does he really mean by Islam? He simply writes that "it is difficult to generalize about Islam; and the word *Islam* denotes more than fourteen centuries of history, a billion and a third people, and a religious and cultural tradition of enormous diversity". (Lewis 2003, 3) With so heavy an emphasis on Muslim societies rather than on Islam as a set of doctrines, the term "Islam" used in the title of the book should be read in a very cautious way; or at least the term Islam in Lewis' application is interchangeable with the terms "Muslim", or "Islamic".

Despite this misleading use of the term "Islam", Lewis is wise when he discusses the clash between the Muslim world and the West. He is right when he states that the Muslim world is far from unanimous in its rejection of the West, nor have the Muslim regions of the third world been alone in their hostility towards the West. There are still significant numbers, in some quarters perhaps a majority, of Muslims with whom the West shares certain basic cultural and moral, social and political beliefs and aspirations.

With that qualification in mind, Lewis tries to answer the key question that occupies many Western policy makers at the present time; "Is Islam, whether fundamentalist or other, a threat to the West?" (Lewis 2003, 20) Lewis then categorizes two schools of thought. The first school of thought suggests that after the demise of the Soviet Union and the communist movements, Islam and Islamic fundamentalism have replaced them as the major threat to the West and the Western way of life. The second group responds that Muslims, including radical fundamentalists, are basically decent, peace-loving, pious people, some of whom have been driven beyond endurance by all the dreadful things the West has done to them. The West chooses to depict them as enemies because the West has a psychological need of an enemy to replace the defunct Soviet Union.

According to Lewis, these answers are mostly misleading; and both are dangerously wrong. Both views, however, contain elements of truth. Lewis argues that Islam as such is not an enemy of the West. More importantly, there are growing numbers of Muslims, both in the Muslim world and in the West, who desire nothing better than a closer and friendlier relationship with the West and the development of democratic institutions in their own countries. At the same time, however, a significant number of Muslims – notably but not exclusively those who are called fundamentalists – are hostile and dangerous, not because the West needs an enemy but because they do.

There is yet another group of Muslims who – while remaining committed Muslims and well aware of the flaws of modern Western society – nevertheless also see its merits, among others; its inquiring spirit, which produced modern science and technology and its concern for freedom, which created modern democratic government. This group of Muslims, furthermore, while retaining their own beliefs and their own culture, seeks to join the West in reaching toward a freer and better world.

HARSH ENCOUNTER

The theme of the crisis of Islam, or more appropriately, the crisis of Muslims has been the subject of numerous studies. Thus, Lewis' arguments outlined here about the root causes of the crisis among Muslims are not really new. One can refer to the writings of such scholars as John Esposito, John Voll, Bruce Lawrence, Gilles Kepel, and many others. What makes Lewis different from others is that he uses the subject 'we' in referring to the opposition to Muslims. He is then explicitly taking sides with the West, and has diverged from the neutral position one usually finds in academic writings.

The root causes of the crisis among Muslims are complex; there could be factors both from within Muslim societies and from without–in this case, from the Western world – that leads Muslims to their continued crisis. Simple and sweeping generalizations will result not only in the perpetuation of inaccurate perceptions of Islam, but consequently also in the growing conflict between Muslims and Westerners.

Internally, the crisis of Muslims originated in the disintegration of Muslim political entities which, in consequence, also resulted in social-economic stagnation. At the same time, Europe – and later in contemporary times also the US – continued to progress in science and technology, which, in turn, produced imperialism and colonialism, and made the Muslim world succumb to their power and influence.

The European onslaught on the Muslim Middle East began with the campaign of a young French general named Napoleon Bonaparte in 1798. Within a remarkably short time, Bonaparte and his small expeditionary force were able to conquer, occupy and rule the great Muslim heartland. The fact that a small European force was able to invade one of the heartlands of Islam caused a profound shock among Muslims in general. This is the beginning of "soul searching" and of "defeatism" among many Muslims as well as of growing resentment against the Europeans.

In the end, as Lewis points out, the Ottoman Sultanate, the last of the great Muslim empires, was finally defeated by European powers in 1918. Its capital Constantinople, was occupied; its sovereign held captive, and much of its territory was partitioned between the victorious British and French empires. Worse still, the Arabic speaking former Ottoman provinces of the Fertile Crescent were divided into three new entities, with new names and frontiers. Two of them, Iraq and Palestine, were under British mandate; the third under the name Syria was given to the French. Later, the French subdivided their mandate into two, calling one part Lebanon and retaining the name Syria for the rest.

The dismemberment of the Muslim region under the Ottoman Empire continued. The British divided Palestine, creating a division between the two banks of the Jordan; the eastern segment was called TransJordan, later simply Jordan; while the Western part was kept under the name Palestine. The only Muslim power that was able to check European imperialist ambitions was the Turks. Led by an Ottoman general named Mustafa Kemal – better known as Kemal Ataturk – the Turks eventually succeeded in liberating their homeland. In retrospect, the success is, however, lamented by the Islamists since he fought not in the name of Islam, but rather in the name of secular nationalism. As he fought successfully to liberate Turkey from Western domination, he adopted Western ways and, abolished the Ottoman sultanate in November 1922.

The abolition of the sultanate – referred to by some Muslims until the present day as "caliphate" – is mourned by the Islamists. Even though most of the Ottoman sultans were repressive and dictatorial, they were widely recognized among Muslims as *caliph*, the political head of all Sunni Islam. During its nearly 13 centuries, the caliphate had gone through many vicissitudes, but it remained a potent symbol of Muslim unity, and even identity. Its abolition, under the double assault of foreign imperialists and their domestic Westernizers like Kemal Ataturk, was bitterly felt throughout the Muslim world, including in the Netherlands Indies (Indonesia).

Because of its political and religious centrality among some Muslims, the disappearance of the "Ottoman Caliphate", was only the beginning of the attempts to reestablish the caliphate. Various Muslim monarchs and leaders had attempted to claim the caliphate but to no avail. In the contemporary times, the idea and attempts to reestablish the caliphate are taken over by a number of Islamist movements, the most prominent being the Hizb al-Tahrir ("Party of Liberation"). The Indonesian public, for instance, can clearly see that the theme advocating the reestablishment of the caliphate has recently been clearly and boldly written in its pamphlets during its mass anti-US rallies in many Indonesian cities and towns. For Hizb al-Tahrir and some other Islamist movements, the establishment of a single and universal caliphate is the only answer and solution to the Muslim disunity and predicament vis-à-vis the West.

The impact of European imperialism on the Muslim lands was more than just its political defeat. In the eyes of many Muslims, the impact of imperialism had been immense and far-reaching. There were certainly major negative consequences of imperialism and, more broadly, of European or Western influence. Notable among the effects of modernization or westernization were the strengthening of un-Islamic ideologies and state authority by the reinforcement of the apparatus of surveillance, repression and indoctrination. At the same time, there took place the weakening or elimination of intermediate powers that, in the traditional order, limited the effective power of autocratic rulers who were supported by Western powers. Rapid social change and the breakdown of old social relationships and obligations, brought continuous harm to Muslim society.

Muslim resentment towards the Western powers grew rapidly with the rise of the US on the international scene soon after World War II. With the demise of European colonialism, anti-American sentiment grew steadily among Muslims in the Middle East in particular. This can be attributed to several causes: economic exploitation, often described as the pillaging of the Muslims' natural resources; the support of corrupt local tyrants who served American interests by oppressing and robbing their own people; and more importantly, American support for Israel, first in its conflict with Palestinian Arabs, then in its conflict with the neighboring Arab states and the larger Muslim world. With its increased involvement in the Middle East since the 1950s at the expense of the Arab Muslim, America has, in the words of Lewis, become the archenemy, the incarnation of evil, the diabolical opponent of all that is good, and, especially for Muslims, of Islam.

There is little doubt that the list of Middle Eastern Muslims' grievances and resentments toward the US has grown even more steadily since the late 1970s with the American support of the despotic ruler of Iran, Shah Reza Pahlevi. On the eve of his successful Islamic Revolution, Ayatullah Ruhullah Khomeini complained that the whole Muslim world was caught in America's clutches. He called upon the Muslims of the world to unite against their enemy. It was about this time that he began to speak of America as the "Great Satan" and of the Egyptian President Anwar Sadat and Iraqi President Saddam Hussein as servants and agents of America. In a much later development, Osama bin Laden called President George W. Bush the Pharaoh of the present day who is supported by his loyal allies among Middle Eastern Muslim rulers.

CONCLUSION

Looking at the historical roots outlined above, Lewis is right when he states that the phenomenon of militant and radical Muslims – who now are increasingly resorting to terrorism – is not new. Since the beginning of their harsh encounters with the West and the increasing impact of the West in the nineteenth century, there have been religiously-expressed, militant opposition movements among Muslims. Their failure not only at the hands of the Western powers, but more importantly at the hands of their own repressive regimes supported by the US and its allies produced even more bitter resentments, which made them more readily resort to terrorism for "martyrdom" in the name of "Islam".

All different militant and radical groups justify and sanctify their violent acts through references to Islamic texts, particularly the Qur'an and the Prophet tradition (*hadith*). They claim to be the representatives of a truer, purer, and more authentic Islam than that currently practised by the vast majority of Muslims. Muslims and Westerners alike should, of course, not be misled by their claims.

In the end, the problem of radicalism and terrorism among Muslims should be addressed not only by mainstream Muslim leaders, but also by the Western world. Moderate Muslim leaders must not condone any kind of violent acts, and should make it clear that Islam is against any kind of violence. At the same time, the US or the Western world in general should also address the root causes of the resentment and bitterness among Muslims. Cracking down only on violent groups will only lead to a vicious circle of violence and terrorism.

Part Three
THE DYNAMICS
OF ISLAMIC MOVEMENTS

CHAPTER 12

INDONESIAN ISLAM AFTER THE BALI BOMBING

Religious life is often colored by myths. In fact many religions have their roots in the myths, originating from the enchantment of human beings with gods and nature. Revealed religions like Islam, Christianity and Judaism (all are Abrahamic religions), however, are opposed to myths. Known as a strict monotheistic religion, Islam strongly emphasizes the need to keep the faith clear of any kind of myth, especially those relating to God, since it could lead to "associationism" (*shirk*), which is one of the cardinal sins in Islam.

The perception of Islam among both Muslims and non-Muslims is also often colored by misperception, if not by myths. Furthermore, there are also a great deal of misperceptions and myths among outside observers about Islam and Muslims in general, because of historical, sociological and political factors. For the purpose of this paper, a few of these myths that specifically relate to Southeast Asian Islam will be mentioned and critically assessed.

The first myth, which is still strong among Western scholars and observers, is that Southeast Asian Islam is not real Islam. The very term "religion of Java" that was used by the American anthropologist Clifford Geertz as the title of his book (1968) to describe Islamic life among the Javanese, reflects the reluctance to recognize the Islamicness of Islam in Java, or even in Southeast Asia in general. Through his distinction of *santri* (strict and practicing Muslims) and *abangan* (nominal Muslims), Geertz argues that the majority of

Muslims in Java were *abangan* only. Thus, Southeast Asian Islam historically, sociologically, culturally and politically is regarded as only a marginal and peripheral Islam vis-à-vis Middle Eastern Islam. Southeast Asian Islam is viewed as an obscure phenomenon and, as Van Leur once asserted, only a "thin veneer of symbols attached to a supposedly solid core of animistic and Hindu-Buddhist meaning" (Van Leur 1955). In short, Islam is regarded as having no significant impact on Southeast Asian culture.

It is true than Southeast Asian Islam is the least Arabicized owing to the process of Islamization that was generally peaceful, and gradual; but one should not be misled by the "myth" of *abangan*. The reality is that while older local beliefs and practices resisted the continued process of Islamization, a purer and more orthodox form of Islam did, nevertheless, steadily penetrate deeper into parts of the region. A number of scholars have not failed to observe this tendency. As early as 1950s, Harry J. Benda maintained that the Islamic history of Indonesia [as elsewhere in Southeast Asia] is essentially a history of *santri* cultural expansion and its impact on Indonesian religious life and politics (1958:14). Two decades later, Federspiel (1970:3) concluded that over the past four hundred years, Indonesia [as well as Islam in Southeast Asia in general] has slowly been moving towards a more orthodox form of religion, while its heterodox beliefs and practices have declined considerably over the same period. Later research by such scholars as Woodward (1989), Pranowo (1994), Ricklefs (1998) and others have further confirmed the strong tendencies towards Islamic orthodoxy and the blurring of the distinction between *santri* and *abangan*.

The tendency towards new attachment – if not to Islamic rejuvenation – can be observed clearly among Muslims in Southeast Asia, particularly in Indonesia and Malaysia, in the last two decades at least. New tendencies in religious observance, new institutions, new Muslim groups, and new Islamic life-styles have been increasingly adopted by many Muslims in this period. More and more new mosques with new architecture have been constructed, and their congregations are full, mostly with youth. At the same time, more and more Muslims have undertaken the pilgrimage; in fact, the number of pilgrims (some 225,000 people) from Southeast Asia is the largest compared to those from other areas of the Muslim world. In addition, more religious alms and donations (*zakat, infaq and sadaqah* – ZIS) have been collected and distributed for the poor and deprived Muslims. New institutions for collecting ZIS have been formed, like the Dompet Dhua'fa *Republika* in Indonesia, which has been phenomenally successful.

The changing political policies of the regimes in both Indonesia and Malaysia during the 1990s, that have tended to be more conciliatory to Islam and Muslim groups, have greatly contributed to the rise of new Islamic institutions such as Islamic banks, Islamic insurance (*takaful*), Islamic people's credit unions (BPR-Syari'ah, or *Bank Perkreditan Rakyat Syari'ah*, and BMT or Bait al-Mal wa al-Tamwil). Malaysia had, of course, developed these Islamic institutions earlier than Indonesia, but now in Indonesia "conventional banks" – following the Malaysian example – have also opened Syari'ah divisions or branches.

In addition, new quality Islamic educational institutions have been established either by private Muslim foundations or by the state. This includes the formation of the International Islamic University Malaysia (IIUM) by the Malaysian Government, followed by a number of other Islamic universities and colleges in Malaysia. In addition, Islamic higher education now consists of fourteen State Institutes for Islamic Studies (*Institut Agama Islam Negeri* – IAIN), thirty-three State Islamic Colleges (*Sekolah Tinggi Agama Negeri* – STAIN) and four State Islamic Universities (*Universitas Islam Negeri* – UIN) in various cities throughout Indonesia. In the meantime, new quality schools and *madrasahs*, such as the Sekolah Islam al-Azhar, SMU Madania, SMU al-Izhar, and the like have also been established. At the same time, the *madrasahs* – that are now equivalent in status to "secular schools" – and *pesantrens/pondoks* have been modernized as well, adopting the national curricula of 1994 issued by the Ministry of National Education. The *pesantrens* are now also established in urban areas; in the past, the *pesantrens* have been associated mostly with rural areas.

All of these new developments are representative of some much wider changes within Southeast Asian Muslim society. Since the 1980s one can observe the rise of a new Muslim middle class. While there is no specific term used to denote them in Indonesia, in Malaysia this rising Muslim middle class is called the "new Malay". Even though this new Muslim middle class is heavily dependent upon the governing regimes, there is little doubt that they have played a significant role in the construction of, and support for, the new Islamic institutions. Furthermore, they are very instrumental in the spread of new life-styles such as the widespread use of the *jilbab* (head-dress) by women, or of *baju koko* (Muslim shirts); or even a new tradition of conducting religious discussions, seminars and ceremonies in hotels and other prominent places.

Despite all of these new attachments to Islam, it is important to point out that, by and large, they have not led to significant changes in political attitudes. The majority of Muslims in Southeast Asia continue to hold fast to the political paradigm that has been achieved in the period since independence following World War II. It is true that after the fall of Soeharto, many Islamic parties have been established in Indonesia but they failed to win significant votes in the 1999 general elections (Azra, 2000). In Malaysia, while PAS has been able to increase its power in the last elections, it is clear that the position of UMNO remains impregnable. It seems that it is almost a myth that the Islamists would be able to wrest political power in either Indonesia or Malaysia and the strength and influence of the Islamists in the region should, therefore, not be over-estimated.

It is clear that, in addition to the internal dynamics of the respective states that contribute to the increased momentum of the new attachment to Islam, global influences have played an important role. As I argued elsewhere, the tendency toward orthodoxy in Southeast Asia had its origins in the intense religio-intellectual contacts and connections that commenced in the sixteenth century between Malay-Indonesian students and their co-religionists and *ulama* in the Middle East, particularly in the Haramayn (Mecca and Medina). Returning students or scholars implanted a more *shari'ah*-oriented Islam in the Malay-Indonesian archipelago, which forced the so-called "pantheistic" (or "*wujudiyyah mulhid*") Sufism to cede ground (Azra, 2003b). This is the beginning of the rise of a more scriptural Islam, or in Reid's term, "scriptural orthodoxy" in Southeast Asia (1988).

The intense contacts between Southeast Asian Islam and that of the Middle East continued in the nineteenth century onwards. By the end of the nineteenth century, new globalizing waves of Muslim discourse reached the shores of the Malay-Indonesian archipelago. These waves were brought into the archipelago not only by returning students, but also by *haj* pilgrims who from the 1870s traveled in ever increasing numbers to the Holy Land.

The most important discourse in the Malay-Indonesian archipelago arising from this wave was pan-Islamism. Other waves came in the early twentieth century. This was a new kind of wave that originated from Cairo and which has been categorized by many observers as "Islamic modernism". The spread of this new discourse had led to the formation of such modernist Muslim organizations as the Muhammadiyah (1912), al-Irsyad (1913), and Persis (in the early 1920s) (Azra, 2002a; Laffan, 2002).

In more contemporary times, the globalizing waves that influence Muslim discourse in Southeast Asia no longer stem only from the Haramayn or even from Cairo. In fact, the respectable position of the Haramayn (or Saudi Arabia as a whole), so far as the discourse on Southeast Asian Islam is concerned, has been in decline for the last few decades. In fact, Wahhabism originated from Arabia in the late eighteenth century. The official religious ideology of Saudi Arabia, Wahhabism remains an anathema for many Muslims in Southeast Asia. The brand and tradition of Islam in Southeast Asia are simply incompatible with Wahhabism. One can therefore, not exaggerate the influence of Saudi Arabian Wahhabism in Southeast Asia. Even though there are some traces of Wahhabism in the region, they are surely too insignificant to influence the course of Southeast Asian Islam (Azra, 2002a).

Other places in the Middle East, or elsewhere in the Muslim world, have recently come to the forefront and, in turn, have left their impact on Muslim discourse in Southeast Asia. Thus, since the 1980s, the discourse developed by such scholars as Abu al-A'la al-Mawdudi, Sayyid Qutb, Taqi al-Din al-Nabhani and Middle Eastern movements like al-Ikhwan al-Muslimun (and its splinter groups), Hizb al-Tahrir and the like began to spread in Southeast Asia. The Iranian Ayatullah Khomeini's Islamic revolution in 1979 has further inspired the Islamists in the region to assert their existence. Once again, however, religious, sociological and political realities give only a very limited room for such discourses and movements to play in Southeast Asia in general. It is also a myth, therefore, to assert that Muslim radicalism in the Middle East would find fertile ground in Southeast Asia.

It is probably almost a cliché that Southeast Asian Islam is a distinctive Islam, having a different expression compared with Islam in the Middle East or elsewhere in the Islamic world. In fact, in the 1990s Southeast Asian Islam was dubbed by leading international media such as *Newsweek* magazine as

"Islam with a smiling face" (*Newsweek*, 23 September 1996). Islam in the region has been generally regarded as a brand of peaceful and moderate Islam that has no problem with modernity, democracy, human rights and other tendencies of the modern world.

But now, for foreign observers as well as international media, the face of Southeast Asian Islam is undergoing significant changes. Islam in the region is now increasingly regarded as being in a rapid process of radicalization and, worse still, the Muslim region of Southeast Asia is now perceived by some as a potential "hotbed of terrorism". This latest term, I would argue, is also a kind of myth. There is, of course, the potential for the radicalization of Southeast Asian Muslims, but it is far to early to view the region as a "hotbed of terrorism".

One has to admit, however, that the rapid political changes that have been taking place at the national, regional and international levels, especially after the September 11, 2001 tragedy in the US, have indeed witnessed the rise of Muslim radicalism in the region. The arrest of a number of individuals and groups in Southeast Asian countries, such as Malaysia, Singapore, Philippines and Indonesia has increasingly indicated the existence of regional links between them as well as with international terrorist groups.

The investigation by Indonesian police of the Bali bombings on 12 October 2002, for instance, so far seems to have disclosed the complex connections between individuals and groups that carry out violent and terrorist activities. A clearer picture of the radical networks has appeared. There are at least two conspicuous patterns that have been uncovered by the police investigation of the Bali bombings. Firstly, some of the perpetrators of the bombings are alumna of the Ngruki *Pesantren*, the head of which is Abu Bakar Ba'asyir, who is widely regarded as the spiritual leader of Jama'ah Islamiyyah, the core of radical groups in Southeast Asia. Secondly, some of the perpetrators had been living in Malaysia in the period of Abu Bakar Ba'asyir's self-exile, escaping President Soeharto's harsh repression. (ICG, August 2002; ICG, December 2002; Nursalim, 2001).

The perception of the rise of radicalism among Southeast Asian Muslims appears rapidly after the tragic events of 11 September 2001 in New York and Washington DC. The perception grows stronger in the successive events that occurred in the aftermath of "Nine-Eleven", especially the Bali bombings that left almost two hundred innocent people dead. The bombings at a McDonalds outlet and Haji Kalla car show room in Makassar, South Sulawesi, on the eve of 'Id al-Fitr (5 December 2002), has furthermore confirmed the tendencies towards terrorism among certain radical individuals and groups in Indonesia. This is the result of police investigations in Indonesia that shows that perpetrators of these terrorist acts are individuals who have been known to be members of, or associated with, certain radical persons and groups.

Again, there is little doubt that the 11 September 2001 tragedy has rapidly radicalized certain individuals and groups among Muslims in Southeast Asia, particularly in Indonesia. The subsequent American military operation in Afghanistan has, unfortunately, given momentum to the radicals to assert themselves more clearly. The Bush administration threat to attack Iraq has further fueled bitter resentment among the radicals. Furthermore, the arrests of a number of suspected radicals in Malaysia, Singapore and Philippines has added fuel to their anger and bitterness toward the US and symbols that they consider to be representative of American imperialist arrogance such as McDonalds or Kentucky Fried Chicken outlets.

One should not be misled, however, by these current developments; in fact, radicalism among Indonesian Muslims in particular is not new. Even though Southeast Asian Islam in general has been viewed as moderate and peaceful Islam, the history of Islam in the region shows that radicalism among Muslims, as will be discussed shortly, has existed for at least two centuries, when the Wahhabi-like Padri movement, in West Sumatra in late eighteenth and early nineteenth centuries held sway and forced other Muslims in the area to subscribe to their literal understanding of Islam. The violent movement aimed at spreading the pure and pristine Islam as practised by the Prophet Muhammad and his companions (the *salaf*). The Padri, however, failed to gain support from the majority of Muslims and, as a result, the Padri movement was the only precedent of Muslim radicalism throughout Southeast Asia.

The Padri movement was a shift in the continued influence of Middle Eastern Islam on the course of Southeast Asian Islam. As I argued elsewhere (Azra, 2003b), from the sixteenth century up to the eighteenth century, Islam in the Middle East exerted a very strong influence on Islamic intellectualism and religious life in Southeast Asia, mainly through complex networks of Middle Eastern and Malay-Indonesian *ulama*. As mentioned above, the Malay-Indonesian *ulama*, in turn, played a crucial role in the peaceful reforms of Islamic intellectualism and life in Southeast Asia. Toward the end of the eighteenth century, however, the discourse on *jihad* (war) was introduced by such prominent Malay-Indonesian scholars as 'Abd al-Samad al-Palimbani and Daud ibn 'Abd Allah al-Patani as a response to the increased encroachment of European colonialism in Southeast Asia; the *jihad* was not directed against other Muslims. It is, therefore, the Padri of West Sumatra who set the precedent in Southeast Asia by launching the *jihad* against their fellow Muslims.

POLITICO-RELIGIOUS ROOTS OF RADICALISM AND TERRORISM

The root causes of radicalism among Muslims are very complex. The complexity is even greater at the present time, because of the many driving factors that are working to influence the course of Muslim societies as a whole. In the past, before the modern period, the causes of radicalism were mainly internal, that is, as a response to internal problems that were faced by the Muslims such as the rapid decline of Muslim political entities and conflicts among Muslims. Many Muslims in the pre-colonial time strongly believed that the sorry state of the Muslim world had a lot to do with the socio-moral decay of Muslims themselves, resulting from their wrong religious beliefs and practices; they had simply abandoned the original and real teachings of Islam.

As a result, some Muslims felt it necessary to conduct *tajdid* (renewal) or islah (reform) not only through peaceful means, but also by force and other radical means they considered to be more effective, by declaring *jihad* (war) against Muslims who were regarded as having gone astray. Islam, of course, emphasizes the need for Muslims to renew their beliefs and practices; in fact, in one of his *hadith* (tradition), the prophet Muhammad states that there would be a reformer or renewer (*mujaddid*) of Islam, coming at the end of every century to renew and revitalize Islam. But at the same time, it is clear that there are Qur'anic injunctions that prohibit the use of radical and violent means in the efforts to renew and reform Islam.

One of the strongest tendencies in the discourses and movements in Islamic renewal and reforms is the orientation towards pure and pristine Islam as practised by the Prophet Muhammad and his companions (the *salafs*). That is why most of the Islamic renewal movements are called "*Salafiyyah*" (or Salafi, or Salafism). There is a very wide spectrum of Islamic discourse and movements that can be included in Salafiyyah. One can make a distinction between "classic Salafiyyah" and "neo-Salafiyyah"; or "peaceful Salafiyyah" and "radical Salafiyyah". The Wahhabi movement in the Arabian Peninsula that gained momentum in the late eighteenth century can be categorized as both classic and radical Salafiyyah. The case is also the same with the Padri movement in West Sumatra in the successive period as described briefly above. The Wahhabi-like Padri movement can be conveniently categorized as the "classic Salafism", in which the internal factor with the Muslim *ummah* was its driving force.

The spectrum of "neo Salafiyyah" discourse and movements is certainly very complex. The term "neo" in the first instance refers to the modern period, beginning with the harsh encounters between Muslim societies and Western colonial powers from the seventeenth century onwards. During this period, the external factors – associated mostly with the Western world – that could incite radicalism became increasingly dominant. In fact, the West has been accused by many Muslims of being responsible for many problems that Muslims have been facing in the last few centuries. Confronting continued Western domination and hegemony, many Muslims were afflicted by a kind of defensive psychology that led to, among others, a belief in the so-called "conspiracy theory".

There were, of course, outbursts of Muslim radicalism in Southeast Asia in the nineteenth century and early twentieth century in the period prior to World War II during the heyday of European colonialism in the region. This was a different kind of radicalism and in fact, constituted *jihads* to liberate Muslim lands (*dar al-Islam*) from the occupation of the hostile infidel Europeans coming from the lands of war (*dar al-harb*). According to classical Islamic doctrines, *jihad* against hostile infidels is justified and, in fact, it is considered to be a just war; *jihads* of this kind are believed to be wars in the way of God (*jihad fi sabil Allah*).

Looking at the whole history of radicalism among Muslims, I would argue that radicalism among Muslims is more political than religious. In some instances, the original motive could be religious, but soon becomes very political. Political developments in Southeast Asia, particularly in Indonesia after World War II, had been important factors in the rise of a new kind of radicalism among Muslims. Disappointed with the Indonesian military policies of rationalization of paramilitary groups following Indonesian independence on 17 August 1945, Kartosuwirjo in the name of Islam rebelled against the government. This was the origin of the Islamic State (*Dar al-Islam* – DI) or the Islamic State of Indonesia (*Negara Islam Indonesia* – NII,) and Indonesian Islamic Army (*Tentara Islam Indonesia* – TII) that aimed at establishing an Islamic state, *dawlah al-Islamiyah*, in Indonesia. Even though the rebellious movement spread to South Sulawesi and Aceh in the 1950s, it failed to gain support from the majority of Indonesian Muslims who, after a bitter struggle in the last year of the Japanese occupation, had finally accepted *Pancasila* ("five pillars") as the national ideology. As a result, the Indonesian army was able to crush these radical movements.

The idea of the establishment of an Islamic state (*dawlah al-Islamiyyah*) is one of the most crucial issues among certain groups of Muslims in Indonesia. Certain groups among the moderates, such as the Masjumi party under the leadership of Mohammad Natsir, for instance, also attempted to transform Indonesia into a *dawlah al-Islamiyyah*. It is important to point out that the attempts were carried out through legal and constitutional ways, more precisely, through parliament avenues but they were unsuccessful, mainly because Islamic parties were involved in quarrels and conflicts among themselves and, therefore, had failed to gain a majority in the parliament at the national election of 1955.

It is important to note that, with that failure, the moderate Muslim leaders had not resorted to illegal means, such as armed rebellion, to transform Indonesia into an Islamic state. In contrast, there was a growing tendency among them to accept *Pancasila* as the final political reality. At the same time, however, there remain individual and Muslim groups who keep the idea of establishing an Islamic state in Indonesia alive. Depending on the political situation in certain times, these people can operate underground or openly in achieving their goals. They may also collaborate with certain dissatisfied elements of the military or even with other radical groups which, in terms of ideology, are incompatible with theirs; this awkward collaboration can be called a "marriage for convenience", or in Islamic terms as "*nikah mut'ah*". One should, therefore, be very careful in an analysis and perspective of radical groups; some of them could be genuine, motivated mostly by religious reasons, but some others could be "engineered" radicals sponsored by certain individuals and groups of people for their own political ends.

The Soeharto New Order regime, at least in the period of the 1970s and 1980s, was not on good terms with Muslim political forces in general. In fact, there was a lot of mutual suspicion and hostility between the two sides. President Soeharto took very harsh measures against any expression of Islamic extremism. But at the same time, it is widely believed that certain military generals such as Ali Murtopo and Benny Moerdani recruited ex DI/TII supporters to form "Komando Jihad" (Jihad Command), conducting subversive activities in order to discredit Islam and Muslims (Ausop, 2003).

CONTEMPORARY MUSLIM RADICAL GROUPS

The fall of President Soeharto, after more than three decades in power, has unleashed the dormant Muslim radicalism. The euphoria of newly found democracy and the lifting of the "anti-subversive law" by President B.J. Habibie, have provided very good grounds for the radicals to express their extremism and radical discourse and activities in a more visible manner. The lack of effective law enforcement because of the demoralization of the police and military (TNI) has created a kind of legal vacuum that, in turn, has been used by the radical groups to take the law into their own hands.

Some of the most important radical groups should be mentioned in this account. They are the Lasykar Jihad (LJ), formed by the Forum Komunikasi Ahlussunnah Wa al-Jamaah (FKAWJ) under the leadership of Ja'far Umar Thalib; the Islamic Defense Front (*Front Pembela Islam* – FPI) led by Habib Rizq Shihab; the Council of Indonesian Jihad Fighters (*Majelis Mujahidin Indonesia* – MMI) led by Abu Bakar Baasyir; the Jamaah Ikhwan al-Muslimin Indonesia (JAMI) led by Habib Husein al-Habsyi; and the Indonesian Party of Liberation (*Hizb al-Tahrir Indonesia* – HTI) (Bamualim et. al. 2001; Azra, 2003; Fananie et. al. 2002).

It is clear that all of these radical groups are independent and have no connection with established organizations like the Nahdlatul Ulama (NU),

Muhammadiyah, etc; nor are they affiliated with any Islamic political parties. This indicates that these radical groups do not trust any other established Muslim organizations, be they socio-religious or political in nature. This is mainly because, in the view of these radical groups, established Muslim organizations are too accommodative in their political and religious attitude vis-à-vis Indonesian political and religious realities. Political struggles and conflicts among fragmented political groups as well as among the pro- and anti-status quo groups, that also involves elements of the Indonesian military (TNI) in the aftermath of President Soeharto's fall, provides another impetus for the radicals to assert themselves.

I would suggest that these radical groups fall into two categories; the first group constitutes those radical groups that are basically homegrown; this includes the Lasykar Jihad, FPI and some other smaller groups. The second group consists of the Middle Eastern affiliated- or oriented groups, like the JAMI – which has its origins in the al-Ikhwan al-Muslimun in Egypt – and Hibz al-Tahrir, which was initially founded in Jordan by Syaikh Taqi al-Din Nabhani in the 1950s. Despite this distinction, all of these radical groups have a very strong Middle Eastern oriented ideology that they believe to be the most genuine world-view. In terms of religious outlook, therefore, they subscribe to the ideology of radical Salafism; and in terms of political view, they are believers in the ideology of *khilafatism* which includes among its important aims the establishment of a single, universal *khilafah* (caliphate) for all Muslims in the world.

Even though these radical groups aim to establish a *dawlah Islamiyah* of *khilafah* in the region, they are quite different to the old DI/NII movement in Indonesia. Due to conflicts and splits among the ex-DI/NII members resulting from the Indonesian intelligence operations mentioned above, the present radical groups tend to operate independently from older groups (Ausop, 2003).

Looking at the whole phenomenon of radicalism among Muslims in Southeast Asia, or in Indonesia in particular, it is clear that it has a long and complex history. The history of radicalism among certain Muslim groups, furthermore, shows that there are many factors that are responsible for their radical tendencies. There is a strong tendency for the motives of their radicalism to be political rather than religious. It is also conspicuous that their radicalism has a lot to do with the disruption of political and social systems as a whole. The absence or lack of law enforcement is certainly an important reason why the radicals have taken the law into their own hands in the name of Islam.

"BLESSING IN DISGUISE?"

The terrorist bombing of Kuta, Bali, on 12 October 2002 is certainly a sad human tragedy in contemporary Indonesia. In fact, the bombing reflects a new phase of violence and terror in the country. This can be seen not only in the relatively large number of victims, but also in the use of lethal weapons by the terrorists to inflict the greatest psychological impact, both domestically and internationally. Worse still, there is suspicion that one of the perpetrators was a suicide bomber, reminding one of the Palestinian suicide bombers. It is difficult for Indonesian people in general to accept that certain individuals among them are increasingly becoming so ruthless and inhumane.

However, after an intensive police investigation, the Bali bombing, for several reasons, could be a "blessing a disguise". First, police have been able to not only catch the alleged perpetrators of the bombing, but also to reveal some fresh insights into the networks of radicals in Indonesia and Southeast Asia in general. The exposure of the networks has been crucial in confirming suspicions that radicals have been working in Southeast Asia, or in Indonesia in particular, over the last few years to achieve their ends, the most important of which is supposedly an "Islamic State of Nusantara" that would consist of Indonesia, Malaysia, Brunei Darussalam, Singapore and, probably also the Muslim area of the southern Philippines.

A great deal of credit, then, must be given to the police who have been working tirelessly to investigate the case and have been successful in uncovering the links between the conspirators. After a series of unsolved bombings since the fall of President Soeharto in 1998, the police, with the help of their counterparts from Australia, have been able to uncover the links between the Bali bombing with a number of other bombings in the last two years at least.

Second, the exposure of the networks of the radicals by the police has, in an apparently convincing way, silenced most of the skeptics who, from the very day of the Bali blast, have maintained that the bombing was simply a US or Western plot to discredit Islam and destroy the image of Muslims in the country. The "skeptics", some of whom are prominent Muslim leaders, seem to believe in the so-called "conspiracy theory" and have, in fact, accused President Megawati's Government of being slavishly pandering to the pressures and wishes of President Bush of the US.

The disclosure of the radical's networks seems to show that the "conspiracy theory" does not ring true. The statements of Amrozi, Imam Samudra and their accomplices, who were involved in the Bali and other bombings, make it clear that the bombings have been motivated by both "genuine" radicalism and hatred of the US and other Western powers. The fact that the perpetrators show no remorse for the innocent victims has further strengthened the belief that they have been strongly motivated by their own violent ideology rather than by anything else.

Third, it points to the fact that there are, indeed, terrorists among Indonesians, ant that they happened to be Muslims who are more than happy to use violent means to achieve their ends. Before the police disclosure, there had been widespread reluctance among leaders of Indonesian Islam to admit that there are terrorists among Indonesian Muslims who have misused the teachings of Islam to justify their terrorist activities. In fact, some prominent Muslim leaders have issued statements that could give the public the wrong impression that they are not only defending the radicals, but are also condoning violence and terrorist acts.

CONCLUSION

It is now the right time for Southeast Asian Muslim leaders, the majority of whom are moderates, to sincerely admit that there is a serious problem of radicalism among certain Muslim individuals and groups. This problem should be fairly addressed by moderate Muslim leaders hand in hand with law enforcement agencies for the sake of the image of Islam as a peaceful religion and of Southeast Asian Muslims as the "Islamic people with a smiling face" (*Newsweek*, September 23, 1996). The problems of the radicals are to be seen at two levels; first, the abuse and manipulation of certain Islamic doctrines to justify radicalism and terrorism. The abuse undoubtedly comes from a literal interpretation of Islam. The second problem is the use of violence and terrorism, which undoubtedly runs contrary to Islam.

It is therefore time for moderate Muslim leaders to speak more clearly and loudly that a literal interpretation of Islam will only lead to extremism that is unacceptable to Islam, and that Islam can not condone, let alone justify, any kind of violent and terrorist act. There is absolutely no valid reason for any Muslim to conduct activities that harm or kill other people, Muslims and non-Muslims alike. Any kind of resentment and deprivation felt by any individual and group of Muslims cannot, and must not, justify any kind of desperate and inhuman act.

Furthermore, the moderate Muslim leaders should not be misled by the claims and assertions of the radicals. The radicals are shrewd, not only in abusing Islamic doctrines for their own ends, but also in manipulating Muslim sentiment through the abuse and manipulation of the mass media, particularly television. The claims that the arrest of certain radical leaders means the suppression of Islam and the *ulama* (Muslim religious scholars) are very misleading. Similarly, the claims that the police investigation in Indonesia of certain *pesantren* (Islamic traditional boarding school) in the search for the perpetrators of the bombings is the initial step of hostility and suspicion against the whole *pesantren* network are even more misleading.

The identification of radical leaders and groups with Islam and *ulama* is again very misleading. In fact the radicals are only a very small fraction of the multitude of moderate Muslims who, from their sheer numbers, can be fairly regarded as the epitome of the peaceful nature of Southeast Asian Islam. The moderates should, therefore, be very careful not to support any impression that could lead to the identification of the radicals with Islam and Muslims at large.

Some have argued that the defensive attitude of certain moderate Muslim leaders, particularly in Indonesia, originates from the trauma of political engineering and abuses by the police and military of the Muslims during the Soeharto period. This argument, I believe, does not seem to be relevant to the current political situation. There is no evidence that the Megawati Soekarnoputri regime is hostile to Islam and Muslims. In fact, President Megawati seems to be very sensitive to Muslim issues compared, for instance, to President Abdurrahman Wahid. Lacking Islamic credentials, President

Megawati, in fact, prevents herself from making statements, let alone policies, that could spark opposition from Muslims in general.

There is, of course, a lot of criticism of President Megawati Soekarnoputri who is regarded as being very hesitant and indecisive in taking any harsh measures against the radicals, because she is worried – it seems – at the possible backlash from the Muslim public. It appears that she does not realize that the moderate Muslim leaders and organizations are more than willing to rally behind her in opposition to any kind of religious extremism and radicalism. This has been made clear by the statements of Hasyim Muzadi (national Chairman of the NU) and Syafii Maarif (national Chairman of Muhammadiyah) in the aftermath of the 11 September 2001 tragedy in the US that Indonesian Islam cannot accept any kind of religious extremism. Furthermore, the two largest Muslim organizations, representing some seventy million Indonesian Muslims, have reached an accord to tackle religious radicalism through their various policies and programs.

As for the police force, it becomes increasingly difficult for them to commit human rights abuses as in the past. The fall of an authoritarian regime and the rise of democracy in Indonesia have forced police to be more sensitive to human rights issues and to the protection of the rights of the alleged perpetrators of any kind of violence and terrorism. This is not to suggest, however, that the police are free from heavy-handedness and insensitivity. It is, therefore, the duty of the public to monitor police investigations closely in order not only to prevent possible wrongdoings and mishandlings of the suspected criminals by the police, but also to establish credible procedures and the due process of law.

Moderate Muslim leaders, while maintaining a watchful eye over the police efforts to bring to justice all perpetrators of violent and terrorist acts, should also support police in their investigations. I suggest that one of the most important root causes of violence and terrorism in present day Indonesia is the almost total absence of effective law enforcement and, worse still, impunity from repercussions for those deficiencies. In fact, the vacuum of law enforcement and of decisive action by the police have been an important *raison d'etre* for certain radical groups to take the law into their own hands through unlawful activities such as the raids on discotheques, nightclubs, and other places the radicals believe to be places of social ills.

Above all, the future of moderate and peaceful Southeast Asian Islam is very dependent on the fair, objective, pro-active attitude of the moderate majority in responding to any radical developments among Muslims in the region. A reactionary and defensive attitude is not going to help in the efforts to show to the world that Islam is a peaceful religion and that Muslims are peace-loving people. Again, it is time for the moderates to be more assertive in leading the way to reestablish the peaceful nature of Southeast Asian Islam.

CHAPTER 13

GLOBALIZATION AND INDONESIAN MUSLIM MOVEMENTS

INTRODUCTION

Globalization is, for sure, a new "pet theme" among scholars today. With respect to the history of Islam in Indonesia, however, "globalization" is not really a new phenomenon. In fact, there has been a continuous "globalization" of Indonesian Muslim discourse since relatively early in the history of Islam in the region. The center of the global system that Indonesian Islam was a part of, both religiously and intellectually, was the Haramayn, i.e. the Two Protected Cities, Mecca and Medina.

As I have shown elsewhere, intense religio-intellectual contacts and connections between Malay-Indonesian students or scholars ('ulamā', in Malay ulamā), and their co-religionists and 'ulamā' in the Haramayn had a vivid reforming impact on the course of Islam in the archipelago, especially from the seventeenth century onwards (Azra, 2004). Returning students or scholars, although they were also Sufi thinkers and shaykhs, implanted a more shari'ah-oriented Islam in the Malay-Indonesian Archipelago, which forced the so-called "pantheistic" (or "wujudiyyah mulhid") Sufism to cede ground. This is the beginning of the rise of a more scriptural Islam, or, in Reid's terms, "scriptural orthodoxy" in Indonesia (Reid, 1993). The most important proponents of this new tendency throughout the seventeenth and eighteenth centuries were Nūr al-Dīn al-Rānīrī, 'Abd al-Ra'ūf al-Sinkilī", Muhammad Yūsuf al-Maqassarī, 'Abd al-Samad al-Palimbānī, Muhammad Arshad al-Banjarī, and Dāwūd b. 'Abd Allāh al-Patānī.

By the end of the nineteenth century new globalizing waves of Muslim discourse reached the shores of the Malay-Indonesian Archipelago. These waves were initially brought into the archipelago mostly by *haj* pilgrims who, from the 1870s, travelled in ever increasing numbers to the Holy Land. Returning to their villages, these new *hajis* spread not only the spirit of pan-Islamism, but most importantly distributed Islamic literature of various kinds. No less important was the significant role played by the many established *pesantrens* (traditional Islamic boarding schools) in the "intensification of Islam".

Other waves came in the early decades of the twentieth century (Roff, 1989). This was a new kind of impact which has been categorized by many observers as "Islamic modernism". As might have been expected, these waves originated not from the Haramayn, but Cairo instead. Heavily indebted to modernist Muslim thinkers like Jamal al-Din al-Afghani and Muhammad 'Abduh, a new Muslim discourse developed in Indonesia, which was later on crystallized in the establishment of such "modernist" Muslim organizations as the Muhammadiyah (1912), al-Irsyad (1913), and Persis (in the early 1920s).

Nowadays, the globalizing waves that influence Muslim discourse in Indonesia no longer stem only from the Haramayn or even from Cairo. In fact, the respectable position of the Haramayn, so far as Indonesian Muslim discourse is concerned, has been in decline for the last few decades (Azra, 1992; Azra, 1995a; Azra, 1995b; Azra, 1995c; Abaza, 1994). Other places in the Middle East, or elsewhere in the Muslim world, have recently come to the forefront and, in turn, have left their impact on Muslim discourse in Indonesia. It might certainly be argued, therefore, that the historic religio-intellectual contacts and relations between Indonesia and the Middle East have been characterized by a combination of continuities and changes.

This text is a preliminary attempt to delineate briefly the contemporary globalization of Muslim discourse in Indonesia by way of tracing religio-intellectual connections between Indonesia and the Middle East in particular. Special attention will be paid to the impact of such religio-intellectual connections upon contemporary Muslim movements in Indonesia.

INTERNAL RESURGENCE OF ISLAM

The contemporary globalization of Muslim discourse in Indonesia is not an isolated phenomenon. Rather, it is a consequence of some interrelated developments at both the domestic and the international level.

At the domestic level, Islam in Indonesia has undergone several tremendous developments and changes during the last three decades. There is no doubt that the failure of the *Partai Komunis Indonesia* (PKI – Indonesian Communist Party) has stimulated some kind of "Islamic resurgence" in Indonesia. During the period of Soekarno's honeymoon with the communists, with the exception of the Nahdlatul *Ulamā* (NU – Awakening of the '*Ulamā*', i.e. Islamic religious scholars), Muslim groups were marginalized, if not suppressed. Some prominent Muslim leaders, including Mohammad Natsir, former leader of the Masjumi (Majelis Sjura Muslimin Indonesia – Indonesian Muslim Deliberation Council), and Professor Hamka, a prominent '*alim* and writer who later became the first Chairman of the Majelis *Ulamā* Indonesia (MUI – Indonesian Council of Religious Scholars), were put into jail by the regime. Not many Muslims dared to identify themselves openly as Muslim; being a Muslim was therefore a handicap, particularly in Indonesian politics.

The fiasco of the alleged PKI coup d'etat (1965) gave new impetus to Muslim life in Indonesia. The pre-eminent role of Muslim organizations in counter-actions against communist elements brought Islam back into the socio-political arena. Despite some political disappointment among Muslims in the early years of the post-1965 New Order era, Islamic religious life was blossoming. Muslim activists who had been pushed behind closed doors during the communist heyday, now steadily began to not only establish mosques, particularly on university campuses and government offices, but also to form *kelompok pengajian* (Islamic discussion groups), or *majelis taklim* (Islamic learning groups). With these the process of "*santrinization*" of Indonesian Muslim society began to take place.

The resurgence of Islam in Indonesia during the first half of the 1980s did not proceed smoothly. It was somewhat restrained by the continuing tensions between Muslim groups and the government. Muslims felt that certain government policies, including the forced fusion of Islamic parties into the PPP (*Partai Persatuan Pembangunan* – United Development Party;

1973), the controversial Marriage Bill of 1974, and lastly the implementation of the *Pancasila* as the sole ideological basis for all social and political organizations (imposed from 1985), were intended to uproot Islamic influences in Indonesian public life. Some Muslims even considered such policies to be part of a systematic "de-politicization" of Indonesian Islam. In spite of the objection of many Muslims, the government succeeded in putting all those policies into effect.

As far as the development of Islam in Indonesia is concerned, the acceptance of the *Pancasila* as the sole ideological basis has led to somewhat surprising consequences, even for Muslims themselves. With its acceptance, the path for Islamic resurgence proved to have been cleared. The relatively long mutual suspicion and tension fostered between the government and Muslim groups now became something of the past. Henceforth, Muslims were able to carry out various activities without any restrictions or hindrance. Since then, the rapprochement between the Muslim population and the Soeharto Government gathered momentum and eventually led to what some observers call the "honeymoon" between the two sides.

The "honeymoon" period, it seems, began openly with the establishment of the ICMI (*Ikatan Cendekiawan Muslim se-Indonesia* – All-Indonesian Association of Muslim Intellectuals) in late 1990. Chaired by the Minister of Research and Technology, BJ. Habibie, the formation of the ICMI was supported by President Soeharto personally. Since its foundation, the ICMI has been playing a predominant role, not only in the establishment of various new Islamic institutions such as the Bank Muamalat Indonesia (Islamic Bank), the *Republika* daily, and the CIDES (Center for Information and Development Studies, an ICMI "think tank"), but supposedly also in the appointments of ICMI leaders to high offices such as cabinet ministries or provincial governorships. There have been other favorable developments for Muslims, such as the enactment of laws on national education and on Islamic courts, which put Islamic institutions like the *madrasah* (Islamic school) and *peradilan agama* (Islamic court) on the same footing as their "secular" counterparts, that is, the *sekolah umum* (public school) and *peradilan negeri* (state court) respectively.

The resurgence of Islam arrived with some significant improvements in Muslim socio-economic life. The liberalization and globalization of the

Indonesian economy which began in earnest in the late 1970s have steadily improved the economic conditions of the Muslim population as a whole. As a result, by the end of the 1980s, an increasing number of Muslims were able to afford the relatively high expenses of the *haj* pilgrimage; and in the last few years Indonesia has sent the largest *haj* contingent from outside of Saudi Arabia. During this period, mosques and other places of Islamic worship have been built in ever-increasing numbers; the *majelis taklim* began to gather in prestigious hotels; and more and more Islamic schools and *pesantrens* have been established in urban areas, no longer just in rural areas as in the past. Keeping pace with these developments, the number of middle class Muslims was also increasing; many of them received their advanced education abroad, and are holding important social, political and economic positions that allow them to enjoy some economic benefits of middle class success.

All these phenomena point to the fact that Islam in Indonesia has become more "*santrinized*", more urbanized and, indeed, more cosmopolitan. Islam is no longer associated with rural culture and backwardness.

THE GLOBAL DIMENSION OF "MAINSTREAM" MOVEMENTS

In many respects, all these developments indicate the rise of a new orientation of Muslim dynamics in the country. Indonesian Muslims, by and large, now employ a socio-cultural rather than a political approach to the development of Islamic life – the latter orientation being so dominant during the Soekarno and early New Order periods. This socio-cultural approach has been strongly advocated since the early 1970s by such leading proponents of the *Kelompok Pembaruan* (renewal group) as Nurcholish Madjid, Harun Nasution, and later Abdurrahman Wahid and Munawir Sjadzali.

The rise of this new orientation of Islam, which, to a great extent, accords with the so called "de-politicization" of Indonesian Islam mentioned above, has puzzled a number of scholars. The Malaysian scholar, Muhammad Kamal Hassan, argues that the *Kelompok Pembaruan* has been stage-managed by the New Order. I would argue, however, that the ideas put forward by leading *pembaruan* thinkers, like Nurcholish Madjid or Harun Nasution, were genuinely conceived by themselves. Nurcholish's ideas of "Islam yes, Partai Islam no" and "secularization and de-secularization", or Harun Nasution's "neo-

Mu'tazilite theology" are clearly in line with the ideas of progress and economic development proposed by the New Order government; but this does not mean that they were simply "engineered" by the regime (Muzani, 1994).

The global dimension of the discourse of the renewal groups is obvious. Nurcholish Madjid was well-versed in various streams of both classical and modern, Muslim as well as Western thought, even before he embarked on advanced studies under the late Fazlur Rahman at the University of Chicago from 1978 to 1984. Since that time, he is said to have been strongly influenced by both Fazlur Rahman and Ibn Taymiyyah. Before long, like his mentor, Nurcholish was being categorized as belonging to the "neo-modernist" group, together with other members of the renewal group (Barton, 1995). In contrast, Harun Nasution, was heavily influenced by the rational and liberal thought of the Mu'tazilah, particularly as this was reformulated in the modern context by the leading Egyptian modernist, Muhammad c Abduh. The most eclectic among these scholars is, of course, Abdurrahman Wahid, whose thought has been influenced by various sources ranging from "traditional Islam" (his NU roots) and liberal Islam (his education and intellectual environment in the Middle East) to contemporary Western intellectual tendencies.

The strongest opposition to, or perhaps more appropriately disapproval of, the "neo-modernist" group has come from the *Dewan Dakwah Islamiyah Indonesia* (DDII – Indonesian Council for Islamic Propagation), which has more recently become also known as the "Kramat Raya Group". This group was once led by the late Mohammad Natsir, the prominent leader of the banned Masjuini and prime minister during the early years of the Soekarno period. After the death of Mohammad Natsir, the leadership of the DDII passed into the hands of Muhammad Rasjidi, whose activities were greatly limited by his advanced years. His inactivity meant that the effective leader of the DDII was Anwar Harjono, a member of the Petisi 50 opposition group. It is important to note, however, that in the second half of the 1990s Anwar Harjono and the Soeharto regime began a reconciliation process. The transformation of the DDII from being a strong critic to a supporter of the regime was accelerated by younger DDII leaders, particularly Ahmad Sumargono, who had close relationships with several generals, such as Prabowo Soebianto, R. Hartono, and Faisal Tanjung. Ahmad Sumargono, the chief leader of the KISDI (Komite Indonesia untuk Solidaritas Dunia

Islam – the Indonesian Committee for Solidarity with the Muslim World), and Husein Umar and K.H. M. Khalil Ridwan became the actual leaders of the DDII because of Anwar Harjono's frail health (Hefner, 1999).

Since the time of Mohammad Natsir, the DDII has shown its disapproval of the renewal group. Though Mohammad Natsir never condemned the renewal group publicly, he was obviously disappointed, particularly with the controversial ideas of Nurcholish Madjid. Nurcholish himself was once dubbed the "young Natsir", but he later took a different path. The fiercest public opposition to both Nurcholish Madjid and Harun Nasution came from Muhammad Rasjidi, who wrote special books to express his criticism of each of them (Barton, 1995; Azra, 1994).

The DDII aversion to the renewal group was once again expressed in 1993. This time it was triggered off by Nurcholish Madjid's public lecture entitled *Penyegaran Paham Keagamaan di Kalangan Generasi Muda Mendatang* (Refreshing the Religious Belief of the Future Young Generation). In this lecture Nurcholish proposed, among other ideas, a new meaning of "islam" (with lowercase i), not only as the religion preached by the Prophet Muhammad ("Islam" with uppercase I), but also as "the attitude of submitting oneself to the Truth". According to this definition, Nurcholish argued, the followers of 'islam' are not confined to those who believe in Muhammad's teachings, but also include other people who believe in the perennial Truth of God (Madjid, 1993: 4-25). This point and other opinions to which he gave voice soon became very controversial issues. The DDII group took the leading role in heated public controversies, and Nurcholish together with his renewal group were pejoratively labelled the "Gerakan Pengacau Keagamaan" (GPK – Movement Creating Religious Confusion) by the DDII group.

Why was (and latently is) the DDII so critical of the *Kelompok Pembaruan*? What are the religio-intellectual sources of the DDII? Does it have any global connection? I would argue that the roots of the DDII criticism and opposition lie in its strong religio-intellectual tendencies towards Salafism. It is well-known that before founding the DDII in 1967, Mohammad Natsir was a leader of the Persis (Persatuan Islam – Islamic Union), a strict Salafite reformist movement established by Ahmad Hassan, of mixed Indian and Indonesian parentage, who was brought up in Singapore. This Salafite orientation was consolidated even more by

Muhammad Rasjidi, a long time prominent member of the Muhammadiyah, the largest Salafite organization in Indonesia. As might have been expected, with its pronounced Salafism – called "fundamentalism" by some (Muzani, 1993: 126-42) – the DDII has strong connections with the Rābitah al-'Ālam al-Islāmī, the Saudi-sponsored Muslim international organization. Besides this doctrinal link, there is some evidence that the DDII also subscribes to certain ideas of Sayyid Qutb and al-Mawdūdī, two of the most influential leaders of Salafite inspiration.

GLOBAL MUSLIM "SPLINTER" MOVEMENTS

Over and above this "mainstream" discourse of Indonesian Muslims, since the 1950s Indonesia has seen the rise of some unprecedented movements. Most of these movements have their origins abroad.

One important factor behind this phenomenon is the spread of new Islamic literature in Indonesia. In the wake of the fascination engendered by the historic success of the Iranian revolution of 1979, many books written by Iranian "secular" intellectuals as well as 'ulamā' began to be translated into Bahasa Indonesia. Since this epoch it has been easy to find Indonesian versions of books by such authors as 'Alī Shari'ātī, Seyyed Hossein Nasr, Ayatullah Khumaynī, Muhammad Husayn Tabātabā'ī, Murtadā Mutahharī, and Muhammad Bāqir al-Sadr. Indonesian translations of various works written by revivalist authors like Mawdudī, Hasan al-Bannā, Sayyid Qutb, Muhammad Qutb, Abū al-Hasan al-Nadwī, Muhammad al-Ghazālī, and Maryam Jameelah are also available. These have been followed by translations of books by M.M. Azami (Muhammad Mustafā al-A'zamī), Yūsuf al-Qaradāwī, Mutawalī Sha'rāwī, and 'Abd Allāh Nasīh 'Ulwān. Another group of translations is represented by works of Fazlur Rahman, Naguib al-Attas, Isma'īl al-Farūqī, Akbar S. Ahmed, Muhammad Asad, Mohammed Arkoun, Bassam Tibi, Ziauddin Sardar, Fatima Mernissi, and Alija Izetbegovic. Not least in importance, some books produced by "orientalists" have also been translated. The list includes works by Montgomery Watt, Bernard Lewis, N.J. Coulson, G.E. von Grunebaum, Edward Said, W.C. Smith, I. Goldziher, Annemarie Schimmel, Maxime Rodinson, John Esposito, Edward Mortimer, and C.E. Bosworth (Azra, 1995d; von der Mehden, 1993).

There is no doubt that the publication of these books contributed significantly to the increasing plurality of Indonesian Muslim discourse. It indicates that the religio-intellectual discourse of Islam in Indonesia is becoming more widely exposed to global perspectives irrespective of their own nature, not only those propounded among Muslim scholars themselves, but also those put forward by outsiders (non-Muslim intellectuals) who have sometimes been the object of darkest suspicion in Muslim circles. In the final analysis, the publication of translated works has stimulated the rise of a new breed of Muslim movements in Indonesia.

The publication of translated works, however, is not the only factor in the rise of the new Muslim movements in Indonesia that will be discussed in detail below. Cultural exchanges between Indonesian Muslims both at home and abroad also play a significant role. As Mona Abaza has convincingly shown us, many Indonesian students in Cairo in the last two decades have been increasingly pulled into the "fundamentalist" lap (Abaza, 1994: 91-101). At the same time, many Indonesian Muslim students, pursuing advanced studies in Western countries, for various reasons, have also undergone a kind of intensification of Islam. Many of them are now also attracted to Islamic ideas unpopular or even unknown in Indonesia in the past.

When these students have returned home ever since the early 1980s, they introduced what they had gained abroad. They have adopted not only these unfamiliar Islamic ideas, they have also embraced the framework and methodology of Muslim movements they saw and became involved in abroad. Many returned with a new Islamic way of dress, particularly the *jilbāb* (veil) and *jalabiyyah* (long robe for men). They have also introduced organizations of a new style known as "*usrah*", under the leadership of an "*imam*" or "*amir*". There is a strong tendency among them not simply to question the belief and practice of mainstream Muslims, but also to reject government authority. This attitude is manifested by phenomena such as their refusal to return the *salam* (that is, the Islamic greeting "*Assalamu'alaykum warahmatullahi wa barakatuh*") of other Muslims; their conducting of marriages only through their "*imam*" or "*amir*" without formal registration with the office of Muslim marital affairs; and their burning of resident identification cards.

Another important factor in the development of new movements is the cultural exchange that occurred in Indonesia itself through the visits of foreign Muslims, either for missionary reasons or otherwise. These foreigners have established their organizations or networks among Indonesian Muslims. It appears that one of the most active foreign Muslim groups in Indonesia is the Tablīghī Jamāʿat, which originates from India.

At this point it is apposite to introduce a discussion of some of the most important contemporary movements in Indonesia which have clear global connections.

SHI 'ISM

For a long time a number of scholars supposed that Shi'ism used to have a strong influence in Indonesia, particularly in the early years of the spread of Islam in the country. I have argued that there is insufficient evidence to support this assertion (Azra, 1995e: 4-19). Were there some "Shi'ite" influences, they would have been very superficial. Undoubtedly, Shi'ism has become popular in Indonesia only recently, particularly after the Iranian revolution, which, as mentioned above, was followed by Indonesian translations of works by Shi'ite intellectuals and scholars.

Many observers and government authorities assume that Shi'ism has gained followers, particularly among young Indonesian Muslims. Ahmad Barakbah, a Qum graduate, claims that there are some twenty thousand Shi'ites in Indonesia today (Dewi Nurjuliyanti and Subhan, 1955; Alkaff, 1998). It is difficult, however, to assess the exact number. It is said that one of the leading "Shi'ite" intellectuals in Indonesia is Jalaluddin Rahmat, a celebrated lecturer at the Padjajaran University of Bandung. Despite the fact that Jalaluddin Rahmat himself has never openly admitted that he is a Shi'ite, he plays a pivotal role in explicating Shi'ite doctrines to various circles. Furthermore, he has been involved in heated debates with certain Sunnite individuals and groups who considered the increasing popularity of Shi'ism a menace to Sunnite orthodoxy.

A further indication of the increasing popularity of Shi'ism in Indonesia is the growth of some forty "Shi'ite" institutions in Jakarta, Bogor, Bandung, Malang, Jember, Bangil, Samarinda, Pontianak, and Banjarmasin. It appears that the center of these institutions is Jakarta, which reportedly has at least twenty-five Shi'ite institutions. All these institutions are devoted to missionary and educational activities. The most prominent among them is perhaps the Mutahhari Foundation in Bandung. This foundation, led by Jalaluddin Rahmat, has an Islamic senior high school called "SMA [senior high school] Mutahhari", which has become one of the most favorite schools in Bandung in the last few years (Sarnapi, 1966: 25). Besides its educational activities, the Mutahhari Foundation issues the journal *Hikmah*, which publishes many translated articles written by Shi'ite *'ulamā'* and intellectuals.

Another noted Shi'ite institution in Bandung is the Jawad Foundation. In addition to conducting regular courses on Ja'farite *fiqh*, the Jawad Foundation first published a "magazine" called *Bulletin al-Jawad*; this name was later changed to *al-Ghadir* (Dewi Nurjulianti and Subhan, 25). Yet another important institution often associated with Shi'ism in Bandung is the Mizan publishing house, which publishes many translations of books written by Shi'ite intellectuals and scholars. In the middle of 1996, at a book launch sponsored by another publisher in Jakarta, there were calls for a boycott of Mizan's allegedly Shi'ite-oriented publications. So far, Mizan itself appears to have remained aloof from such allegations and actions, and it also publishes many works by non-Shi'ite authors.

One of the leading Shi'ite institutions in Jakarta is the Muntadzar Foundation which was established in 1991. Like the Jawad Foundation in Bandung, the Muntadzar Foundation was established by some Shi'ites. The initial programme of the foundation was the study of the "*madhhab* [*fiqh* school] of the *ahl al-bayt* [lit. the family (of the Prophet Muhammad)]", i.e. Islamic jurisprudence in the Shi'ite tradition. The Muntadzar Foundation now claims to have at least four hundred members from all over Jakarta. Its activities are not confined to studying Shi'ite *fiqh*, but also include education at the kindergarten, primary school and junior and senior high school level.

In Bogor, a Shi'ite institution called the Mulla Sadra Foundation was founded in 1993. Like other such institutions, the Mulla Sadra Foundation originally devoted itself to studying the *fiqh ahl al-bayt* school. The foundation later expanded its activities to include education and the provision of various social and health services. *Pesantren* al-Hadi in Pekalongan, a town in Central Java, has a similar background. This *pesantren* was established by Ahmad

Barakbah in 1989. The *pesantren* adopted the educational system of Qum. All nine of its teachers were graduates from Qum in Iran and *Pesantren* al-Hadi now has 112 students, most of whom come from outside Java.

Jama'ah Tabligh

The Tablīghī Jamā'at or Jama'ah al-Tablīgh wa-al-Da'wah was founded in India by Shaykh Mawlana Muhammad Ilyas in 1930. It is believed to have been introduced into Indonesia in 1952, but it only began to gain momentum in this country in the early 1970s, especially after the construction of its mosque in Kebon Jeruk, Jakarta, in 1974. Now, according to Ahmad Zulfakar, the chief leader of the Jama'ah Tabligh – as it is called in this country – in Indonesia, the movement has branches in all twenty-seven provinces of the pre-1999 administrative division. My own observation tends to confirm this. At a recent observation in Sawangan, a suburb in South Jakarta, I found a small community of Jama'ah Tabligh, living in peaceful co-existence with other Muslims. According to a local resident, the movement was brought to their village by some Pakistani and Bangladeshi Muslims who later on married local women.

The Jama'ah Tabligh is known for the distinctive appearance of its adherents. Most – if not all – Jama'ah Tabligh members wear Middle Eastern style clothes; men wear *jalabiyyah*, and women wear a fully closed veil. Men also let their beard grow. The adherents also take a *siwāk* – a kind of vegetable toothbrush believed to have been used by the Prophet Muhammad – everywhere they go. They have also adopted what they believe to have been the Prophet's way of eating; a communal meal served in a *nampan* (common dish), using only the hands to eat.

Distinguishing itself from most other contemporary Muslim "splinter" movements that tend to be more political, the Jama'ah Tabligh is a completely non-political movement. It is said that its only concern is to spread what its members believe is the correct Islamic way of life through missionary activities. In their eyes talking about politics is *harām* (impermissible); the same goes for talking about *khilāfiyyāt* ("minor differences") between Muslims, asking for charity, or condemning the government. Every member of the Jama'ah Tabligh has the obligation to conduct *khurūj* (lit. "go outside") at least once a year in order to spread their message, e.g. by door-to-door propaganda. The expenses for the *khurūj* are the responsibility of the participants themselves. Also once a year they have an *ijtimā'* or meeting. It is during this great gathering that prominent leaders from other countries, mainly from India and Pakistan, give what they call *ceramah pencerahan* ("enlightening speeches").

Darul Arqam

This is undoubtedly the most politically controversial Muslim movement not only in Malaysia – where it was firstly established – but also in Indonesia. Founded in Kuala Lumpur, Malaysia, in 1968, by Imam Ashari Muhammad al-Tamimi, since the late 1970s the Darul Arqam movement has increasingly acquired followers from among the middle and higher classes of Malaysian Muslim society, including many students and a number of high-ranking officials or members of their families. The main objective of the Darul Arqam is the application of a total Islamic way of life. Towards this end, the Darul Arqam established exclusive communities, where it could implement its teachings, not only religiously, but also socially and economically. It was relatively successful, particularly in its economic enterprises, which, according to some observers, were well on the way to becoming a challenge to UMNO's political and economic ventures (Meuleman, 1996: 43-78).

It is difficult to know exactly when the Darul Arqam began to spread in Indonesia. Nevertheless, there is no doubt that the movement became increasingly popular in this country throughout the 1980s and early 1990s. It appears that the Darul Arqam spread all over Indonesia, with prominent centers in Jakarta (Depok), Bogor and Bandung. The followers of the Darul Arqam are mainly young people and university graduates. Until 1990, the Darul Arqam was, by and large, not regarded as a national threat, mainly because mainstream Muslim organizations in Indonesia had not yet questioned its interpretation of Islam or its activities. The controversy began publicly only on 17 April 1990 when the Indonesian Council of 'Ulamā' (MUI) for the province of West Sumatra issued a *fatwa* declaring that the teachings of the Darul Arqam were deviating from Islam and therefore asked the authorities to ban the movement. The Fatwa Commission of the national

MUI soon followed suit; in 1991 it issued a similar *fatwa*, and on 13 August 1994, the national MUI declared the Darul Arqam doctrine to be deviant and, therefore, proposed that the Indonesian Attorney General should ban the movement. The office of the Attorney General was reluctant to do so and left it to each provincial prosecutor's office to decide whether or not to issue a ban. Most provinces chose to do so (Meuleman, 1996; Azra, 1994).

As far as the Darul Arqam controversy is concerned, it is important to note a marked difference of opinion between various Muslim mainstream organizations in Indonesia on the issue of whether or not the Darul Arqam was a deviant movement and, therefore, whether or not measures should be taken against it. Some organizations believed that the Darul Arqam had strayed from the path of Islamic teaching and, therefore, should be banned. This group consisted of the Muhammadiyah, the DDII, and the Ikatan Masjid Indonesia (Association of Indonesian Mosques). A second group, consisting mainly of organizations affiliated to the Nahdlatul *Ulamā*, were of the opinion that there was nothing wrong with the teachings of the Darul Arqam. If the Darul Arqam were to be banned, they argued, this should not be for religious reasons, but for reasons of national security or in order to preserve the harmonious relationship between different elements of the Muslim population (Meuleman, 1996).

It is highly questionable whether the provincial bans were effective. Subsequent observations have confirmed that Darul Arqam has remained very much alive and relatively unhampered in its activities The New Order authorities seemed to ignore it to the extent that it caused no further "disruption" to inter-religious harmony, which indeed is one of the principles of religious policy in Indonesia.

After the fall of Soeharto Darul Arqam seems to have regained momentum. Although it adopted a low profile after the controversy mentioned above, its adherents are now coming out more into the open. At present their distinctive dress can be observed in many mosques in various Indonesian cities, including the Istiqlal Mosque and the Grand al-Azhar Mosque in Jakarta. They now publish their own tabloid entitled *Kebenaran*, which is sold in many mosques, particularly on the occasion of the Friday congregational prayers.

Hizb al-Tahrir

This group was perhaps introduced into Indonesia in 1978. Before long, it had gained some popularity among students on university campuses in Jakarta, Bandung, Surabaya, Yogyakarta and Bogor. The Hizb al-Tahrīr was established in 1952 in Lebanon by Shaykh Taqī al-Dīn al-Nabhānī. Al-Nabhānī himself was known as a thinker and politician with certain connection with the Egyptian al-Ikhwan al-Muslimun revivalist movement, who formerly worked as a judge at the Supreme Court in Jerusalem.

The main objectives of the Hizb al-Tahrīr are to perpetuate what they regarded the true Islamic way of life globally and, most importantly, to re-establish the *khilafah* (caliphate), which is believed to have been the most suitable and effective political system by which to achieve Muslim unity (Dekmejian, 1995). To achieve these goals, the Hizb al-Tahrīr seems to have little difficulty in resorting to radicalism. This is why it soon became one of the most popular movements among disenchanted students and young people, not only in the Middle East, but also among Muslim students pursuing their degrees in Western countries.

In Indonesia, however, the Hizb al-Tahrīr – as it is called here – appears to have moderated its attitude. In other words, it has had to accommodate to, and compromise with, the conditions of Indonesian *Realpolitik*. That is why the Hizb al-Tahrīr has not yet been regarded as an enemy by the government authorities. This probably also has something to do with the fact that the Hizb al-Tahrīr does not insist on its members adopting a particular distinguishing form of outward appearance such as wearing a beard or a *jalabiyyah*. Hizb al-Tahrīr members are apparently critical of established Muslim organizations, such as the Nahdlatul *Ulamā* and the Muhammadiyah, which they consider not to be real *da'wah* (propagation of the Islamic faith) movements. The Hizb al-Tahrīr asserts that "the concern of NU and Muhammadiyah is not to transform Indonesia into a fully Islamic society; what they have been doing is simply to improve Muslim education."

Besides all those groups mentioned above, there is still a large number of smaller groups which are loosely organized in *kelompok pengajian* or as *usrah*. In terms of their origins, most of them have been inspired by similar groups operating outside Indonesia, but a small number of them are some kind of "splinter group" of established mainstream organizations, including the Muhammadiyah, the NU, and the Himpunan Mahasiswa Islam (HMI – Association of Muslim University Students). Most of them are politically motivated and oriented in one way or another, though sometimes in a very subtle way, but a minority is more religiously oriented, like student Sufi groups.

FROM QUIETISM TO ACTIVISM: RADICALISM IN THE POST-SOEHARTO ERA

Most of the Muslim splinter movements discussed above restrained themselves and shunned the limelight during much of the Soeharto era. In fact, they made some adjustments to their ideological position – at least temporarily – for two reasons. Firstly, splinter movements – especially those with a political orientation – domesticated themselves in order to survive the repression of the New Order political machine which would not tolerate any movement it believed could create religious, social or political conflicts. Within the framework of the notorious *SARA* policy and the introduction of the *Pancasila* as the sole ideological basis of all Indonesian religious, social and political organizations, the Soeharto regime did not allow Indonesians to confront sensitive issues regarding ethnicity, religion, race and social class. The Soeharto regime also took harsh measures against organizations that adopted any other "ideology" – including Islam – instead of the *Pancasila*. Secondly, non-political movements such as the Shi'ite group and the Jama'ah Tabligh tended to adopt a kind of *taqiyyah* being discrete in their religious beliefs and practices. This was done mainly to avoid controversies and conflicts with mainstream Muslim organizations.

The fall of President Soeharto in May 1998, following the monetary, economic, and political crises, was undoubtedly a great stimulus for the splinter movements that had survived his regime and induced them not only to appear in public, but also to consolidate and spread their organizations. Moreover, new "hardline" groups proclaimed their existence publicly, creating a new tendency among Muslim movements in Indonesia and widespread concern among mainstream Muslims (Azra, 2005; Azra, 2001). Some of the most prominent of these numerous new groups are the Lasykar Jihad (Jihad Troops), the *Front Pembela Islam* (FPI – Islamic Defence Front), and the Angkatan Mujahidin Indonesia (Indonesian Troop of Mujahidin – i.e. *jihād*, or "holy war" fighters). Of the older Muslim splinter movements, the Hizb al-Tahrīr organized an international conference on its favorite theme, the caliphate, in Jakarta in 2000.

It appears that all these movements, now emerging from the closet, are independent of any connection with any of the Muslim political parties that have proliferated in post-Soeharto Indonesia (Azra, 2000). In contrast, there are rumors that certain hardline groups have been sponsored by, or at least are in close connection with, certain circles of the Indonesian military and have received financial support from a number of ambitious entrepreneurs who had amassed large fortunes during the *ancien régime*. Obviously, it is very difficult to verify these rumors. The extremist nature of these groups cannot, however, be denied. The Lasykar Jihad, for instance, has become known for dispatching its fighters to Maluku in defence of the Muslims against alleged Christian violence and expansionism. The FPI has aroused public concern by its frequent attacks on discotheques, nightclubs and other dens of alleged social iniquity (Azra, 2001; Bamualim et al, 2001).

The information available and analyses of this tend to show that domestic transformation processes and conflicts, both at the national and at the regional levels, are the primary factors in the emergence of these radical groups, but international dimensions do exist. A case in point is the Indonesian Hizb al-Tahrīr, which is part of an international organization. The leader of the Lasykar Jihad, Ja'far Umar Thalib, studied in the Middle East and he, as well as various of his followers, have reportedly received guerrilla training in Afghanistan (Bamualim, 2001). This Afghan training, believed to have been set up originally by United States secret services in order to combat the Soviet influence in this Central Asian country, is known to have played a role in various countries in the formation of groups that use violence in the name of Islam. More pertinent to our theme, Noorhaidi Hasan, referring to analyses by Olivier Roy of what this French author calls "radical neo-fundamentalism", indicates the international discourse of the movement designated by this term as one of the constituent elements of radical Muslim groups in contemporary Indonesia. This international discourse throws into question the nation-state, which has great difficulties preserving national solidarity while facing globalization. Noorhaidi too, however, considers domestic factors the primary ones in the emergence of these radical groups in Indonesia (Hasan, 2001).

It is important to point out that not all splinter movements consist of hardliners or radicals. The Shi'ites and the Jama'ah Tabligh, for instance, seem to remain non-political, despite the fact that the Shi'ites have publicly declared the foundation of a nation-wide organization that aims to spread Shi'ism in the country. The Darul Arqam has also become increasingly visible, but it appears that it puts more emphasis on the religious and spiritual well-being of the Muslim population than on political activities. The Jama'ah Tabligh has remained as peaceable as before.

In passing, it is worth mentioning that some of the Muslim parties and organizations have created or revived martial arts youth wings which have the potential to transform themselves into radical organizations. The *Partai Kebangkitan Bangsa* (PKB – National Awakening Party) and the Nahdlatul Ulamā (NU), for instance, have consolidated their *Banser Ansor* (*Bantuan Serba Guna Ansor – Ansar or* Assistance Units for All Purposes); the *Partai Persatuan Pembangunan* (PPP) has reinvigorated its *Gerakan Pemuda Ka'bah* (Ka'bah Youth Movement). This phenomenon is not characteristic of Muslim organizations only. The *Partai Demokrasi Indonesia-Perjuangan* (PDI-P – Indonesian Democratic Party of Struggle) has also formed groups known as the *Satgas* (*Satuan Tugas* – Task Force) PDI-P or by other names, whereas the *Pemuda Pancasila* (*Pancasila* Youth) and other organizations closely related to the central social-cum-political organization of the Soeharto era, the *Golkar* (*Golongan Karya* – Functional Groups), have functioned as pressure groups on various occasions since the New Order.

CONCLUDING NOTES

The sudden proliferation of splinter and hardline groups in contemporary Indonesia should lead one to question the reasons behind this new tendency. For students of Indonesian Islam, this new tendency is not only unexpected, it could even lead them to question the image of the moderate and "smiling" face of Indonesian Islam. In their eyes, the new tendency seems to bring Indonesian Islam closer to Middle Eastern Islam, in which the existence and proliferation of such groups was considered characteristic. Furthermore, the rise of such groups is thought to threaten the future of democracy in Indonesia (Azra, 2001).

I would suggest that the proliferation of these splinter groups is closely related to two important phenomena. Firstly, the euphoria of political Islam after a long period of repression during the Soeharto regime stimulated the development of these groups. The liberalization of Indonesian politics since the *interregnum* of President Habibie provided further impetus to such groups to establish themselves. Secondly, the continued political struggle between fragmented political groups and disappointment at the delay in economic recovery during the presidency of Abdurrahman Wahid is another factor. The weakness of the Abdurrahman Wahid Government seriously limited law enforcement. This, in the final analysis, makes it easier for hardline groups to hold sway in society.

Looking at the *raison d'etre* of hardline groups in particular, I am not pessimistic about the future of both moderate Islam and democracy in Indonesia. These groups are not supported by the mainstream of Indonesian Muslims. Even though these groups are henceforth free to preach their ideas and practices, they are failing to attract a significant following. Lastly, their sudden proliferation, visibility and radicalization are taking place only in the time of uncertain transition towards democracy. Once Indonesia attains a new equilibrium in this painful transition, most – if not all – of these hardline groups will lose momentum.

Chapter 14

MUSLIM LEADERSHIP IN CONTEMPORARY INDONESIA

The fall of President Soeharto in May 1998 following a series of monetary, economic and political crises has brought a great deal of rapid and dramatic change in Indonesia. One of the most obvious changes is evident not only in Indonesian political leadership, but also particularly in Muslim leadership. The unfolding of these various crises in Indonesia has, however, brought the Muslim leadership onto center stage. When President Soeharto felt unable to cling to his long-held power, he handed over the presidency to Vice President B.J. Habibie, an engineer-cum-politician, who was also the Chairperson of the All-Indonesia Association of Muslim Intellectuals (*Ikatan Cendekiawan Islam se-Indonesia* – ICMI).

Following the 1999 general election, the Habibie *interregnum* ended with the election of Abdurrahman Wahid, Chairman of the Nahdlatul Ulama (NU), by the Peoples' Consultative Assembly (*Majelis Permu syawaratan Rakyat* – MPR), as Indonesia's new president in October 1999. In addition to Wahid, two other Muslim leaders were also elected to high positions; Amien Rais, former chairman of the Muhammadiyah who is Chairman of National Mandate Party (*Partai Amanat Nasional* – PAN), as the Chairman of the MPR; and Akbar Tanjung, former Chairman of the Muslim University Student Association (*Himpunan Mahasiswa Islam* – HMI) who is Chairman of the Golkar Party, as the Speaker of the House of Representatives (*Dewan Perwakilan Rakyat* – DPR) (Azra, 2000; 2001a).

The rise of Muslim leaders to such lofty positions has brought much hope from the Muslim community. But given the heavy burden of the crises, some observers are skeptical that the Muslim leadership could bring Indonesia to a peaceful transition to democracy in the shortest time possible. This is also mainly because the Muslim leadership, when it comes to politics, has been marred by continued internal competition, struggles and conflicts. This is, of course, not unique to Indonesia. As Dale Eickelman and James Piscatori observe, a central feature of Muslim politics throughout the Muslim World – including Indonesia – involves the competition and contest over both the interpretation of symbols and control of the institutions, both formal and informal, that produce and sustain them (Eickelman & Piscatori, 1996:5).

One of the most important challenges for the Muslim leadership in Indonesia today and in the future is, therefore, how to reconcile the different visions and translations of Islam within its ranks, especially in the political realm. Another important challenge – which has arisen because the Muslim leadership in today's Indonesia is in power – is how they can contribute to the building of a democratic and civil Islam in Indonesia.

This chapter attempts to briefly discuss the challenges and opportunities that the Muslim leadership confronts in today's Indonesia. It will also discuss their role in the current transition of Indonesia to democracy and how Muslim leadership can contribute to the development of a democratic and civil Islam in Indonesia.

MUSLIM LEADERSHIP REDEFINED

The concept of "Muslim leadership" in Indonesia is neither static nor constant. The meaning of the concept of Muslim leadership has undergone a change over time because of the changes in the sociological and political factors at work in Indonesia as a whole. In other words, the meaning and even the actualization of the Muslim leadership in Indonesia has changed over time depending mostly on Indonesia's political situation, especially on the kind of relationship between Islam and the regime in power.

From the time of the Indonesian struggle against Dutch colonialism up to the end of the 1980s, the meaning of "Muslim leadership" was very narrow and restricted to Muslim leaders who came from *santri* backgrounds. The term *santri* originally and literally refers to Muslims who study, teach and live in the *pesantren*, a traditional Javanese Islamic educational institution. In a much wider sense *santri* means "practicing" or "committed" Muslims, that is, those believers who adhere to Islam in a strict way, who do not necessarily live in the *pesantren* surroundings, but in society at large. They are called *santri* Muslims as opposed to *abangan* Muslims who are nominal Muslims and also popularly known as "ID card Muslims" (*Muslim KTP*).

By this definition, Indonesia's Muslim leadership, in a conventional and restricted sense, is identical with the *santri* leadership that comes from Islamic institutions such as *pesantren*, Muslim/Islamic social-religious organizations, Muslim/Islamic political parties, and the like. The social origin of the *santri* leadership was admittedly limited, despite the fact that almost ninety per cent of Indonesia's total population was (and still is) Muslim. As a result, Indonesia's political leadership had tended to be dominated by the *abangan* leaders and this left the *santris* in despair. Worse still, this unfortunate situation had produced a syndrome of "majority with minority complex", that is, the feeling of the Muslim majority as a minority group because of their disadvantage in Indonesian national politics both during the colonial and independent periods vis-à-vis the *abangan* and nationalist leadership which dominated the political course.

With respect to the strict meaning of Muslim leadership, it is now easier to understand that the Muslim leadership during the colonial period was represented mostly by such figures, among others, as Haji Tjokroaminoto and Haji Agus Salim (both were leaders of Sarekat Islam); Kiyai Haji Ahmad Dahlan (leader of Muhammadiyah); Kiyai Haji Hasyim Asy'ari (leader of the Nahdlatul Ulama/NU). In the early years of Indonesian independence, the Muslim leadership was again represented only by *santris* such as Mohammad Natsir, Mohammad Roem (both from the Masyumi Party) and Wahid Hasyim (NU).

It is important to note that the *santri* leadership was also deeply divided. In fact Muslim leaders have long been involved in continued quarrels, conflicts and struggles among themselves, particularly when it comes to politics and power. I would argue – as we will see below – that power and politics are the main sources of conflict and struggle among Muslim leaders. Before long, conflict among the leadership produced negative impacts on relations among Muslims at the grass-roots level.

Religious matters used to be one of the most important sources of the conflict between Indonesian Muslims. There were a lot of quarrels and conflicts among them on "trivial" (furu'iyyah) matters, not on major religious issues. In the last three decades at least, there has no longer been much quarreling among Muslims on religious matters. In fact, there now exists a kind of religious convergence among various schools of Islamic thought and practice in Indonesia.

The root of religious differences almost certainly lies in their different understanding of Muslim doctrines as well as their different attitude to Islam reform in Indonesia. Generally speaking, there are at least two significant divisions within the *santri* communities in Indonesia. Firstly, are the modernists, who are mainly represented by the Muhammadiyah (est. 1912), the Sarekat Islam (est. 1911) and the Persis (*Persatuan Islam*) and, secondly, the traditionalists, who are represented by the NU (est. 1926), al-Washliyah and the Nahdlatul Wathan (NW).

The contests between the modernists and traditionalists initially took place in the religious field. The modernists, heavily influenced by Middle Eastern reformist thinkers such as Jamal al-Din al-Afghani, Muhammad Abduh and Rashid Rida, devote themselves to reforming religious and social lives of the Muslims. This is carried out through the reforms and renewal of the religious field. The modernists appeal to their fellow Muslims to return to the Qur'an and the *hadith* of the Prophet Muhammad; abandon unwarranted innovations (*bid'ah*) in Muslim belief and practices; and discard blind obedience (*taqlid*) to the *ulama*. The modernists also urge Muslims to use their reason in order to produce their own *ijtihad*, religious consideration and decision.

The traditionalists, on the other hand, hold fast to what they believe to be the most valid Islamic traditions that have developed since the time of the Prophet to the present. They feel that all the modernists' efforts have been aimed at abolishing their religious beliefs and practices. It is no surprise that the traditionalists, from the foundation of the Muhammadiyah in 1912, consolidated themselves and were finally able to found the NU in 1926 (cf Noer, 1978).

Since then, these two wings of Indonesian Islam have been involved in religious controversies; even though – as argued above – there have been less religious differences between them in the last three decades. Before long, their differences made their presence known in Indonesian politics. It appears that both of them were able to put aside their political differences during their involvement in the Indonesian Islamic Supreme Council (*Majelis Islam A'la Indonesia* – MIAI), a body that had been established in the early 1940s by the Japanese during their occupation in order to support their own aims. Later, the MIAI was replaced by the Masyumi, which was envisaged by the Japanese as a federation of Islamic organizations. On 7 November 1945, not long after Indonesia gained its independence, the Masyumi was transformed into a political party. Muslim hopes that the Masyumi would become the sole Islamic party were short-lived, however, when the NU withdrew its membership in the Masyumi in 1952 and established itself as an independent party. The main reason for NU's withdrawal, as one might expect, was the fact that the leadership of the Masyumi party had been dominated by the modernists at the expense of the traditionalists (cf. Noer, 1987).

The split in the Muslim political leadership in the 1950s was clearly reflected in the 1955 general election. The election produced four big parties: the Indonesian Nationalist Party (*Partai Nasionalis Indonesia* – PNI) which won 22.3 per cent of the total vote; Masyumi (20.9 per cent); NU (18.4 per cent); and the Indonesian Communist Party (*Partai Komunis Indonesia* – PKI) with 15.4 per cent. In the final analysis, the combined vote of all Islamic parties won less than half of the total vote and, as a result, failed to gain the upper hand in the parliament. In the ensuing struggle over the issue of whether Indonesia remained a "*Pancasila* state" or became an "Islamic state", the Islamic parties lost out in the parliament to the *abangan* parties. With this defeat, the legal and constitutional attempts of the Muslim leadership to transform Indonesia into an Islamic state came to an end.

While the Muslim political leadership has been deeply divided, Muslim leaders excluded the *abangan* Muslims, represented, for instance, by Soekarno (Indonesia's first president), and Soeharto (second president); and "nationalist" Muslims, represented by Mohammad Hatta (Indonesia's first vice president), for example, from their ranks. Even though these leaders were Muslim, they were clearly not Islamic oriented in their political attitudes and behavior and, thus, were rightly not considered by the *santri*s as Muslim leaders.

Given the division within this leadership, Indonesian politics has been marked by bitter and continued struggles, conflict and contests between the *santri* leadership on the one hand, and the *abangan* and nationalists on the other. This division within the Indonesian leadership and politics is referred to by many as the "*aliran*" politics (*politik aliran*), the division of politics based on "*aliran*", religious beliefs and practices that were in many cases influenced by the social origins of each leader (cf. Liddle, 2002:64-5).

The *politik aliran* has been a salient feature of Indonesian politics since the time when Indonesia's leaders were making preparations for Indonesia's independence in the first half of the 1940s. The *abangan* and nationalist leadership, however, were able to take advantage of this *aliran* politics by exploiting the competition and conflict within the *santri* leadership. In the late 1950s, President Soekarno developed a very close relationship with the traditionalist *santri* leadership at the expense of the modernists. While bringing the NU, as the representative of the *agama* (religious) group, into the triangular axis known as Nasakom [*nationalis-agama-komunis*], Soekarno put a number of the most prominent leaders of the modernist *santri* into jail.

NEW MUSLIM LEADERSHIP

The division within the *santri* leadership continued when Soeharto began to take firm control of Indonesian politics after the fall of Soekarno in the aftermath of the abortive communist coup d'etat in the late 1965. In the early years of the New Order government under President Soeharto, the Muslim leadership was sidelined and marginalized or, even worse, was suppressed. The root of the conflict was mutual suspicion that led to increasing hostility between the two sides. Even though both of them had joined forces to crush communism in the aftermath of the abortive PKI (Indonesian Communist Party) coup d'etat of 1965, Muslims soon became a target of military suspicion when they attempted to revive the Islamic Masyumi Party that had been banned by President Soekarno in the early 1960s.

From the early 1970s, however, President Soeharto's policies of political stability and economic development had brought him closer to certain elements of modernist Muslims. The traditionalist *santri* who had enjoyed a very close relationship with the Soekarno regime, were now sidelined. The modernists who possessed better technocratic skills needed for economic development began to be recruited in earnest by the Soeharto Government. Soon, however, the number of modernist *santri* in the government grew steadily. This in the end has resulted in their increasing influence in the Indonesian bureaucracy; they in turn played a significant role in Soeharto's changing attitude toward Islam; from hostility to an attitude that was more reconciliatory in nature.

Up until the late 1980s, Soeharto was clearly still an *abangan* Muslim who formulated and implemented various policies that, by and large, contained an element of hostility toward the *santris* in general. In the late 1970s in the religious field, for instance, Soeharto formalized within Indonesia's legal system the "*Aliran Kepercayaan*"; local Javanese religious beliefs and practices, despite strong opposition from *santri* communities.

In passing it is worth mentioning that in the early 1980s a new trend arose within Indonesia's Islamic movement and leadership. Clearly influenced by the phenomenal rise of the Ayatullah Ruhullah Khomeini and his Islamic Republic of Iran, a number of new Islamic movements began to gain momentum in Indonesia. Having observed the disunity of Indonesian Muslim leaders, these new movements appealed for the unity of the Muslim leadership. For that reason, they introduced the concept and practice of *imamah* and *amir* that were popular among some Islamic movements in the Middle East. They argued that only by adopting this kind of leadership would Indonesian Muslims be able to not only solve the problems of the Muslim leadership, but also to bring progress to Muslims (Azra, 2001b).

The arguments of these new movements seem to be very appealing. They failed to attract a significant following among Indonesian Muslims, however, largely because of their literal attitude to their understanding of Islam, but also because of the fact that the sociological, cultural and political nature of Indonesian Islam did not provide good grounds for such movements.

One of the most significant changes in the Indonesian Muslim leadership began to take form in the late 1980s. Simultaneously with the changes within the Soeharto regime, there appeared a new kind of Muslim leadership that went beyond the traditional meaning of the Muslim leadership as defined above. In fact, political changes that have taken place since the late 1980s have been crucial to the rise and decline of the Muslim leadership. Beginning in the late 1980s, President Soeharto took a more reconciliatory attitude to the Muslim leadership. It is hard to imagine that without this change of attitude, it would have been possible, for example, for Muslims to establish ICMI in 1990, an organization that was led by B.J. Habibie, a close confidant of Soeharto.

The rise of ICMI was very crucial not only in terms of its political impact, but also, more importantly, in Muslim leadership. In a similar way to my argument above, Hefner has persuasively argued that ICMI's creation was the result of a complex convergence of social forces. These factors, according to Hefner's observation, were; the Islamic revival; the growth of an educated and prosperous middle class; and, in the late 1980s, President Soeharto's interest in courting a base of support beyond the armed forces. Taken together, all these developments have pushed Islam to the center of Indonesian politics from which it had been barred for some twenty-five years (Hefner, 1999: 49; 2000:140-60).

It is no secret that ICMI was bitterly opposed by many in the military and by some leaders of the NU. The majority of other Muslim leaders, however, welcomed ICMI's establishment. Many Muslims hoped that ICMI would bring about a heightened state commitment to Muslim enterprise and Muslim representation – called *proporsionalisme* in Bahasa Indonesia – in the state bureaucracy. To cite Hefner once again, *proporsionalisme* in government and the economy was to become one of ICMI's lasting contributions to Indonesian political discourse (Hefner, 2000:140). As soon as it became apparent that ICMI had won the unqualified favor of President Soeharto, the organization became one of the most important access points to power.

There is little doubt that the rise of ICMI had brought about changes in Indonesia's Muslim leadership. As mentioned above, the Muslim leadership in the past was usually identified with the leaders of Muslim organizations and political parties. Now, however, leaders of ICMI who had never been known to have a *santri* background or any involvement in any Muslim organization, were increasingly regarded as Muslim leaders as well. Technocrats like

Habibie, the chairman of ICMI, or Wardiman, the General Secretary of ICMI, were accepted by many Muslims as their leaders while President Soeharto himself was increasingly also regarded as a Muslim leader.

POLITICAL FRAGMENTATION

The election of Abdurrahman Wahid, Amien Rais and Akbar Tanjung to the highest positions of national leadership has undoubtedly created a lot of euphoria among Muslims as a whole. Leaving aside Akbar Tanjung, former national leader of the Muslim University Student Association, who is the Chairman of the Golkar Party, both Wahid and Rais were top leaders of the NU and Muhammadiyah respectively. Generally regarded as Muslim leaders par excellence, their election seems to represent the revival of Muslim leadership in Indonesia.

It would soon become clear, however, that their election was, more than anything else, a result of political expediency rather than of genuine political unity among Muslims. In contrast, there is a lot of political fragmentation among Muslims in post-Soeharto Indonesia. The appearance of more than twenty Islamic/Muslim parties during the Habibie presidency seems to have been motivated by a lust for power of the Muslim political elite rather than by genuinely religious motives. At the 1999 general election, Islamic/Muslim parties failed to poll well, with most voters opting for secular parties such as the Indonesian Democratic Party of Struggle (PDI-P) and Golkar Party. Islamic parties, such as the United Development Party (*Partai Persatuan Pembangunan* – PPP), the Moon and Crescent Party (*Partai Bulan Bintang* – PBB), and the Justice Party (*Partai Keadilan* – PK), or Muslim-based parties like Abdurrahman Wahid's National Awakening Party (*Partai Kebangkitan Bangsa* – PKB) and the National Mandate Party (*Partai Amanat Nasional* – PAN) led by Amien Rais, gained far fewer votes. It is not surprising that many Muslims felt that this marked the end of "Islamic politics" (Azra, 2000).

In a certain way, the failure of Islamic or Muslim-based parties at the poll can be viewed as a "blessing in disguise" for Muslim political leaders. It led not only to much soul searching among them, but also to a search for ways to put aside their differences and create a unified vision. They increasingly

realized that they would have to forge their own political front by establishing
a unified coalition popularly known as the *Poros Tengah* (Middle Axis). The
Middle Axis did indeed play a crucial role in the election of Wahid to the
presidency by beating Megawati Soekarnoputri, whose party (PDI-P) had
won the most votes in the election. It is also through the Middle Axis that
Amien Rais and Akbar Tanjung were elected as the Chairman of the MPR
and Speaker of the DPR respectively.

Despite this encouraging rise of the Muslim leadership, it is also clear
that Muslim leaders failed to put an end to their political fragmentation.
Owing much to President Wahid's erratic and eclectic attitude that created
much controversy, most of the Islamic/Muslim based parties, together with
PDI-P and Golkar, forged a grand coalition against him. As a result, the DPR
has been able to censure him, producing his imminent impeachment in the
MPR Special Session to be held in August.

What can we learn from this case of Muslim leadership in today's
Indonesia? For one thing, it is clear that the Muslim leadership represented
by President Wahid has failed to live up to the peoples' expectation. Worse
still, it could be a stigmatizing experience for Indonesia if a Muslim leader
is not able to fulfill the promise of the best Islamic leadership. Even though
this "stigma" cannot, and should not, be the whole truth – since there are still
many able Muslim leaders – Muslims are challenged to prove that Muslim
leadership is a blessing for all universe (*rahmah li al-'alamin*).

Muslim leaders, as Hefner convincingly shows, have contributed a great
deal to the growth of democracy and civil society since the last decade of
Soeharto's presidency and have played a significant role in forcing Soeharto to
resign in disgrace. It now remains to be seen whether or not Muslim leaders
will be able to continue to do so at this crucial time in Indonesia's history.
Wallahu a'lam bi al-sawab.

POSTSCRIPT

INDONESIAN ISLAM, ELECTION POLITICS AND BEYOND

Indonesian Islam, no doubt, since its early history in the late 12th century is basically a moderate and tolerant Islam. This is due not only to the peaceful penetration and spread of Islam in the Indonesian archipelago, but also to social and cultural systems of the Indonesian people. Therefore, social, cultural, and political expression of Islam in Indonesia is quite distinctive if one compares with Islam somewhere else.

Despite its cultural, social, and political distinctions, Indonesian Islam is no less Islamic compares with Islam in other areas of the Muslim world. Indonesian Muslims subscribes to the very same fundamental beliefs of Islam as laid down by the Qur'an and the tradition of the Prophet Muhammad, which later were elaborated and formulated by authoritative and recognized 'ulama' (Muslim religious scholars). Indonesian Muslims also practice Islamic rituals like Muslims in other areas. If there are some differences, they are only in small or even trivial matters (furu'iyyah), not in fundamental teachings of Islam.

Therefore, it is wrong to assume that Indonesian Islam is theologically, doctrinally, and ritually peripheral vis-à-vis Islam anywhere else. It is true that Indonesian Muslims live in a region far away from the places – precisely Mecca and Medina – where Islam was firstly revealed and developed. But that should not lead one to argue that Indonesian Islam is also a 'peripheral Islam', a kind of impure Islam, or 'bad Islam', and the like.

Indonesian Islam is very rich, not only in terms of its cultural and social expressions, but also in terms of institutions. Indonesian Islam has two big wings, the Muhammadiyah (founded in 1912), and NU (Nahdlatul Ulama, founded in 1926), which since their foundations have operated in what is often called as 'cultural Islam' – as opposed to 'political Islam'. They perfectly represent moderate Islam in Indonesia. These organizations together with many other mainstream Muslim organizations throughout the country own thousands of educational institutions ranging from elementary *madrasahs* and schools to *pesantrens* and university. In addition, they operate hospitals and clinics, orphanages, people's credit banks (Bank Perkreditan Rakyat/BPR of Baitul Mal Wattamwil/BMT), cooperatives, NGOs, and many others.

Not least important role of these mainstream Muslim organizations is in the civic life and civic culture. In fact they are religious-based civil society organizations. They perfectly fit in with the definition of civil society organizations that is, independent from the state, self-regulating, and self-financing, that work as mediating and bridging force between the state on the one hand and the society on the other. As civil society organizations, they work for the better ordering of society as a whole.

Politically speaking, Indonesia is clearly not an Islamic state; nor is Islam the official religion of the state. Despite the fact that almost 90 per cent of country's total population is Muslim, Indonesia is the *Pancasila* ('Five Pillars) state. The very first pillar of *Pancasila* is the belief in One Single God, which according to virtually all Muslim leaders is in conformity with the Islamic belief in *tawhid*, unity of God. That is also true with the other four of pillars of *Pancasila*, that is, humanity, unity of Indonesia, democracy, and social justice. That is why Indonesia is neither a theocratic nor a secular state.

That is why, *Pancasila* as common platform of the plural Indonesia, has been accepted by mainstream and moderate Muslim organizations mentioned above. That is also one of the reasons why these Muslim organizations do not support the appeal and efforts of certain fringe groups among Muslim for the transformation of Indonesian state into an Islamic state, nor do they support the implementation of *shari'ah* (Islamic law) in the country.

There is no doubt that Muslims played a great role in the rise and decline of the Indonesian state. Likewise, Indonesia has also experienced the rise and decline of democracy. Since the time of independence on 17 August, 1945, Indonesian people have accepted democracy. And since then, one can observed various kinds of democracy implemented. It is only, after the fall of President Soeharto came the so-called 'period of reforms' (*masa reformasi*), during which time Indonesia has been trying to implement a more genuine and authentic democracy. The last experience in this regard was parliamentary and presidential elections in 2004.

COMPATIBILITY OF ISLAM AND DEMOCRACY

The long and tiring election year in Indonesia in 2004 is finally over in surprisingly peaceful manner. To recall once again, the elections began with the legislature general election on April 5th, followed by First Round Presidential election on July 4th, and finally Second Round of Presidential election on September 20th. Despite bomb blast on September 9, 2004, at the front of Australian embassy, the final run off of Presidential election run smoothly with Susilo Bambang Yudhoyono (SBY) and Muhammad Jusuf Kalla (MJK), respectively Presidential and Vice Presidential candidates, as the clear winners defeating Megawati Soekarnoputri, the incumbent President, and Hasyim Muzadi.

The completion of the election and the formation of new government soon will arguably accelerate the peaceful transition of Indonesia from authoritarianism to democracy; only six years ago the autocratic Soeharto regime was forced to abruptly end its long-held power for more than three decades. Following the introduction President BJ Habibie – who replaced President Soeharto – of liberal and multi-party politics since 1998, hopes for a smooth transition to democracy have seemingly withered away in the aftermath of the 1999 general election with continued political fragmentation and conflict among political elites and parties.

In fact the democratically elected President Abdurrahman Wahid was impeached in 2001 for mismanagement and erratic attitude, and was replaced by President Megawati Soekarnoputri. President Megawati was able to bring political stability and improved Indonesian economy. Despite of a great deal of criticism towards her government, the successful 2004 general election was, one should admit, the greatest achievement of President Megawati Soekarnoputri. With the same token, her greatest weakness was her failure to address the spread of ever rampant KKN (*korupsi, kolusi, nepotisme* or corruption, collusion and nepotism).

The fair, free and peaceful elections have shown to the world that Indonesia – being the largest Muslim nation in the world – that Indonesian Islam is indeed compatible with democracy. As a largest Muslim country Indonesia is neither Islamic state nor is Islam the official religion of the state. Since its independence on August 17, 1945, Indonesia tried to adopt democracy; what was implemented, however, was a kind of quasi-democracy, which was called "Guided Democracy" (*Demokrasi Terpimpin*) during the period of President Soekarno and, "*Pancasila* Democracy" (*Demokrasi Pancasila*) during the era of President Soeharto.

Therefore, Indonesian citizens have very little knowledge of and experience with real and genuine democracy. That is way in the early years of the Indonesian experience in democracy in the so-called period of reforms (*masa reformasi*) there is a lot of signs of the "breakdown" of democracy; indeed what has happened was a kind of "demo-crazy" since democracy seems to be understood by certain segments of Indonesian society as mass-demonstration that often ended on chaos and anarchy.

The success of Indonesia to hold general elections in peaceful way should silence the skeptics who wrongly believe that democracy can not have strong root in a dominant or pre-dominant Muslim country. The case is probably true in particular Muslim countries elsewhere, but that should not be taken into sweeping generalization. The Indonesian case shows that Islam is not inherently undemocratic or incompatible with democracy. In fact there is a lot of Islamic principles and teachings that compatible with democracy.

The seemingly incompatibility between Islam and democracy is a result of literal understanding of certain verses of the Qur'an, or of taking only certain aspect of Islam and ignoring other at the same time. In addition, the failure of democracy is many Muslim countries due mainly to a number of internal and external factors that inhibit the growth of democracy; some of the most important inhibiting factors are, among others, weak economic condition, backwardness in education, lack of socio-cultural capital and, not least important, the support of Western powers towards undemocratic regimes in Muslim countries.

Furthermore, the Indonesian exercise in democracy has shown the fallacy of the so-called "democratic trap" theory which argues that the democratic opening in Muslim countries would result only in the rise to power of the Islamists, not to say Muslim fundamentalists. In line to this theory, certain regime, supported by certain Western countries, annulled the results of the election when the Islamists or Islamic parties would seem to win the election. The classic example of the interference in democracy is the Algerian case in early 1990s; the West-supported regime annulled the election when the Islamic party FIS seemed to win the elections and, thus, would replace the Western-supported ruling regime.

This unexpected interference has in fact alienated the proponents of democracy in Muslim countries from democracy; the double-standard attitude of some Western countries has produced some disillusionment among Muslims who love to see democracy becomes the order of the day in their country. The democracy trap argument has proven wrong in Indonesian case. The Indonesian elections have in fact shown that Islamic parties or the Islamists have not been able to ride the waves of the democratic opening nor to create a "democratic trap".

ISLAM AND TRANSFORMATION OF INDONESIAN POLITICS

As far as Islam is concerned, the results of the 2004 general elections in Indonesia indicate a number of interesting political developments, not only in the Presidential election, but also in the legislature one. All in all, I would argue, Islam and Islamic issues – such as the possible implementation of shari'ah or Islamic law – did not become central and big issues throughout general elections. Indonesian people in general, in contrast, were concerned mostly with issues they face in real life, such continued economic hardship, more rampant corruption, lack of law enforcement, increased insecurity, continued spread of narcotics and other forms of social ills.

The best example in this is *Partai Keadilan Sejahtera* (PKS or Prosperous and Justice Party), the most Islamically-oriented conservative party that was able to substantially increase its gains the last election from less that two percent in the 1999 election to seven percent. The party succeeded in getting more voters not because they campaigned for the implementation of *shari'a* or the transformation of Indonesia into an Islamic state, but rather for the fight against corruption and creation of good governance.

The first direct Presidential elections have substantially transformed Indonesia politics. Some of the most important tendencies are; firstly, political parties have not been able now to dictate their will on the members let alone the masses as a whole. Even though big parties like Golkar party – which won the legislature elections – PDIP, PPP and others forged the so-called "Nation Coalition" (*Koalisi Kebangsaan*) to contain the momentum of SBY-JK – who in contrast formed what they called "People Coalition" (*Koalisi Rakyat*) – this pair won the elections any way. More than that, the appeal of Hasyim Muzadi – the non-active national leader of NU, who was also the Vice-Presidential candidate of Megawati Soekarnoputri – to the *kiyai* and their masses to vote for his favor has also failed. These indicate that the Indonesian voters are now becoming more independent and more rational in their political and voting behavior; they can not now be dictated by their party leaders or by their *kiyai*; now decide themselves.

Secondly; the election of SBY-JK also shows the continued decline of the so-called "*politik aliran*" theory. According to this theory – based on Clifford Geertz' divisions of "*santri*" (strict Muslims), "*abangan*" (nominal Muslims) and "*priyayi*" (aristocracy) – Indonesian politics was heavily divided along religious line and traditional loyalty. Sociological and religious changes that have been taking place since that last decade of Soeharto's rule have contributed to the rapid demise of the *politik aliran*. Indonesian politics, since the the reform era, has been characterized by less and less *politik aliran*. In contrast what has characterized Indonesian politics since then is "interest politics" if not "opportunist politics". The election of SBY-JK clearly shows that religious line is no longer relevant. Though SBY has been called by some international media as a "secular" person, he is known in Indonesia as good and practicing Muslim; while JK on the other hand has long been known as having more Islamic credentials, being the former leader of HMI (Association of University Muslim Students), for instance.

Thirdly; despite the 9/9 bomb blast, Indonesian Islam remains moderate and tolerant Islam. The bomb has in fact contributed to a more resolute and stronger attitude among Indonesian Muslims in general to confront radicalism; more and more Muslims abandon the defensive and apologetic attitude towards the ruthlessness of the perpetrators of the bombing. The belief among some people of the so-called "conspiracy theory" seems to decreasing. Virtually all Muslim leaders issued statements in strongest terms ever to condemn the bombing.

The police investigation of the bombing makes it clear that the "intellectualist actors" of the bombings in Indonesia in the last several years are Malaysian – DR Azahari and Noordin M. Top – who recruited some misled Indonesians. While Azahari was killed during a siege by Indonesian police in Batu, Malang, East Java, on November 9, 2005, Noordin remains at large; he is, for sure, will continue recruit potential suicide bombers, and create security problems in Indonesia.

Looking at Azahari and Noordin case, therefore, there is strong tendency that radical and militant groups or terrorist groups are foreign-led, rather than home-grown ones. This again, confirms that Indonesian Muslims are basically moderate and tolerant Muslims; but they must be aware of negative foreign influence brought in by foreign Muslims, especially on young Muslims.

With that kind of development both at the societal and government levels, the bomb blasts in Kuningan, Jakarta, and Bali II on October 1, 2005, has forced other radical groups to further lay low. It is no secret that a good number of suspected people have been arrested by the police after the disclosure of the networks of the perpetrators of Bali bombing I three years ago; more alleged terrorists were detained and brought to justice after Marriott bombing in Jakarta; and more of them have been put into police custody in the aftermath of the Kuningan and Bali II bombings.

Therefore, one of the most important keys to address terrorism in Indonesia is more stringent law enforcement; the professionalism and credibility of the police in the investigation of the perpetrators of bombing and other kind of terrorism is very crucial in addressing terrorism. With public support, the police are now in a better position to decisively act in the war against terrorism.

Not least important is the support of civil society organizations – particularly moderate Muslim organizations – in the fight against terrorism. An encouraging development took place in the aftermath of Bali bombing

II. In conjunction with the post-Ramadhan and Id al-Fitr celebrations, Vice President MJK met at his official residence with a number of Muslim leaders, including from the NU, Muhammadiyah and MUI (*Majelis Ulama Indonesia*/the Council of Indonesian *'Ulama*), and representatives from other organizations. During the meeting, Vice President also showed a video tape of the perpetrators of Bali blast II who had military training and messages for their families before they conducted the suicide bombing.

The end result of the meeting was the formation of the Team of Anti-Terrorism (*Tim Penanggulangan Terorism*/TPT) led by KH Ma'ruf Amin, a respected *'ulama'* from the MUI. He is assisted by a number of vice-chairpersons from the NU, Muhammadiyah, DDII (Dewan Dakwah Islamiyah Indonesia/the Indonesian Council of Islamic Preaching) and Ministry of Religious Affairs. The team has decided to launch a number programs; firstly, disseminating the true teaching of *jihad* from national to grass-root levels through Muslim organizations, and educational institutions; secondly, researching literature on misleading concept on *jihad* in order to provide counter-discourse; developing cooperation with related institutions in countering terrorism.

CONCLUSION

There is a lot of signs that Indonesia under President SBY is more likely to be more stable. The expectation towards the new national leadership basically continues to run high in Indonesia. One of the most important keys for President SBY and Vice-President MJK to get stronger support from the people is their ability to form a cabinet that could win the widest possible public acceptability. For many, it is disappointing that SBY-JK cabinet consists of some ministers that are lacking of credibility and professionalism in their field. President SBY seemed to have been very compromising with political parties in particular. President SBY also failed to satisfy public in general when he did a partial reshuffle of his cabinet in early December, 2004.

Despite this problem, so far is still quite good for President SBY; and it seems that he is able to lead Indonesia on the right way. One of his greatest challenges is the possible tension and conflict between him and the "Nation Coalition" which dominates the seats in the Parliament (DPR). But, one has to admit, that the Nation Coalition is indeed very fragile. The interest or opportunist politics among Parliament members and party politics, however, makes it possible for the SBY government to run with minimum opposition from and conflict with the DPR.

The SBY theme of K2A (*Konsiliasi, Konsolidasi, Aksi,* or Conciliation, Consolidation, and Action) could be very appropriate and a smart move for President SBY to anticipate maneuvers against him from the DPR. Furthermore, the election of Vice-President MJK as the chairperson of Golkar Party that has the largest number of seats in DPR, has significantly reduced the possible head on collision between President SBY administration and the DPR.

With regards to consolidation, the period of President SBY is indeed the period of consolidation for Indonesia. The SBY government needs not only to consolidate efforts to solve Indonesia's huge internal problems, but also to reconsolidate the very fabric of Indonesian society. There is now an increasing need to reconsolidate civil society and NGOs as a pillar of democracy. In the last election – as the case since the fall of Soeharto – civil society and NGOs at large have also been pulled into power politics. This is particularly true with the NU when its national chief Hasyim Muzadi decided to run as Vice-Presidential candidate of Megawati Soekarnoputri. Tension and conflict resulted from Hasyim's candidacy need to be resolved. Otherwise, this largest Muslim organization in Indonesia can not function effectively for a better ordering of Indonesian society as a whole.

In addition, President SBY is expected to continue with fight against rampant corruption. There are some good signs on this; a good number of public official both from the executive and legislative branches have been brought to justice. But there is still a lot of things to be done before Indonesian public can see a significant results of anti-corruption campaign. But, with the same token, Indonesian public in general, should also show their concrete support to President SBY anti-corruption campaign.

The anti-corruption campaign, no doubt, is very crucial for the creation of good governance in Indonesia. President SBY has repeatedly talked about the need for Indonesia to develop good governance. Again, there is a lot of reforms needed in public institutions and bureaucracy in order for Indonesia to be able to have a good governance. It is difficult to imagine a better future of Indonesia, unless good governance becomes the order of the day.

ORIGINAL SOURCES
OF CHAPTERS

Part One

Indonesia, Islam, and Democracy

1. **Islam and the Indonesian Transition to Democracy:**

    Chapter of "Democracy Project" Discourses and Practices of Democracy in Southeast Asia: Globalization, National Governance, and Local Responses, Editor Taufik Abdullah. Part of this paper is published in Islamic Perspective on the Millennium edited by Amin Saikal and Virginia Hooker, Singapore: ISEAS, 2004.

2. **The Islamic Factor in Post-Soeharto Indonesia:**

    Published in "Indonesia Assessment Series, Research School of Pacific and Asian Studies, The Australian National University" edited by C. Manning and P. Van Diermen., Indonesia in Transition: Some Aspects of Reformasi and Crisis, Singapore and London, 2000.

3. **Civil Society and Democratization during the Presidency of Abdurrahman Wahid:**

    Paper presented at Workshop on "Towards Good Society? Civil Society Actors, the State, and the Business Class in Southeast Asia", Heinrich Boell Foundation, Berlin, 26-27 October 2004 and published under the same title by the Heinrich Boell Foundation, 2005. Part of this paper was originally published in Civil Society in Asia edited by D.C. Schack and W. Hudson, Aldershot and Burlington, 2003.

4. **The Megawati Presidency: The Challenge of Political Islam:**
   Paper for Forum on Indonesia "The First 100 Days of President Megawati: Political and Economic Perspectives", held jointly by ISEAS & CSIS Orchard Hotel, Singapore, 1 November 2001. A shorter version is published in Governance in Indonesia: Challenges Facing the Megawati Presidency edited by S. Hadi, A.L. Smith and H.M. Ling, Singapore, 2003.

5. **Communal Riots in Indonesia's Recent History:**
   Originally published in Communal Conflicts in Contemporary Indonesia by The Center for Languages and Cultures, UIN Syarif Hidayatullah, Jakarta in cooperation with The Konrad Adenauer Foundation (KAF), 2002.

Part Two
Indonesia, Islam, and the International Order

6. **Islam in Indonesian Foreign Policy:**
   Paper presented in the Workshop on "Islamic Revivalism and State Response", Singapore, Institute of Southeast Asian Studies (ISEAS), Singapore, 2-3 June 1997. Published in Studia Islamika, Vol. 7, No. 3, Jakarta, 2000.

7. **The Bosnian Crisis and the Indonesian Response:**
   Published in The Bosnian Crisis and the Islamic World edited by R. Bulliet and M. Imber-Goldstein, New York, Middle East Institute Columbia University, 2002.

8. **Indonesian Islam in a World Context:**
   Paper originally presented at the conference "Islam and Democracy in Indonesia" hosted by The Asia Foundation and USINDO, Washington DC 7 February 2002, and later delivered at the conference "Islam in Indonesia and the West" McGill University, Montreal, Canada, 28-29 October 2002; also published in Kultur: The Indonesian Journal for Muslim Cultures, Vol. 2, No. 1, Jakarta.

9. **Islam and the West Revisited:**
   Originally written as an essay for the monograph Islamic Reformation Global Policy Exchange, Alexandria, VA, USA, 2004. Parts were presented

as pointers at the symposium "What Now? A Debate on America and the World" New York University, 10 May 2003, and at "US-Islamic World Forum" hosted by the Brookings Institution and the Government of Qatar, Doha, Qatar, 10-12 January 2004.

10. **Indonesia's Role in the Muslim World and International Affairs:**
Paper for International Seminar "A Portrait of Contemporary Indonesian Islam: Remapping and Responding to the Worldwide Social Agenda", Center for Languages and Cultures, Syarif Hidayatullah State Islamic University, Sahid Hotel, Jakarta, December 14-15, 2004; published Chaider S. Bamualim (ed.), A Portrait of Contemporary Indonesian Islam, Jakarta, 2005

11. **The Historical Roots of Muslim Crisis:**
A shorter version was published as book *The Jakarta Post*, 6 May 2003.

Part Three
The Dynamics of Islamic Movements

12. **Indonesian Islam after the Bali Bombing:**
Paper presented at Workshop "After Bali: The Threat of Terrorism in Southeast Asia" Institute of Defense and Strategic Studies (IDSS) Nanyang Technological University, Singapore, 27-28 January 2003; published in Kumar Ramakrishna & See Seng Tan (eds), After Bali: The Threat of Terrorism in Southeast Asia, Singapore & London, 2003.

13. **Globalization and Indonesian Muslim Movements:**
Published in Johan H. Meuleman (ed.), Islam in the Era of Globalization Muslim: Attitudes Towards Modernity and Identity, Jakarta, INIS, 2001; published also by Routledge Curzon, London, 2003.

14. **Muslim Leadership in Contemporary Indonesia:**
This paper was initially presented at an International Seminar on "Towards the Establishment of an Ideal Islamic Leadership of the Twenty-First Century", Akademi Pengkajian Islam, Universiti Malaya, Kuala Lumpur, 19-20 June, 2001.

Postscript: Indonesian Islam, Election Politics and Beyond:
This paper, presented at public lecture sponsored by The Embassy of the Republic of Indonesia, in Athens, Greece, is a substantive revision of

contribution to discussion on "Islam and the Promotion of Democracy, Good Governance and Pluralism", in honor of the visit of the Speaker of the Canadian Senate, Dan Hays in Jakarta (January 11, 2005). An early brief version in the form of pointers was presented at "Canada-Indonesia Symposium – The New Shape of Government in Indonesia and Implications for Bilateral Relations", UBC Center for Southeast Asia Research, Simon Fraser University International and the Consulate General of the Republic of Indonesia, Vancouver, October 12, 2004.

BIBLIOGRAPHY

BOOKS AND PAPERS

Abaza, Mona, 1994, *Islamic Education, Perceptions and Exchanges: Indonesian Students in Cairo*, Paris: Cahier d'Archipel, No. 23.

Abdulgani, Roeslan, 1985, "Sekitar Konperensi Asia-Afrika dan Maknanya bagi Politik Luar Negeri Indonesia", *Analisa*, 4, (Jakarta: CSIS).

Abdullah, M. Amin, 2001, 'Muhammadiyah's Experience in Promoting Civil Society on the Eve of the 21st Century'. In *Islam and Civil Society in Southeast Asia* edited by Mitsuo Nakamura, Sharon Siddique, and Omar Faruk Bajunid (Singapore: ISEAS).

Abu-Rabi', Ibrahim M., 1996, *Intellectual Origins of Islamic Resurgence in the Modern Arab World*, (Albany, NY: State University of New York Press).

Alfian, Ibrahim, 1987, *Perang di Jalan Allah* (Jakarta: Sinar Harapan).

Alkaff, Thohir Abdullah, 1998, "Perkembangan Syiah di Indonesia", in Abduh and Away (eds.), *Mengapa Kita Menolak Syiah*, (Jakarta: Gema Insani Press).

Ausop, Asep Zainal, 2004, *NII: Ajaran dan Gerakan* (1992-2002), doctoral diss., Universitas Islam Negeri (Jakarta: UIN Syarif Hidayatullah).

Azra, Azyumardi, 1992, "The Transmission of Islamic Reformism to Indonesia: Networks of Middle Eastern and Malay-Indonesian 'Ulama in the Seventeenth and Eighteenth Centuries", Ph.D. dissertation, Columbia University.

— 1992, "'Ulamā' Indonesia di Haramayn", *Jurnal Ulumul Qur'an*, III, 3 (July-Sept);

— 1994, "Guarding the Faith of the Ummah; Religio-Intellectual Journey of Mohammad Rasjidi", *Studia Islamika, Indonesian Journal for Islamic Studies*, Jakarta, I, 2 (April-June).

— 1995, "The Bosnian Crisis in the Eastern Islamic World: The Case of Indonesia", paper presented at the Conference on "The Bosnian Crisis and the Islamic World', Middle East Institute, Columbia University, March 10-11, 1995.

— 1995a, "Melacak Pengaruh dan Pergeseran Orientasi Tamatan Kairo", *Studia Islamika, Indonesian Journal for Islamic Studies*, II, 3 (July-Sept).

— 1995b, "Two Worlds of Islam: Interaction between Southeast Asia and the Middle East", *Journal of Islamic Studies* (Oxford), 6.

— 1995c, "Dari Haramayn ke Kairo", in Aswab Mahasin, et. al. (eds.), *Ruh Islam dalam Budaya Bangsa*, (Jakarta: Yayasan Festival Istiqlal).

— 1995d, "Perbukuan Islam di Indonesia", paper presented at the Istiqlal Festival II, Jakarta.

— 1995e, "Syiah di Indonesia; Antara Mitos dan Realitas", *Jurnal Ulumul Quran* (Jakarta) VI, 4 (October-December),

— 1996, *Pergolakan Politik Islam: Dari Fundamentalisme, Modernisme hingga Post-Modernisme*, (Jakarta: Paramadina).

— 1999, Menuju *Masyarakat madani*, (Bandung: Rosda Karya).

— 2000, "Islam in Indonesian Foreign Policy: Assessing Impacts of Islamic Revivalism during the Soeharto Era", Studia Islamika: *Indonesian Journal for Islamic Studies*, Vol. 7, No. 3.

— 2000a, *Islam Substantif: Agar Umat Tidak Jadi Buih* (Bandung: Mizan).

— 2000b, "The Islamic Factor in Post-Soeharto Indonesia". *In Indonesia in Transition: Social Aspects of Reformasi and Crisis* edited by C. Manning and P. van Diermen (Canberra and Singapore: Zed Books Ltd.).

— 2000c, "Islam and Christianity in Indonesia: The Roots of Conflict and Hostility", paper presented in International Conference on "Religion and Culture in Asia-Pacific: Violence or Healing?', RMIT University, Melbourne, 22-25 October,.

— 2000d, "Islamic Perspective on the Nation-State: Political Islam in Post-Soeharto Indonesia", paper at International Conference on "*Islamic Perspectives on the New Millennium*", The Australian National University (ANU), Canberra, 20-21 November, published in Amin Saikal and Virginia Hooker (eds.), Islamic Perspectives in the New Millennium, (Singapore: ISEAS, 2005).

— 2000e, 'In Search the Man behind the Image', in *Questioning Gus Dur, The Jakarta Post* (Jakarta,).

— 2001, "Sustaining the Transition from Authoritarian Rule to Democracy: a Special Reference to Indonesia", paper presented at the International Conference of the International Council on Human Rights Policy, Jakarta, 16 March.

— 2001a, "Consolidating Reforms in Indonesia: Challenges and Opportunities", paper presented in Panel Discussion on "Crucial Reforms for the Development of a More Humane Civil Society in Indonesia", *The Jakarta Post*, Jakarta, 5-6 December.

— 2001b, "Civil Society and Democratization in Indonesia: Transition during President Wahid's Rule and Beyond", paper originally presented at Workshop on "Civil Society in Asia", Griffith University, Brisbane, Australia, 10-12 July; revised version in *Refleksi*: Jurnal Kajian Agama dan Filsafat (Jakarta, 2001), Vol III, No. 3.

— 2001c, "Globalization of Indonesian Muslim Discourse: Contemporary Religio-Intellectual Connections between Indonesian and the Middle East". In *Islam in the Era of Globalization: Muslim Attitudes towards Modernity and Identity* edited by J.H. Meuleman (Leiden and Jakarta); published also by Routledge-Curzon, 2003, London.

— 2002a, "Indonesian Islam in a World Context", paper presented in Conference on "Islam and Democracy", The Asia Foundation and USINDO, Washington DC, 7 February 2002 and published in "Indonesian Islam in a World Context", *Kultur: The Indonesian Journal for Muslim Cultures*, Vol. 2, No. 1.

— 2002a, "The Bosnian Crisis in the Eastern Islamic World: The Case of Indonesia", in Bulliet, Richard & Martha Imber-Goldstein (eds.), *The Bosnian Crisis and the Islamic World*, New York: Middle East Institute Columbia University, Occasional Papers 3.

— 2002b, *Konflik Baru Antar-Peradaban: Globalisasi, Radikalisme & Pluralitas* (Jakarta: Grafindo Persada).

— 2003a, "The Megawati Presidency: The Challenge of Political Islam". In *Governance in Indonesia: Challenges Facing the Megawati Presidency*, edited by H. Soesastro, A.L. Smith and H.M Ling (Singapore: ISEAS).

— 2004, *Japan, Islam, the Muslim World and Indonesia: Past and Present*, (Jakarta: The Japan Foundation Lecture) Series 3.

— 2004, *The Origins of Islamic Reformism in Southeast Asia* (Crows Nest, Honolulu, Leiden: AAAS & Allen-Unwin, University of Hawaii Press, KITLV Press).

— et. al., 1996, *Sistem Siaga Dini untuk Kerusuhan Sosial* (Jakarta: Litbang Dept Agama RI).

Bamualim, Chaider et. al. (eds.), 2001, *Laporan Penelitian Radikalisme Agama dan Perubahan Sosial di DKI Jakarta*, Jakarta.

Barters, Dieters, 1977, "Guarding The Invisible Mountain: Inter-village Alliance, Religious Syncretism, and Ethnic Identity among Ambonese Christian in the Moluccas", Ph.D diss., (Cornell University).

Barton, Greg, 1995, "Neo-Modernism: a Vital Synthesis of Traditionalist and Modernist Islamic Thought in Indonesia", *Studia Islamika, Indonesian Journal for Islamic Studies*, Jakarta, II, 3 (July-Sept 1995).

Baso, Ahmad, 1999, *Civil Society versus Masyarakat madani: Arkeologi Pemikiran "Civil Society" dalam Islam Indonesia* (Bandung: Pustaka Hidayah).

Benda, Harry J., 1958, *The Crescent and the Rising Sun: Indonesian Islam under the Japanese Occupation* 1942-1945, (The Hague and Bandung: W. van Hoeve Ltd.).

Bush, Robin, 2001, 'Islam and Civil Society in Indonesia: The Case of Nahdlatul Ulama', unpublished paper.

Carey, P. & G. Carter Bentley eds., 1995, *East Timor at the Crossroads: The Forging of a Nation* (Honolulu: University of Hawaii Press).

Chaidar, A.I. et. al., 1999, *Aceh Bersimbah Darah: Mengungkap Penerapan Daerah Operasi Militer (DOM) di Aceh 1989-1998* (Jakarta).

Culla, Adi Suryadi, 1999, *Masyarakat madani: Pemikiran, Teori, dan Relevansinya dengan Cita-cita Reformasi* (Jakarta: Rajawali).

Dahl, Robert A., 1971, *Polyarchy: Participation and Opposition* (New Haven: Yale University Press).

— 1989, *Democracy and Its Critics* (New Haven: Yale University Press).

Dam, Syamsumar & Erni Budiwanti, 1999, "Aceh: Otonomi atau Merdeka?", in *Indonesia di Ambang Perpecahan*? edited by S. Haris (Jakarta).

Dekmejian, R. Hrair, 1995, *Islam in Revolution: Fundamentalism in the Arab World* second edition (Syracuse, New York: Syracuse University Press).

Departemen Luar Negeri R.I., 1971, *Dua Puluh Lima Tahun Departemen Luar Negeri 1945-1970*, Jakarta: Kawal.

Di Palma, Guiseppe, 1990, *To Craft Democracies: An Essay on Democratic Transitions* (Berkeley: The University of California Press).

Dipoyudo, Kirdi, 1981, "Indonesia's Foreign Policy towards the Middle East and Africa", in *Trends in Indonesia*, Jakarta: CSIS.

— 1985, "Indonesia's Foreign Policy towards the Middle East and Africa", *The Indonesian Quarterly*, XIII, No. 4.

Djalal, Hasjim, 1996, *Politik Luar Negeri Indonesia Menghadapi Abad ke 21*, (Bandung: Universitas Padjadjaran).

Djiweng, Stephanus ed., 1996, *Manusia Dayak: Orang Kecil Yang Terperangkap Modernisasi* (Pontianak: Institute Dayakologi).

Effendy, Bahtiar, 1998, *Islam dan Negara: Transformasi Pemikiran dan Praktik Politik Islam di Indonesia* (Jakarta: Paramadina).

Eickelman, Dale F. & James Piscatori, 1996, *Muslim Politics* (Princeton: Princeton University Press).

El Ibrahimy, M. Nur, 1982, *Tengku Daud Beureueh: Peranannya dalam Pergolakan di Aceh* (Jakarta) re-published and revised in 2001, *Peranan Tengku Daud Beureueh dalam Pergolakan Aceh* (Jakarta: Media Dakwah).

Eliraz, Giora, 2004, *Islam in Indonesia: Modernism, Radicalism, and the Middle East Dimension*, (Brighton: Sussex Academic Press).

Esposito, John L. and John O. Voll, 1996, *Islam and Democracy* (New York: Oxford University Press).

Falaakh, Mohammad Fajrul, 2001, 'Nahdlatul Ulama and Civil Society in Indonesia'. In *Islam and Civil Society in Southeast Asia* edited by Mitsue Nakamura, Sharon Siddique and Omar Faruk Bajunid (Singapore: ISEAS).

Fananie, Zainuddin, Atika Sabardila and Dwi Purnanto, 2002, *Radikalisme Agama & Perubahan Sosial* (Surakarta).

Fealy, Greg, 2000, "Islamic Politics: A Rising or Declining Force?", paper presented to "Rethinking Indonesia Conference", Melbourne, 4-5 March.

Federspiel, Howard M., 1970, *Persatuan Islam: Islamic Reform in Twentieth*

Century Indonesia (Ithaca, New York: Cornell University Modern Indonesia Project).

Geertz, Clifford, 1960, *The Religion of Java* (New Haven & London: the University of Chicago Press Ltd.).

Haris, Syamsuddin and M. Riefki Muna, 1999, "Dilema Penyelesaian Kasus Timor Timur", in *Indonesia di Ambang Perpecahan*? edited by S. Haris (Jakarta).

Hasan, Noorhaidi, 2001, "Islamic Radicalism and the Crisis of the Nation-State", ISIM Newsletter, 7 (Leiden, March).

— 1999, "Islam and Nation in the Post-Soeharto Era". In *The Politics of Post-Soeharto Indonesia* edited by A. Schwarz and J. Paris (New York: Council of Foreign Relations Press).

— 2000, *Civil Islam: Muslims and Democratization in Indonesia* (Princeton: Princeton University Press).

— 2001, 'Cooptation, Enmitization, and Democracy: The Modernist Muslim Dilemma in Indonesia', paper presented in Conference 'Consolidating Indonesian Democracy', Ohio State University, Columbus, 11-13 May.

Hein, G., 1986, "Scenario's Foreign Policy: Second Generation Nationalism in Indonesia", Ph.D. Diss., UC Berkeley.

Hill, Hal. ed., 1996, *Unity and Diversity: Regional Economic Development in Indonesia since 1970. West Kalimantan: Uneven Development*? (Canberra)

Huntington, Samuel P., 1984, 'Will More Countries Become Democratic?' *Political Science Quarterly*.

Huntington, Samuel P., 1997, *The Clash of Civilizations and the Remaking of World Order* (New York: Simon & Schuster).

ICG (International Crisis Group), 2001, *Indonesia: Violence and Radical Muslim* (Jakarta/Brussels).

— 2002, *Al-Qaeda in Southeast Asia: The Case of the "Ngruki Network" in Indonesia* (Jakarta/Brussels).

— 2002, *Indonesian Backgrounder: How the Jemaah Islamiyah Terrorist Networks Operates* (Jakarta/Brussels).

Inbaray, Sonny, 1995, *East Timor: Blood and Tears in ASEAN* (Chicung: Silkworm Books).

Kadir, Suzainah, 2001, "Indonesia's 'Democratization Dilemma': Political Islam and the Prospects for Democratic Consolidation", paper presented at Conference "Consolidating Indonesia's Democracy", Columbus, Ohio State University, 11-13 May.

Karni, Asrori, 1999, *Civil Society dan Ummah: Sintesa Diskursif "Rumah" Demokrasi"* (Ciputat, Jakarta: Logos).

Kusumaatmadja, Mochtar, 1983, *Politik Luar Negeri Indonesia dan Pelaksanaannya Dewasa Ini*, eds. Eddy Damian and Budiono Kusumohamidjojo (Bandung: Alumni).

— 1994, "Politik Luar Negeri Indonesia: Suatu Evaluasi", *Analisis* CSIS, Vol. XXIII, No. 2, Jakarta: CSIS.

Laporan Hasil Musyawarah Adat (Musdat) Pertama Dayak Kabupaten, 1986, (Sambas: Bengkawang).

Lawrence, Bruce B., 1998, *Shattering the Myth: Islam beyond Violence* (Princeton: Princeton University Press).

Leifer, Michael, 1981, "The Islamic Factor", in *Trends in Indonesia*, (Jakarta: CSIS).

— 1983, "The Islamic Factor in Indonesia's Foreign Policy: A Case of Functional Ambiguity", in Adeed Dawisha (ed.), *Islam in Foreign Policy*, (Cambridge: Cambridge University Press).

Lewis, Bernard, 2002, *What Went Wrong: The Clash Between Islam and Modernity in the Middle East*, (New York: Harper Perennial).

— 2003, *The Crisis of Islam: Holy War and Unholy Terror*, (London: Random House)

Liddle, William and Saiful Mujani, 2000, "*Islam, Kultur Politik, dan Demokrasi: Sebuah Telaah Komparatif Awal*", unpublished paper.

— 2002, "The Islamic Challenge to Democratic Consolidation in Indonesia", paper presented at International Conference "The Challenge of Democracy in the Muslim World", Jakarta, PPIM IAIN Jakarta & The Mershon Center, Ohio State University, 19-20 March.

Lipset, Seymor Martin, 1959, 'Some Requisites of Democracy: Economic Development and Political Legitimacy', *American Political Science Review*.

Lokollo, J.E. et. al., 1997, *Seri Budaya Pela Gandong dari Pulau Ambon* (Ambon).

Madjid, Nurcholish, 1993, "Beberapa Renungan tentang Kehidupan Keagamaan untuk Generasi Mendatang", *Jurnal Ulumul Qur'an* (Jakarta), IV, I (January-March).

Mehden, Fred R von der, 1992, *Two Worlds of Islam: Interaction between Southeast Asia and the Middle East* (Gainsville, Florida: University of Florida Press).

Mering, Ngo, 1997, "Perilaku Kekerasan Kolektif: Kondisi dan Pemicu Kalimantan Barat", unpublished paper (Jakarta).

Meuleman, Johan H., 1996, "Reactions and Attitudes towards the Darul Arqam Movement in Southeast Asia", *Studia Islamika, Indonesian Journal for Islamic Studies*, Jakarta, I, (January-March).

Moore, Barrington, 1966, *Social Origins of Dictatorship and Democracy: Lord and Peasant in the Making of the Modern World* (Boston: Beacon Press).

Morris, Eric, 1978, *Islam and Politics in Aceh*, Melbourne.

Muzani, Saiful, 1993, "Di Balik Polemik Anti-Pembaruan Islam. Memahami Gejala Fundamentalisme Islam di Indonesia," *Islamika* (Jakarta), I (July-September).

— 1994, "Mu'tazilah Theology and Modernization of the Indonesian Muslim Community," *Studia Islamika, Indonesian Journal for Islamic Studies*, Jakarta, I, 1 (January-April).

Nakamura, Mitsuo, Sharon Siddique and Omar Faruk Bajunid eds., 2001, *Islam and Civil Society in Southeast Asia* (Singapore).

Norton, August Richard, ed., 1996, *Civil Society in the Middle East*, (Leiden, 1995 and 1996), 2 vols.

Nugroho, Bimo ed., et. al., 1997, *Sisi Gelap Kalimantan Barat: Perseteruan Etnis Dayak-Madura 1997* (Yakarta: Institute Dayakologi).

Nurjuliyanti, Dewi and Arief Subhan, 1955, "Lembaga-lembaga Syi'ah di Indonesia", *Jurnal Ulumul Quran* (Jakarta) VI, 4 (October-December).

Nursalim, Muh., 2001, "Faksi Abdullah Sungkar dalam Gerakan NII Era Orde Baru", MA thesis, Universitas Muhammadiyah (Surakarta).

O. Sutomo Roesnadi, 1979, "Hubungan antara Indonesia dan Timur Tengah", *Analisa*, VIII, No. 3.

Pattikayhatu, J.A. et. al., 1997, *Sejarah Asal Usul dan Terbentuknya Negeri-negeri di Pulau Ambon* (Ambon).

Pemda Kalimantan Barat, 1997, *Informasi Kerusuhan Sosial di Kalimantan Barat* (Pontianak: Bappeda Kalimantan Barat).

Pender, C.L.M., 1975, *The Life and Times of Soekarno* (Singapore: Oxford University Press).

Pranowo, M. Bambang, 1994, "Islam and Party Politics in Rural Java", *Studia Islamika, Indonesian Journal for Islamic Studies*, vol. I, No 2.

Reid, Anthony, 1988 and 1993, *Southeast Asia in the Age of Commerce 1450-1680*, (New Haven: Yale University Press) Vol. 1 and Vol. 2.

Ricklefs, Merle, 1998, *The Seen and the Unseen Worlds in Java: History, Literature and Islam in Court of Pakubuwana II, 1726-1749* (Honolulu: University of Hawai'i Press, in association with the Asian Studies Association of Australia).

Roff, William, 1989, "Islam di Asia Tenggara dalam Abad 19", in Azyumardi Azra (ed.), *Perspektif Islam di Asia Tenggara* (Jakarta: Yayasan Obor Indonesia).

Said, Edward, 1978, *Orientalism*, (New York).

Said, Muhammad, 1981, *Jihad Akbar di Medan Area* (Jakarta,).

— 1988, *Aceh Sepanjang Abad* (Jakarta).

Salim, Arskal, 2000, "The Idea of Islamic State in Indonesia", paper presented at the University of Wisconsin-Madison and Northern Illinois University Student Conference on Southeast Asia, DeKalb, Illinois, 3-4 March.

Sarnapi, 1996, "SMU Plus Mutahhari: Setetes Embun di Tengah Kemarau Mutu SMU", *Hikmah*, week 3, May.

Schwarz, Adam and Jonathan Paris (eds.), 1999, *The Politics of Post- Soeharto Indonesia*, (New Cork: Council on Foreign Relations Book)

Soetrisno, Loekman, et. al., 1997, "Kalimantan Barat" in *his Laporan Akhir Hasil Penelitian Pertikaian Antara Komunitas Madura Kalbar Dengan Komunitas Dayak Tahun 1996/1997 dan Antara Komunitas Madura Sambas Dengan Komunitas Melayu Sambas Tahun 1998/1999 di Kalimantan Barat.* (Yakarta, Yogyakarta: Yayasan Ilmu-Ilmu Sosial & Pontianak: Fisipol Untan)

— 1997, "Timor-Timur" in *Perilaku Kekerasan Koleklif: Kondisi dan Pemicu* (Yogyakarta).

Solahuddin, 2002, "Tracing the Roots of Hizbut Tahrir in Indonesia", *The Jakarta Post*, 2 April.

Sorensen, Georg, 1993, *Democracy and Democratization: Processes and Prospects in a Changing World* (Boulder: Westview Press Inc).

Sullivan, Denis J., 1994, *Private Voluntary Organizations in Egypt: Islamic Development, Private Initiative and State Control* (Gainsville: University Press of Florida).

Suparlan, Parsudi, et. al, 1999, *Laporan Hasil Penelitian Kerusuhan Ambon dan Rekomendasi Penanganannya* (Jakarta: Universitas Indonesia).

Taher, Tarmizi, 1997, *Aspiring for the Middle Path: Religious Harmony in Indonesia* (Jakarta: Censis).

Thaba, Abdul Azis, 1996, *Islam dan Negara dalam Politik Orde Baru*, (Jakarta: Gema Insani Press).

Thaib, Lukman, 1995, *The Islamic Polity and Leadership* (Petaling Jaya: Windrush Publishing Services).

The Freedom House Survey Team, 2002, *Freedom in the World 2002: The Democracy Gap* (New York: Freedom House).

Tibi, Bassam 1998, *The Challenge of Fundamentalism: Political Islam and the New World Disorder* (Berkeley: University of California Press).

van Klinken, Gary, 1996, *Akar Perlawanan Rakyat Timor Timur dan Prospek Perdamaiannya*, (Yogyakarta).

van Leur, JC., 1960, *Indonesia Trade and Society*, (Bandung: Sumur Bandung).

von der Mehden, Fred R.,1990, "Malaysian and Indonesian Islamic Movements and the Iranian Connection", in J.L. Esposito (ed.), *The Iranian Revolution: Its Global Impact* (Miami: Florida International University Press).

— 1993, *Two Worlds of Islam, Interaction between Southeast Asia and the Middle East*, (Gainsville, Florida: University Press of Florida).

Wanadi, Jusuf, 1989, "Indonesian Domectic Policy and Its Impact on Foreign Policy", *The Indonesian Quarterly*, Vol. XVII, No. 4.

Woodwark, Mark R., 1989, *Islam in Java: Normative Piety and Mysticism in the Sultanate of Yogyakarta* (Tucson: The University of Arizona Press).

Zada, Khamami, 2002, *Islam Radikal: Pergulatan Ormas-ormas Islam Garis Keras di Indonesia* (Jakarta: Teraju).

NEWSPAPERS AND MAGAZINES

DR, 12 July 1999.
DR, 2 August 1999.
Forum Keadilan, 25 July 1999
Forum Keadilan, 8 August 1999
Forum Keadilan, 15 August 1999
Forum Keadilan, 22 August 1999
Forum Keadilan, 29 August 1999.
Forum Keadilan, 5 September 1999
Forum Keadilan, 24 Oktober 1999.
Gamma, 1 August 1999
Gamma, 15 August 1999.
Gamma, 22 August 1999
Gamma, 19 September 1999
Gamma, 10 October 1999.
Gamma, 17 October 1999.
Gatra, 14 August 1999.
Gatra, 18 September 1999.
Gatra, 16 October 1999.
Panji Masyarakat, 25 August 1999.
Panji Masyarakat, 8 September 1999.
Tempo, 22 March 1999.
Tempo, 15 August 1999.
Tempo, 12 September 1999.

INDEX